Papa's Baby

Papa's Baby

Paternity and Artificial Insemination

Browne C. Lewis

NEW YORK UNIVERSITY PRESS
New York and London

NEW YORK UNIVERSITY PRESS
New York and London
www.nyupress.org

References to Internet websites (URLs) were accurate at the time of writing.
Neither the author nor New York University Press is responsible for URLs that
may have expired or changed since the manuscript was prepared.

Library of Congress Cataloging-in-Publication Data
Lewis, Browne.
Papa's baby : paternity and artificial insemination / Browne C. Lewis.
p. cm.
Includes bibliographical references and index.
ISBN 978-0-8147-3848-1 (cl : alk. paper)
ISBN 978-0-8147-5260-9 (ebook)
ISBN 978-0-8147-5327-9 (ebook)
1. Paternity--United States. 2. Artificial insemination, Human--Law and legislation--United
States. 3. Children--Legal status, laws, etc.--United States. I. Title.
KF542.L49 2012
346.7301'75--dc23   2011052278

New York University Press books are printed on acid-free paper, and their binding
materials are chosen for strength and durability. We strive to use environmentally
responsible suppliers and materials to the greatest extent possible in publishing our books.

Manufactured in the United States of America
10 9 8 7 6 5 4 3 2 1

This book is dedicated to the memory of my brother, Nova Joe Blount, who was a father in every way but biology, and to my niece, Stephanie Monique Lewis, who inspires me to keep standing.

Contents

Acknowledgments

My mother, Josephine, was a gentle woman who threatened more than she punished. I remember the numerous times that she warned, "Wait until your father gets home." Even when I had behaved in a manner that warranted his discipline, I was still excited when my daddy came home. As an adult, I continued to experience pure joy whenever I was blessed with my father's presence. Although my daddy died over nine years ago, sometimes I can hear his voice clearly, giving me direction and encouragement. Joe Lewis was a daddy and not just a father. He would have enjoyed reading this book because it emphasizes the importance of the father-child relationship. I am so grateful that I got to spend the first forty years of my life in his care.

During the course of preparing this book, I endured a funeral and a flood. I could not have completed the book without the grace of God. I give all thanks to Him for enabling me to overcome obstacles to finish the book. I thank my paternal siblings, Emma S., Joe, Batt, Evon, Don, Ora Bell, and Emma L., for sharing their memories of our dad. As single parents, my sisters all raised their children without the benefit of fathers. Nonetheless, they understand that it is critical that children receive support from their fathers. I thank Coré Cotton, my BFF, for sharing her dad with me after my daddy died.

I could not have completed the book without the encouragement and support I received from the members of my scholarship support group at Cleveland-Marshall College of Law: Kris Niedringhaus, Heidi Robertson, Alan Weinsein, Kermit Lind, and Dena Davis. They read the roughest of drafts and still found something positive to say about it. For an entire week, Professor Matthew Green and I stayed at the law school until the wee hours of the morning working on our writing. During that time, Matthew supplied me with the pep talks and candy that I needed to finally bring the book to life. I am also grateful for the financial support that I received from Deans Geoffery Mearns and Phyllis Crocker and from the Cleveland-Marshall Fund.

At New York University Press, I appreciate all of the support I received from editor Deborah Gershenowitz. Debbie encouraged me to turn my idea into a book and waited patiently for me to complete it. Finally, I thank Gabrielle Begue for her calmness and support in the face of my actual and figurative storms.

Introduction

The Cuckolded Husband

Her hands shook. Her voice trembled. Tears stained her cheeks. She slowly turned to her husband and said she was sorry. He gently wiped the tears from her eyes. He proclaimed she was his reason for living. They had just celebrated their seventh year of marriage. The audience booed her and cheered him. The talk-show host raised his hands to calm the audience. A member of the crew slowly raised an enlarged picture behind the stage. In the picture, the woman, the man, and their five-year-old son smiled for the camera. The host turned to the woman and asked her to tell the audience why she was on the show. She sighed and took her husband's hand. She told him she had had an affair with one of his friends, so the little boy might not be his son. He looked at the picture of the little boy, shook his head, and asked her why. She shrugged and looked helplessly at the host. The host told the audience that after years of feeling guilty, the woman decided to come clean. The host asked the man if he was willing to submit to a paternity test to determine whether or not he was the child's father. He hesitated. After looking at the boy's picture again, the man nodded. Later in the show, the host held up the results for the audience to see. The host looked down at the paper. Then, he turned to the couple. The host shook his head and announced that the test excluded the man as the little boy's father. For five years, the law presumed the man to be the legal father of the child. The man's paternity was established by the couple's marital status.

The Fornicating Man

She was a freshman from a small rural town. He was a senior from a big city. She was a geeky book worm. He was an athletic wide receiver on the college football team. The night of the party, she spent the evening leaning on the wall. He spent the evening dancing on the tables. When they finally made eye contact, he turned on the charm. She was shocked and flattered by the attention. He was intrigued by her shyness. He suggested that they go some place quiet, so they could talk. One thing led to another, and, before she could think about it, they were doing more than talking. They never became a couple, but they did conceive a child. She dropped out of college to breast feed and change diapers. He stayed in college to catch passes and score touchdowns. He did not believe that after failing to procreate with his long-term girlfriend, he could conceive a child with another woman after a one-night stand. He pulled a "Billy Jean,"[1] and said, "The kid is not my son." She applied for public benefits. He graduated and got a job doing public relations. The court ordered him to take a paternity test. The paternity test determined that he was the child's father. Based upon genetics, he was adjudicated as the child's legal father. The man's paternity was established by the biological connection between the man and the child.

The Non-Consenting Husband

Sophia dedicated the first half of her adult life to her career. Then, at the age of forty-two, she met thirty-seven-year-old William. As soon as the "I do's" were said, the couple started trying to have a child. After three painful years of infertility, Sophia sought medical help. The doctors concluded that the problem was not Sophia's slightly worn eggs, but William's sluggish sperm. William's low sperm count made it impossible for him to conceive a child. The couple considered all of their options, including adoption. William decided that they should wait for God to bless them with a child. Sophia was impatient. Therefore, she decided to conceive using artificial insemination. Sophia went alone to a local sperm bank. She looked at hundreds of files. Finally, she found a donor who had physical characteristics that were similar to William's. Without his knowledge, Sophia filled out and signed the necessary consent forms. Sophia conceived a child as a result of the artificial insemination with the donor sperm. Since he did not consent to the artificial insemination procedure, William was not legally recognized as the child's father. Although William and Sophia were married, because he did not consent to Sophia's insemination, his paternity was not presumed. The couple's marital status did not lead to an establishment of paternity.

The Fertile Man

On the second day of kindergarten, Jennifer punched Matthew in the eye. After that, they were inseparable. Over the years, they supported each other through broken bones, broken hearts, and broken families. At the age of thirty-two, Jennifer had one ovary removed and discovered that she had fibroid tumors growing inside her uterus. Jennifer's burning desire to have a baby felt like an impossible dream. As always, Jennifer turned to her best friend, Matthew, for help. Matthew thought of Jennifer as a sister, so he could not imagine the two of them having sexual intercourse. Besides, Matthew was happily married with two beautiful children. After discussing it with his wife, Matthew agreed to donate his sperm so that Jennifer could conceive a child. Jennifer gave birth to a baby girl. On the birth certificate, she listed the father as unknown. Even though Matthew supplied the sperm used to create the child, he was not legally recognized as the father of the child. Despite the biological relationship between Matthew and the child, in the majority of the states, Matthew's paternity could never be established.

Sexual intercourse is intimate. It is natural. Society and the law are comfortable with passionate sex being the process through which children are conceived. Children conceived in that manner are considered to be normal because of the circumstances of their conception. Normality entitles those children to special rights and privileges. The legal treatment of children has been colored by that societal perception. As a consequence, children of passion are considered to be the innocent players in the sex games men and women play. That innocence entitles those children to certain legal protections. Regardless of whether children of passion are conceived inside or outside of wedlock, the law provides ways for them to have legal fathers. The men do not have to consent or give permission to have their paternity established. In fact, the lack of a genetic connection between the man and the child may not be a deterrent to the paternity adjudication. Marital children are treated as special, not because they are conceived during the marriage, but because they are the result of passion. By the same token, non-marital children are not protected because society expects men to provide support for their biological children. They are protected because, if a man's sexual activities lead to the conception of a child, society wants him to take responsibility for the child.

With regard to the allocation of paternity, the law treats children conceived by artificial insemination differently from those children conceived by sexual intercourse. This book focuses upon the allocation of paternity between the husbands and partners of women who have been artificially inseminated using donor sperm and the men who donate the sperm to inseminate married and unmarried women. The book compares the manner in which the law adjudicates the paternity of children conceived naturally with the way the law allocates the paternity of children conceived artificially. The problem is that the paternity of children conceived as a result of artificial insemination is unclear. A two-tier system exists—one set of rules for children of passion and another set of rules for the children of science.

The husband of a woman who conceives artificially using donor sperm is legally recognized as the father of the resulting child only if he consents to the procedure. There is no presumption of paternity that results from the marriage. On the other hand, if a married woman becomes pregnant with another man's child as the result of sexual intercourse, her husband is presumed to be the father of the child. Some courts make it difficult to rebut the husband's paternity. The following is a typical case. A child is conceived and born into a marriage as the result of an extramarital affair. The woman's husband is presumed to be the father of the child, and he establishes a relationship with the child. The man with whom the woman had the affair suspects that he is the child's biological father. Thus, he files an action to have his paternity adjudicated. The court will usually conclude that the biological father does not have standing to challenge the husband's paternity in order to preserve the stability of the marriage and to protect the child from a disruptive and unnecessary attack on the father-child relationship. The woman's husband did not have to consent to the affair in order for his paternity to be established by the marital presumption doctrine.

If a man donates sperm to an unmarried woman through sexual intercourse, he is legally responsible for the support of the child. By contrast, if a man donates his sperm to a sperm bank, and a woman is inseminated with it, the man is not legally obligated to provide support for the child. The public seems to find this differential treatment acceptable. For example, in the summer of 2009, when the media reported a story about a twenty-nine-year-old man who was unable to provide financial support for the twenty-one children whom he naturally conceived with eleven different women, the reaction was outrage. In comparison, the response to the story detailing the fact that Nadya Suleman conceived fourteen children using sperm donated by a man whom she knew was relatively mild. The public did not seem to expect that man to support the children financially.

According to one court, "'fatherhood' or 'paternity' is a legally, socially, and politically defined relationship, not a biological fact."[2] Therefore, courts rely on statutes enacted by legislatures in allocating paternal obligations. In other words, nature makes a man a dad; the law makes him a father. Parental determination establishes fundamental emotional, social, legal, and economic ties between parents and children. This book explores the manner in which the legal father-child relationship is created.

The artificial insemination process involves the injection of sperm near the woman's cervix.[3] The procedure may be done by a licensed physician in a medical facility or by a woman at home with a turkey baster.[4] Medically, there are three main types of artificial insemination.[5] The classification of the type of artificial insemination involved depends upon the source of the sperm inserted into the woman.[6] If the woman's husband contributes the sperm that is implanted, the process is called homologous insemination.[7] That type of insemination may also be referred to as artificial insemination by husband (AIH).[8] Initially, this was the only type of artificial insemination performed by doctors.[9] That type of artificial insemination is not the focus of this book.

More and more women are choosing to be inseminated with sperm donated by men with whom they do not have a relationship. There are several reasons for a woman to use donated sperm. A woman who is not in a relationship may want to conceive a child to beat her biological clock. At times, married women use donor sperm to conceive. In those instances, the woman's husband may have a medical condition that prevents him from being able to conceive a child. In others, even if the man is capable of impregnating his wife, he may have a genetic condition that he does not want to pass on to his children. Moreover, recent studies have shown that male fertility declines with age. Thus, a woman married to an older man may need to rely on donor sperm to conceive. The procedure involving the use of donor sperm is heterologous insemination (HI).[10] In some cases, a doctor may inseminate a woman with a mixture consisting of her husband's sperm and sperm from a donor. This process is called confused artificial insemination.[11] The focus of this book is upon the paternal obligations of the men involved in the artificial insemination process when the woman is inseminated with donor sperm.

Why Paternity Matters

For too long, the burden of parenthood has been placed on mothers. The expectation has always been that children are their responsibility. Now, though, the tide is turning. We are bombarded with media images of "deadbeat dads" who do not want to support their children. The days of permitting men to procreate with impunity have come to an end. During his campaign for president, Barack Obama stressed the importance of men taking responsibility for raising their children. On Father's Day of 2009, in an interview published in *Parade Magazine*, President Obama continued this theme, stating that "we need fathers to step up, to realize that their jobs do not end at conception; that what makes a man is not the ability to have a child but the courage to raise one."[12] Paternity matters to children, men, and society. Thus, state legislatures and courts should act to insure that children of science are afforded the same protections as children of passion.

The allocation of paternity impacts the financial, emotional, and physical health of children. Paternity is important because a child has an economic stake in knowing the identity of his or her legal father. In order for a child to have the right to receive financial support from a man, a legal father-child relationship must exist. A higher proportion of children living in poverty comes from homes where the only parent is a mother providing financial support. An adjudication of paternity opens up several avenues for the child to receive financial resources from his or her father. Once paternity is established, the child's father becomes legally obligated to support the child until the age of majority. Even if the father is able to provide only minimal financial support, his doing so will ease the burden on the child's mother and enable the child to have a better quality of life.

An adjudication of paternity survives the death of the man. That fact is important because the intestacy system favors children. If a man dies without a will, his children have the right to inherit his estate. A child will not be considered a child for inheritance purposes unless the court assigns paternity. The establishment of paternity identities the man's legal heirs. The classification as a legal heir makes the child eligible to receive other benefits through his or her father, including Social Security Survivors' Benefits and Veterans' Benefits. Moreover, the allocation of paternity impacts the child's standing to bring tort claims, like wrongful death actions, for the loss of his or her father.

Paternity is important because a child has an emotional and psychological stake in knowing the identity of his or her legal father. In reference to psychological development, Sigmund Freud stated, "I cannot think of any need in childhood as strong as the need for a father's protection."[13] Fathers serve as role models and are crucial to the emotional development of children. Boys need fathers to teach them how to be men; girls need fathers to teach them how to choose husbands. George Santayana stated, "A child educated only at school is an uneducated child."[14] I grew up in a two-parent family with a hard-working father. My father did not have a social life. When he was not at work, he was with my siblings and me. Growing up, I was the only one of my friends who had a father living inside the home. As a result, we were the only family on our street with a telephone and an automobile. I took having a father for granted. An experience I had with my niece changed my opinion about the need for a paternal parent.

My older sister is a free spirit. She does not let much bother her. She dances to her own beat. When I was almost a teenager, my sister left home to find herself, and returned home expecting her first child. There was no mention of the baby's father. During my niece's formative years, she was raised by my parents. She grew up in a house full of people who wanted to meet her every need. She was spoiled rotten. By all outward experiences, she had a great childhood. Nonetheless, twenty-two years later, my niece and I spent three hours on the Internet unsuccessfully searching for her father. Although my niece is a divorced mother of three children, every once in a while, she goes online looking for her paternal parent. Throughout her life, my niece has had father figures, including a grandfather, several uncles, and her mother's long-time boyfriend. The presence of those men has not served to fill the void caused by not knowing the identity of her biological father. Even though she is an adult, for my niece, paternity still matters.

Paternity is important because a child has a physical stake in knowing the identity of his or her father. For years, adopted children have sought to discover the identity of their birth parents. Recently, children conceived as the result of sperm taken from anonymous donors have attempted to find their biological fathers. The desire to discover the identity of one's father may be a practical one. As children get older, it is critical that they have the information necessary to create a complete medical history.[15] Hence, it is important for the child to be able to evaluate the medical history on his or her father's side. That information will enable the child to know if he or she may have a genetic predisposition towards certain conditions such as breast cancer. Furthermore, if the child needs an organ or bone marrow transplant, the pool of possible donors will double if the child knows the identity of his or her father.

The creation of a legal father-child relationship will identify the person obligated to provide for the child in the event that the child's mother dies or becomes incapacitated. The Anna Nicole Smith case provides a good illustration. A few months after she gave birth to a baby girl, Ms. Smith died of an accidental drug overdose. At the time of her death, Ms. Smith was estranged from her mother and her other family members. Since no one had been adjudicated as the child's legal father, no one had a legal duty to take care of the child. In this situation, several men came forward claiming to be the child's father.[16] Nonetheless, things would have been different if no one had stepped forward acknowledging paternity.

As a matter of fact, Father's Day came about as the result of a motherless child. In 1909, Sonora Smart listened to a Mother's Day sermon. The moment was bittersweet to Sonora because her mother was deceased. While listening to the tribute to mothers, Sonora thought about all of the sacrifices her father, William Jackson Smart, made to raise her. As a result, Sonora came up with the idea of setting aside a day to honor fathers. Since her father's birthday was in June, Sonora chose that month to have the celebration. In 1924, President Calvin Coolidge proclaimed the third Sunday in June to be Father's Day. In 1972, President Nixon established a permanent national observance of Father's Day to be held on that date.[17]

Establishment of the father-child relationship benefits a man legally, emotionally, and economically. The growth of the Fathers' Rights Movement and the rise in the number of "unwed fathers"[18] cases indicate that men want to parent their children.[19] An adjudication of paternity protects a man's legal right to parent his child. In 2004, Bruna Goldman took her son, Sean, on a two-week vacation to her native Brazil. While in Brazil, Bruna divorced David Goldman, Sean's biological father, and married a Brazilian lawyer. Bruna later died of complications while giving birth to her second child. For years, Sean's stepfather refused to return him to Goldman. Eventually, Goldman was successful in regaining custody of his child.[20] Goldman's fight was a difficult one. However, if there was any doubt about his paternity, Goldman would have had no hope of bringing his son home from a foreign country.

A man has an emotional stake in being declared the legal father of his biological child. Allocation of paternity is important to men because most men view fatherhood as a blessing. My father was an over-the-road truck driver. He spent most of his life wearing coveralls. Yet, every Father's Day, my siblings and I pooled our money and bought him a tie. He smiled, acted excited, and placed the tie in his dresser drawer. The ritual was repeated every Father's Day for years. As we got older, my siblings and I got more creative, but not more practical, with my father's gifts. Even though we were living in the warmth of the South, at least one of my siblings gave my dad wool gloves every Christmas. Those gloves joined the hats, ties, and socks in the dresser drawer. My father never threw out or gave away any of the gifts he received from his children. He often said that the source of his greatest joy was being a dad.

We often think of paternity tests as a means of forcing a man to pay child support. Sometimes a determination of paternity helps a man by preventing him from being held financially responsible for a child who is not his biologically. Frank Hatley was in a relationship with Essie Lee Morrison. In 1987, Ms. Morrison gave birth to a child and told Mr. Hatley that he was the father. Instead of having a paternity test performed, Mr. Hatley took Ms. Morrison at her word. The couple split up shortly after the child was born. In 1989, Ms. Morrison started receiving public assistance for the child. As a result, the Georgia Department of Human Resources sought reimbursement from Mr. Hatley. Mr. Hatley paid approximately $9,500 towards his financial obligation. When DNA tests were finally conducted in 2000, Mr. Hatley discovered that he was not the father of the child. Thus, as of 2001, Mr. Hatley did not have a duty to provide financial support for the child. Nonetheless, since the father-child relationship had been established, the superior court determined that Mr. Hatley was legally responsible for $16,000 in back payments that started accruing in 1989. After paying $6,000, Mr. Hatley was laid off from his job. In June of 2008, Mr. Hatley was incarcerated for not meeting his financial obligation to the Department of Human Resources. Mr. Hatley remained in jail for over a year for failing to pay child support for a child who was not his biologically.[21] If he had insisted on a paternity test from the beginning, Mr. Hatley might have avoided making unnecessary child-support payments and losing more than a year of his freedom. Stories like this one have led to the paternity fraud movement. Men are going to court to get their paternity disestablished because of alleged fraud on the part of women.

Allocation of paternity benefits society in several ways. President Herbert Hoover correctly asserted that "Children are our most valuable natural resource."[22] Commentators, including Hillary Clinton, have said that it takes a village to raise a child. Nonetheless, children are raised by their parents. Fathers and mothers teach children morals and values so that they do not become menaces to society. Children without fathers are more likely to be at risk. They are more likely to drop out of school, to do drugs, and to commit violent crimes.[23] Fatherless children often live in poverty and continue the cycle of poverty by having children whom they cannot support.[24] The percentage of children in single-parent homes who have children out of wedlock is higher than those of children who grow up in two-parent homes.[25] These adverse circumstances have a detrimental impact on society.

An adjudication of paternity encourages judicial economy. Establishment of the father-child relationship makes it clear who is responsible for making decisions with respect to the child and who is legally responsible for caring for the child. After Michael Jackson's death, there was speculation about the identity of the biological father of his two children. Some persons claimed the children were conceived by artificial insemination using the sperm of Mr. Jackson's dermatologist. Since Mr. Jackson and Ms. Rowe were married when the children were conceived, the speculation never led to a legal dispute. The circumstance of the children's birth was not relevant to Mr. Jackson's paternity. If the children resulted from a sexual relationship between Ms. Rowe and the dermatologist, the children were still Mr. Jackson's legal children because of the marital presumption. Likewise, if the children were conceived by artificial insemination as Ms. Rowe claims, given that Mr. Jackson consented to the artificial insemination of his wife with donor sperm, Mr. Jackson was the legal father of the children.

Children of Passion (Papa's Baby)

Part I of this book examines the mechanisms that are in place to ensure that children conceived by sexual intercourse have legal fathers. The marital presumption makes a man responsible for a child his wife conceives during their marriage. The fact that the conception occurred using another man's sperm may not negate the woman husband's status as the child's legal father. The majority of states have statutes that set forth the conditions that must be satisfied in order for a man to be recognized as the legal father of a child he conceives with an unmarried woman.

In view of these considerations, chapter 1 deals with the paternity of the cuckolded husband. It evaluates situations where a wife has an affair with another man and gets pregnant with his child. The paternity of the woman's husband is usually determined using the marital presumption. This chapter will provide an historical overview of the marital presumption doctrine. Historically, the husband of the woman was considered to be the legal father of all children conceived during the marriage. The man who donated the sperm by having sex with the married woman had no standing to challenge her husband's paternity. The husband could rebut the presumption of paternity by demanding a test proving that he was not the biological father of the child. This chapter will also discuss changes to the marital presumption doctrine. Initially, it was difficult for the woman's husband to rebut the presumption of paternity because he was permitted to challenge his paternity only under very limited circumstances. Eventually, the courts relaxed the evidentiary rules, and the woman, her husband, and the biological father were allowed to challenge the husband' paternity. Recently, the pendulum has swung and some jurisdictions are again making it hard to challenge the husband's paternity. In those jurisdictions, the traditional presumption rule has been replaced with the "best interests of the child" marital presumption. Under this rule, the husband can rebut the presumption only if it is in the best interests of the child to do so.

Chapter 2 focuses upon the paternity of the fornicating man. This is a man who fathers a child without being married to the child's mother. Although this man had sexual intercourse with the mother of his child, he is little more than a sperm donor. In most cases, the only difference between him and a man who donates sperm at a sperm bank is the method used to insert the sperm into the woman's body. Historically, a child born out of wedlock was considered to be the child of no one, so the sperm donor who donated his sperm by having sex with the woman was not legally recognized as the child's father. Under current statutes, a man who conceives a child out of wedlock is the legal father if a paternity test proves he is the biological father. In child-support cases, the man must provide child support if the child satisfies the requirements of the state's paternity statute. With regard to inheritance, the child is eligible to be recognized as the heir of the man if the child meets specific statutory requirements.

Children of Science (Papa's Maybe)

Part II of this book analyzes the legislative and judicial responses to the existence of children conceived using the science of artificial insemination. In a situation where her husband is unable to conceive, a woman may turn to a donor for help to become a mother. Once a married woman conceives a child using the sperm of a man who is not her husband, the court must determine how to allocate paternity. The actions of the husband and the statutory mandates will impact the court's decision. The use of donor sperm within marriage is decreasing because of the advances in reproductive technology. Nonetheless, that reduction does not make the need to address the paternity of husbands in artificial insemination arrangements obsolete. First, from a medical perspective, understanding of the causes of male infertility has expanded.[26] In addition, some causes of male infertility, such as those related to genetic problems or to illness, can never be eliminated. Hence, married couples will continue to conceive using artificial insemination. Second, from a legal perspective, the majority of artificial insemination statutes apply exclusively to married couples. Therefore, courts are going to have to continue to address paternity issues in the context of marriage. The number of women choosing to have a child without waiting to meet "Mr. Right" has increased. Single women who desire to have children on their own utilize donor sperm to conceive. Likewise, women in same-sex relationships rely on donor sperm to have children. Consequently the parental status of the sperm donor must be resolved.

Chapter 3 develops the theme by discussing the paternity of the nonconsenting husband in situations where the wife uses the sperm of a donor to conceive a child. The paternity of the woman's husband is determined by focusing on his actions. In the majority of jurisdictions, if a man does not consent to the artificial insemination of his wife using another man's sperm, he is not the legal father of the resulting child. Most statutes require that the husband's consent be in writing. However, some courts and legislatures have stated that the man's consent may be implied by his actions. A few statutes presume that the woman's husband is the legal father of the child even if he does not consent to the artificial insemination.

Chapter 4 considers the paternity of the fertile man who donates sperm so that an unmarried woman can conceive his child. The donor may be someone whom the woman knows or someone who makes a contribution to a sperm bank. Under most state statutes, the sperm donor is never acknowledged as the legal child of the father. The statutes do not make a distinction between known and anonymous sperm donors. However, in some states, the sperm donor may agree to be a father to the child. Courts will usually recognize these agreements. A sperm donor may also be recognized as the legal father of the child if he does not comply with the state's artificial insemination statute. States without statutes tend to treat known sperm donors differently from anonymous sperm donors. While anonymous sperm donors are generally protected from parental obligations, at least one court has recognized a known sperm donor as the legal father of the children created using his genetic material.

Redefining the Family

A court recently observed, "We have long recognized that there are three ways by which a person may become a parent: conception, adoption or pursuant to the artificial insemination statutes."[27] In some situations, the above statement is inaccurate. There is a saying that children belong to the people who love them, and at least one legislature developed the point as follows:

1. The best interests of a child are promoted by having persons in the child's life who manifest a deep concern for the child's growth and development;
2. The best interests of a child are promoted when a child has as many persons loving and caring for the child as possible; and

3. The best interests of a child are promoted when the child is part of a loving, supportive, and stable family, whether that family is a nuclear, extended, split, blended, single-parent, adoptive, or foster family.[28]

These points highlight two important truths about children and paternity. The first is that families come in numerous different configurations. Therefore, courts should also understand that the manner in which paternity is allocated may be impacted by the status of the child involved in the case. Further, in adjudicating paternity, courts should give a broad definition to "fatherhood." The second truth is that courts must make decisions regarding paternity relying on what is in the best interests of the child. While the issue of the "best interests of the child" will be examined in Part IV of the book, in Part III, on "Redefining the Family," the two chapters address the first concern by examining the expanding definition of "child" and the evolving definition of "parent."

Historically, a family consisted of a man, a woman, and their biological or adoptive children. In the past few decades, the composition of the family has changed dramatically. In light of that evolution, legislatures and courts have to restructure the manner in which the law addresses the needs of children living in non-traditional families.

Chapter 5 discusses the different classes of children and indicates the way their legal treatment has been influenced by the way they are viewed by society. The United States was founded on Christian principles.[29] The majority of persons holding leadership roles in this country still profess to be Christians. Those persons are influenced by their own value systems and the beliefs of the people they must satisfy in order to remain in office. In 2010, an example of the influence morality can have on legal decision-making occurred in Iowa. In that state, three Iowa Supreme Court justices who had run unopposed were voted out of office because they helped to make same-sex marriage legal in the state.[30] This incident shows that members of both the legislative and judicial branches have to be mindful of the public's opinion about certain behaviors. As a result, the legal protections afforded to specific classes of children often correspond to society's views about the manner in which they are conceived. This is important with regard to children of science because understanding these social views helps to predict the manner in which the law may allocate the paternity of the men involved in their conception.

Chapter 6 enumerates the different ways fatherhood can be defined. Typically, the man who has a genetic link to the child is adjudicated as the child's legal father. Nonetheless, in situations involving children conceived by artificial insemination, genetics or biology may not be the optimal way to allocate paternity. Thus, this chapter discusses several theories of fatherhood that have been put forth by courts, legal commentators, and child advocates.

Rethinking Paternity Adjudication in the Best Interests of the Child

Part IV of this book considers the welfare of the child conceived by artificial insemination. It examines the ways in which allocating the paternity of husbands and sperm donors impact those children. It also sets forth the components that the courts must evaluate in order to promote the best interests of the artificially conceived children. In addition, this part of the book details my proposals for changing the mechanisms currently in place for allocating paternity and advocates new approaches to paternity adjudication in cases involving children of science. In the process, I am also mindful of the manner in which same-sex couples are disadvantaged by the current system used to determine the paternity of artificially conceived children. The statutory regimes in most states are designed to respond to situations involving married couples and/or men and women. In addressing the resulting disparity, I indicate that the court's goal when adjudicating paternity is not strictly to designate the child's father, but to ensure that the child has two legal parents. Thus, the child's paternal parent may be a man or a woman. In cases dealing with artificial insemination, courts should make sure that the adult with no biological connection to the child is not treated like a stranger or non-parent. If the circumstances make it appropriate, that person should be recognized as the child's paternal parent.

Hence, chapter 7 sets forth the standard I think courts should use when evaluating whether an adjudication of paternity will serve the best interests of the child. I derived the standard by relying on several legal, economic, and sociological theories. When adopting a "best interests of the child" standard, my focus is mostly upon the economic support the child receives from having a father. Courts are unable to force men to nurture their children. Nonetheless, that fact has not prevented courts from requiring men who conceive children by sexual intercourse to provide financial support for those children. The same should be true with regard to men who consent and/or contribute to the conception of children using artificial insemination. Ultimately, though, my proposal goes further than just economics. I think that it is in the best interests of the child for courts to recognize and respect the relationships that children have developed with the adults in their lives.

Chapter 8 analyzes why equal treatment is necessary in order to promote the best interests of the artificially conceived child. If a woman conceives a child through sexual intercourse during her marriage, her husband is presumed to be the child's father.[31] With regard to children conceived by artificial insemination,[32] if the husband of the woman who conceives using sperm donated by another man[33] does not consent to the process, he is not legally responsible for the resulting child.[34] In order to protect the resulting child, courts have interpreted consent broadly to include both written and non-written consent.[35] When a problem occurs, it is usually when the couple divorces or separates. Thus, the legal status of the child depends upon the relationship between the parents. This may disadvantage a child conceived as the result of artificial insemination. If a child is conceived by sexual intercourse and the child's parents divorce or separate, the child retains the status of a child of the marriage. That status ensures that the child has the legal right to financial support from two legal parents. On the other hand, if the woman's husband is successfully able to argue that he did not consent to his wife's artificial insemination, he may be released from further legal obligations pertaining to the child. As a result, the artificially conceived child may be deemed to be legally fatherless. When a married woman conceives using donor sperm, even if she knows the donor, the man has no legal responsibility for the child. The child is not given the opportunity to receive support from his or her biological father.

I am proposing that the definition of paternity be expanded to include a man or woman who may not be genetically related to the artificially conceived child.[36] In other words, I am suggesting that biology and/or genetics not be the sole indicator of paternity. Courts should apply a series of tests or standards when adjudicating paternity. If the person's paternity can be established under one or more of those tests or standards, he or she should be recognized as the child's paternal parent. As a consequence, that person would be financially obligated to support the child and should be entitled to all of the benefits of the parent-child relationship. This approach is not radical because courts have engaged in a similar analysis in order to decide maternity in cases involving children created as the result of surrogacy arrangements.[37]

Chapter 8 also discusses the ways courts should allocate paternity to the adults involved in the artificial insemination process. The first part of the chapter deals with the paternity of the husbands or partners of women who are inseminated using donor sperm. In order to make sure that the artificially conceived child receives financial support from at least two persons, the court should prevent the husband or partner of the inseminated woman from denying paternity by recognizing that paternity can be established based upon a variety of criteria. The first thing the courts should do is to focus upon the contributions the inseminated woman's husband or partner made to ensure the child's conception. The level of the person's contribution should determine whether or not he or she should be held responsible for the resulting child. It is similar to a "but-for" analysis in torts. If, but for the woman's husband or partner's contributions, the child would not have been conceived, the person should be adjudicated as the child's legal parent based upon consent or presumption.

In order to protect the emotional and physical health of the artificially conceived child, the courts should recognize paternity by estoppel, psychology, and function. Courts applying the estoppel theory should examine the actions of the non-consenting husband or partner prior to the conception and birth of the child. If the husband or partner acted in such a way that a reasonable person would conclude that he or she consented to the artificial insemination and intended to parent the resulting child, he or she should be prevented from denying paternity.[38] Likewise, under those circumstances, the biological mother of the child should be estopped from claiming that her non-consenting husband or partner is not the parent of her artificially conceived child.[39] The court should apply the traditional estoppel principles— representation, reliance, and detriment.[40] Paternity by estoppel should result if the husband or partner, through word or deed, represented the intent to parent the artificially conceived child, the woman permitted herself to be inseminated in reasonable reliance upon that representation, and the woman and/or child will be harmed if the husband is not adjudicated the father of the child. The person seeking to establish paternity by estoppel should have the burden of proving these elements. In deciding whether or not to adjudicate the paternity of the woman's husband or partner based on psychology, function, or economics, the court should consider the actions the parties took after the birth or conception of the child.

The second part of the chapter explores the standards the courts should use when adjudicating the paternity of the known sperm donor. The first way to deem the sperm donor as the legal father is to rely upon biology. Although biology should not be the sole indicator of paternity, it should not be completely discounted. When a man donates sperm to a woman he knows by sexual intercourse, he is legally responsible for the child even if he did not intend to father a child. In some cases, a man may be tricked into conceiving a child naturally. Indeed, there have been suits involving men who accused women of using sperm obtained during oral sex to become pregnant. In one such case, the man argued that since he did not have sexual intercourse with the woman, he should not be held responsible for the child.[41] Nonetheless, the "pregnancy by deception" allegation typically does not absolve the man of his legal duty to the child. The same rationale should be applied to a man who donates his sperm to a woman he knows by ejaculating into a container. Another way a known sperm donor may be adjudicated the child's father is by function or psychology. Under that theory, the focus is upon the actions the man takes after the child is born. If the sperm donor attempts to emulate a father by taking the child into his home, providing child support, and holding the child out as his child, he is the legal father of the child because he functions as the father. This theory would permit the court to recognize the father-child relationship created by function or emotional attachment.

George Foreman named all of his children George because he felt that they were living reflections of him. Nelson Mandela, the former president of South Africa, said, "There can be no keener revelation of a society's soul than the way in which it treats its children." All children deserve to be protected and supported. Regardless of the circumstances of their births, children have the same needs and vulnerabilities. The adults involved in the conception of their children should bear the burden of providing for their emotional, social, and economic needs. The law is ill equipped to force parents to develop relationships with their child. Nonetheless, the makers and enforcers of the law have an obligation to make sure that all children, including those conceived as the result of artificial insemination, have adults who are responsible for supporting them financially. The first step in that process is to adjudicate the paternity of the persons involved in the process.

Children of Passion (Papa's Baby)

The Cuckolded Man

The media seem to be eager to expose cheating men. Sandra Bullock received more press for being the latest victim of a cheating husband than she did for winning her first Academy Award. In addition to enduring the pain of her husband's infidelity, Elin Woods was forced to witness the parade of women who claimed to have had sex with him. Instead of being permitted to deal with her terminal cancer and to raise her small children in peace, Elizabeth Edwards had to endure the media's in-depth analysis of her husband's extramarital affair with a woman who gave birth to his child. It is unclear why the public is so fascinated with stories about unfaithful public figures. Given the fact that cheating appears to be commonplace among public figures, is it really news? Media coverage also makes it seem like the only persons cheating are men.

Women are unfaithful, too, and the consequences for their children may be more severe. For example, John Edwards' affair resulted in the conception of a child. That child's existence did not have any impact on Elizabeth Edwards' legal rights. However, if the tables were turned, the outcome would have been different. Had Elizabeth conceived a child with another man, her extramarital child would have been presumed to be John's legal child. The saga of the cheating spouse would have taken on a new dimension. His cheating heart *might* tell on him, but her cheating body *would definitely* tell on her. A cheating woman might be forced to explain why she gave birth to a child that bore no resemblance to her husband. In some cultures, an admission of infidelity can cause the woman to be ostracized or physically harmed. Thus, a woman may not be so eager to disclaim her husband as the father of her child. A woman who regrets her affair may desire to keep her marriage intact. The existence of the marital presumption of paternity may help the woman to achieve that goal.

Despite the media's portrayal to the contrary, the cuckolded man is not an oddity. Cheating is not a sport that only men play. Women are perfectly capable of taking off their wedding rings and forgetting their wedding vows.

For instance, country singer LeAnn Rimes was caught on camera kissing actor Eddie Cibrian, who was not her husband. Sometimes those extramarital affairs may lead to the birth of a child. On a daily basis, hundreds of men file actions seeking to have their paternity revoked. Organizations like Citizens Against Paternity Fraud are made up mostly of men who claim they were duped into paying child support for children fathered by other men. Members of those groups claim that, as a matter of equity, "misrepresenting moms" should get as much negative publicity as "deadbeat dads." Once a man is presumed to be the father of a child and develops a relationship with him or her, there is no going back. Even if the man does not establish a relationship with the child, it may not be easy for him to have the status of legal father removed. A paternity adjudication places obligations on him. A legal father is financially responsible for the child until the child reaches the age of majority. In some cases, a man may be permanently responsible for a child who has a disability. In light of the heavy burden that a legal father has to bear, it is important that the court gets the matter of paternity and responsibility right. The court's task may be complicated by a woman who engages in intentional deception.

In most cases, marriage trumps biology when it comes to paternity. Courts have concluded that a child cannot have two legal fathers, and courts generally conclude that paternity resides with the woman's husband, rather than with the man who donated the sperm used to conceive the child by having sex with the man's wife. A woman's husband is responsible for all children conceived during the marriage. That man's paternity is usually determined by legal presumption. The law presumes that a man is the father of any child whom his wife conceives during the course of the marriage. That presumption indicates the value that the law places on marriage, which, in turn, may account for the special treatment received by marital children. Those children are automatically given a legal father. If he chooses not to rebut or is prevented from rebutting the presumption, the woman's husband is the child's father. Moreover, in a case where the husband is able to successfully rebut the marital presumption, the court usually adjudicates the paternity of the biological father. In any case, the child of the marriage has a legal father.

Children born in wedlock have always received special treatment. That special treatment comes from the law and society's affinity for marriage. Marital children benefit as result of the union between the woman and her husband. The law has taken steps to insure that children born during the course of the marriage do not become legally fatherless. As long as the child is conceived by "natural" means, the child is entitled to have a legal father. The primary candidate for the job is the husband of the child's mother. The husband is not given a pass because he lacks a biological connection to the child. His obligation to financially support the children his wife conceives stems from his decision to say, "I do." In all jurisdictions, as a result of the adjudication of paternity, the husband is obligated to support the child financially. The law cannot force the man to love and bond with the child. Nonetheless, the law can make the man help take care of the child's basic needs by providing food, clothing, and shelter.

Children and Marriage

Marriage is not simply a union between two individuals. It is an institution based upon religion and sanctioned by the state. Marriage has been recognized as a legal contract, a moral commitment, and a potential life-long partnership. Any one of these classifications of marriage may be used to justify the special treatment given to marital children. Children who are products of legal marriage do not lose their presumptive fathers simply because their mothers are unfaithful. The nature of the marital relationship supports the application of the presumption of paternity.

A man and a woman form a marriage contract by agreeing to create an association. Initially, marriage was considered to be a religious ritual. From a societal perspective, marriage gradually became known as a secular, civil arrangement. Over the years, courts have embraced the principle of marriage as a legal contact. Marriage is now recognized as a true contract in which the parties agree to be bound to one another and to accept the legal obligation to remain together. The mutual exchange of promises through the reciting of the wedding vows serves as legally sufficient consideration and establishes the contract. That was the position taken by the court in *In re Neiderhiser's Estate*,[1] a Pennsylvania case. On August 16, 1976, Robert Neiderhiser and Naomi Nicely obtained a marriage license.[2] A month later, the couple, along with their families and friends, assembled at the Fort Palmer United Presbyterian Church to get married.[3] Reverend Williams Jacobs performed the wedding ceremony.[4] The couple exchanged vows, and Robert placed a ring on Naomi's fourth finger. Then, Robert repeated, "'With this ring I thee wed, in the name of the Father, and of the son, and of the Holy Spirit. Amen.'"[5] Afterwards, Robert fell to the floor. A few moments after Reverend Jacobs pronounced the couple to be husband and wife, Robert died.[6] Three days later, Reverend Jacobs filed the license in the orphan's court. The license had been signed by the couple and attested by the Register of Wills.[7] The court had to decide whether or not to remove Naomi as executor of Robert's estate.[8]

In addressing the issue, the court focused upon the validity of the marriage.[9] The court determined that a valid marriage ceremony was one that contained words that were "sufficient to evidence a present contract."[10] Moreover, the court reasoned that the marriage contract can be formed and proven like any other contract.[11] In this case, the court held that since Robert died after the couple had already exchanged promises, the contract of marriage was established.[12] The death of one of the parties did not negate the contract that made Naomi Robert's legal wife. As Robert's widow, Naomi was entitled to receive letters of administration to serve as executor of his estate.[13]

Some courts have held that there are three parties to the civil contract of marriage: the woman, the man, and the state. Some persons argue that a fourth party should be added to that list: the child. As a product of the marriage, the child should be considered a party to the contract. If the child is characterized as a third-party beneficiary of the marital contract, the child is entitled to the benefits of that contract. Those benefits may include the right to be identified as a legitimate child. The only way for the child to be considered legitimate is if his or her mother's husband is adjudicated to be the child's legal father. The application of the marital presumption of paternity will enable the child to receive that benefit. The status as a legitimate marital child will entitle the child to financial support and other benefits. Courts have expanded the third- party beneficiary theory to include heirs under a will. The potential heirs under a will may bring a cause of action against the attorney who prepared the will. In fact, heirs have been able to argue successfully that their status as third-party beneficiaries of the will give them standing to sue the drafting attorney.[14] Some persons in long-term relationships decide to get married only when they want to have children. Therefore, when they enter into the marriage contract, they intend for their children to have the benefit of that union. One of those benefits is financial support. A man who enters into a marriage contract is bound to provide for the children born during that union. If the child's mother breaches the contract by having an affair, the mother's actions should not be attributed to the child. Marriage is a contract between the man and the woman. The exchange of vows places certain obligations on both parties. Once the child is born during the marriage, the child becomes a third-party beneficiary of the marital contract. That status entitles the child to support from both his or her biological mother and his or her marital father. The man's paternity is established by the marriage, and cannot be terminated just because the marriage ends. The wife's breach of the marital contract may justify the dissolution of the marriage, but it does not warrant the termination of the father-child relationship. Although the man and the woman agree to split up, the child should not lose the support of both of parents. The child cannot do anything to prevent the destruction of the marriage. Consequently, the child of the marriage should not be penalized for the actions of his or her parents. This reasoning led the courts to remove the stigma of illegitimacy from non-marital children. Marital children deserve no less protection. As a result, courts should uphold the marital presumption of paternity to assure that the child has a legal father.

In addition to the secular aspect of marriage, marriage can have a religious component. By exchanging their vows before God, the man and the woman make a covenant. That covenant places moral obligations on them. Some persons think that marriage is more than a civil contract; it is a moral promise/covenant between a man, a woman, and God. This philosophy led some jurisdictions to adopt statutes permitting covenant marriages. In 1997, Louisiana became the first state to officially recognize marriage as a covenant.[15] Parties involved in a covenant marriage are bound by more than a legal obligation. They are bound by moral commitment. By marrying, the man and woman make a covenant between God and themselves. Part of that covenant is the agreement to protect their children from harm. That protection extends to protecting the children from illegitimacy and the emotional pain of being legally fatherless. The moral obligation to the children does not fall solely on the shoulders of the mother. The husband should not be permitted to walk away from his responsibility. When a woman breaks her covenant by cheating, her actions should not be permitted to negate the husband's moral duty to care for the child. The cuckolded husband is a victim of the unfaithful wife. However, the child is also a victim. In the law, when there are two innocent parties, equity mandates that the court protect the more vulnerable of the victims. Marriage, not the manner of conception, should protect the interests of the child.

In the commercial world, a partnership refers to a voluntary association between two persons engaged in a joint enterprise for profit. Beyond commerce, though, a broad definition of profit encompasses more than money. Generally speaking, a profit is a benefit. The persons involved in the partnership seek to improve their individual positions by joining forces. Given the nature of the union, marriage resembles a partnership. The man and the woman usually enter the partnership of marriage with hopes that the collaboration will improve their lives. They seek to profit, or benefit, from the existence of the marital partnership. The benefits of the marital partnership may be financial, emotional, and/or social. By getting married, the couple reduces expenses such as house payments by half. The reduction of living expenses is accompanied by a combining of assets. Thus, the average couple has more resources after the marriage. Since marriage is a partnership between the man and the woman, they both have fiduciary duties to one another. One of those duties is to provide financial support for one another. That was one of the underlying theories used to support the awarding of alimony.[16] Once a child is born into the partnership, the man and the woman have the obligation to support that child financially—an obligation that survives the dissolution of the partnership. When the child is born, the mother acts as the child's agent or representative. Thus, the mother has an obligation to make sure that the child's interests are protected. The woman's husband also owes a duty to the child because the child was born into the partnership. The dissolution of the partnership should not impact the paternal duty.

It does not matter how marriage is characterized with regard to the child's need for support. Paternity is established by the marital relationship because the child is the innocent party in the arrangement. The illicit actions of the mother should not negatively impact the child. Application of the marital presumption will help to protect the child from his or her mother's actions.

Marital Presumption

As a result of a common law rule established in 1823, if a woman was married to a man and a child was conceived during the marriage, the woman's husband was presumed to be the father of the child. As a result of the presumption, parties were prohibited from disputing the paternity of a married woman's children. Courts enforced the presumption for several reasons. The main one was the need to preserve the sanctity of marriage. Judges believed that a marriage could not survive the allegation that a woman had conceived a child with someone other than her husband. Permitting persons to disrupt marriages by accusing women of infidelity would severely damage the institution of marriage. Judges were also trying to protect families and courts from false assertions. Since the science necessary to perform genetic paternity tests did not exist, courts were forced to sort out "he-said, she-said" situations. For instance, if another man claimed to be the father of a married woman's child and she denied the accusation, the court had no clear-cut way to determine which party was telling the truth. Therefore, for the sake of judicial economy, courts relied upon the marital presumption to discourage persons from challenging the paternity of a pregnant woman's husband. Another justification for the marital presumption was the desire to shield children from being labeled as "bastards." If a woman's husband was not the father of her child, the child was classified as illegitimate. As a result of that classification, the child was forced to endure both legal and social hardships.

It could be argued that one of the first marital presumption cases occurred in biblical times. Christians believe that Jesus is the son of God. While she was married to Joseph, Mary gave birth to Jesus. Jesus was presumed to be Joseph's child. For instance, when Jesus returned to His home town to preach, the people referred to Him as the carpenter's son.[17] Since he was married to Mary at the time Jesus was born, Joseph was the presumed father. The fact that Joseph did not have sexual relations with Mary prior to Jesus' birth did not rebut that presumption.

The use of marriage to establish paternity is a long-standing tradition. The concept was derived from Roman civil law and adopted into English common law. A man's status as a father arose because he was married to the woman who gave birth to the child. It did not matter if the man was the dupe of an unfaithful wife. Under early English common law, a child who was conceived during the course of the marriage was presumed to be the legal child of the woman and her husband. According to the doctrine that was referred to as "Lord Mansfield's Rule," if a woman had a child while she was married, the child belonged to the man. Since the woman was considered to be the man's property, it made sense that the child would be treated in a similar manner. A man was not permitted to claim ownership of another man's land and/or livestock. Thus, the law sought to make sure that a man could not claim ownership of another man's child. Biology did not matter. All property a wife had, including her children, belonged to her husband. The underlying goal was not to protect the cheating wife. The law's purpose was to prevent a married man from being deprived of his human property. Consequently, the law made it difficult for a person to challenge the paternity of a woman's husband. In fact, the unfaithful woman was not even allowed to question her husband's paternity. As long as the child was born during the course of the marriage, the husband was presumed to be the child's biological father.

Historically, although the presumption was rebuttable, the law treated it as though it was irrebuttable. The presumption was reinforced through the use of strict evidentiary requirements. The only evidence that was sufficient to rebut the presumption was that it was impossible for the woman's husband to be the child's father. In order to prove that impossibility, the person attempting to rebut the presumption of paternity had to show that the man did not have access to his wife during the crucial period of conception. That lack of access could not be established by evidence that the man and the woman were estranged and not having sexual relations. The law demanded more. The person attempting to challenge the presumption of paternity had to prove that the man did not have access to his wife because he was "beyond the four seas" (outside of the jurisdiction of the king of England).[18] The only persons given standing to rebut the marital presumption were the wife, the husband, and the possible biological father. In order to protect the child, the law made it difficult to rebut the presumption. One court stated, "The presumption of legitimacy arising from birth during wedlock 'is not lightly to be repelled."[19] The court strictly enforced the marital presumption to protect the marriage and the child born therein.

By claiming that the woman's husband was not the child's father, the woman and/or her husband was asking the court to find that the child was illegitimate. Consequently, the child was not entitled to be financially supported by his presumed father. This was especially tragic for the child because married women had very few financial resources. Thus, the child of a woman struggled for basic necessities like food, clothing, and shelter. Moreover, the child was often ostracized by members of the community. The impact on the child was so adverse that one court declared: "[T]he law of England is clear, that the declarations of a father or mother, cannot be admitted to bastardize the issue born after marriage."[20] Courts in the United States adopted Lord Mansfield's Rule and made it difficult for the woman and/or her husband to prove that he was not the father of the child she conceived during the marriage.

While the marital presumption remained in place, it did come under attack. Eventually, in the early 1900s, courts relaxed the evidentiary rules and made it easier for the presumption to be rebutted. The high divorce rates in the country and the introduction of DNA technology contributed to the weakening of the marital presumption of paternity. Further, the removal of the legal consequences and the stigma of illegitimacy lessened the importance of the marital presumption of paternity. The frequency of divorce in this country frustrated one of the key purposes of the marital presumption of paternity. Covering up the actions of the unfaithful wife was no longer necessary to preserve marriages. If a woman had an affair that resulted in the conception of a child, that woman was likely to file for divorce so that she could start a life with the biological father of her child. That was an option because the law removed most of the obstacles to obtaining a divorce. Thus, a woman no longer had to remain in the marriage and hope that her husband would forgive her and accept the child. The marital presumption was not necessary to protect the child from poverty and the stigma of illegitimacy. Moreover, the advances in DNA technology made it possible for social service agencies to identity the biological father of the child. Thus, even if the man was not married to the child's mother, he had to support the child financially. Consequently, the woman's husband did not have to be available to act as a safety net for the child. In addition, as more and more persons had children without the benefit of marriage, society became more accepting of children who were born out of wedlock. In response, the law changed to treat non-marital children on par with marital children with regard to child support and other financial benefits.

The marital presumption of paternity is still good law. The doctrine has been codified in most jurisdictions. The following statute is typical of those enacted.

1. A man is presumed to be the natural father of a child if:

   (i) He and the child's natural mother are or have been married to each other and the child is born during the marriage, or within three hundred (300) days after the marriage is terminated by death, annulment, or divorce or after a decree of separation is entered by the Court.[21]

However, courts have relaxed the evidentiary rules in order to open up the possibility that the husband's paternity might be successfully challenged. Critics argue that the marital presumption is no longer necessary because it is not an effective tool to preserve marriages or to protect the child's best interests. If a man wants to divorce his unfaithful wife, making him legally responsible for the child that results from her infidelity is not going to prevent him from filing for divorce. Furthermore, a presumption that prevents the child from knowing the identity of his or her biological father may not be in the child's best interests. The law should not assist parents who choose to lie to a child about the identity of his or her father. It is in the child's best interest to know the identity of his or her biological father. Adopted children often seek to establish relationships with their biological parents. Despite arguments made by persons advocating the abolition of the marital presumption of paternity, courts have continued to apply the doctrine when it is appropriate. For instance, if a couple attempts to save their marriage, courts will apply the presumption to help preserve the marriage intact. In addition, courts apply the presumption when it is necessary to protect the child's best interests.

Preserving the Couple

Once marriage is formed, society has some interest in preserving it. It cannot be dissolved except by court action. One of the main justifications for the marital presumption of paternity was to preserve marriages. Thus, the courts did not want the woman's infidelity to become public knowledge. A man might ignore his suspicions and parent the child. Nonetheless, if the entire community became aware of the fact that the man was cuckolded, in order to save face, the man might abandon his wife and the child. Courts wanted to discourage that behavior by limiting the circumstances in which the paternity of the woman's husband could be questioned. Once the couple filed for divorce, there was no marriage to preserve. Thus, courts were more lenient when someone challenged the husband's paternity as a part of a divorce action. However, if the marriage was intact, courts made it more difficult to rebut the presumption.

Courts are serious about using the marital presumption to protect marriages. Even if a man suspects that his wife has gotten pregnant by another man, the couple has a chance of staying married if those suspicions are not confirmed. Thus, the court is reluctant to grant the "other man" a forum to air the dirty laundry of the affair. That is a concern when the legislatures and the courts have to decide whether or not to grant the child's potential biological father standing to rebut the paternity of the woman's husband. And, indeed, that is more of a concern than challenges by the man and/or his wife because, if either party of the marriage wants to rebut the husband's paternity, the marriage is probably already over or in serious trouble.

Some state legislatures went so far as to codify the proposition that a third party cannot challenge the paternity of a woman's husband if the marriage is still intact. The third party involved is usually the man claiming to be the child's biological father. Even when that person is permitted to challenge the paternity of the woman's husband, he is not successful if the marital unit is sound. In *Michael H. v. Gerald D.*,[22] the U.S. Supreme Court granted summary judgment in favor of the woman's husband in an action to establish paternity and to obtain visitation brought by a man who had engaged in an adulterous affair with the woman. The Court reasoned that it would sacrifice the parental rights of the alleged biological father in order to preserve the marriage intact. After the affair, the woman reunited with her husband. At the time the case came before the Court, the woman's husband had embraced the child as his own. The Court was not concerned about whether or not the biological father was ready, willing, and able to parent the child. The focus was upon protecting the integrity of the marriage. Another court has stated:

> The public policy in support of the presumption of paternity is the concern that marriages which function as family units should not be destroyed by disputes over the parentage of children conceived or born during the marriage. Third parties should not be allowed to attack the integrity of a functioning marital unit, and members of that unit should not be allowed to deny their identities as parents.[23]

Infidelity can cause heartbreak in a marriage. However, it does not have to signal the end of a marriage. Former President William Clinton's extramarital affair almost caused him his presidency, but it did not end his marriage. The Clintons decided to work through their problems and to fight to save their marriage. *Late Show* host David Letterman admitted to having affairs with several different female employees. In spite of Letterman's admission, his wife decided to remain in the marriage. Once a husband and wife decide to repair their marriage, they should be afforded the opportunity to do so. This is especially true if children are involved. If the man decides to forgive his unfaithful wife and accept the extramarital child as his own, the family should be permitted to live in peace. The appearance of a man claiming to be the child's biological father may ruin any chance the couple has of saving the marriage. The law seeks to reduce the possibility of that happening. According to some courts, if the couple remains married after the woman conceives a child as the result of an extramarital affair, the presumption of paternity is irrebuttable. The *Rodney F.*[24] case illustrates that position.

Karen M. was unhappy in her marriage, so she filed for divorce in May of 1991. In February of 1992, Karen M. had a change of heart and had the divorce action dismissed. A month later, Karen M. re-filed the dissolution action. During the course of her troubled marriage, Karen M. had an affair with Rodney F., one of her coworkers. In order to carry on their affair, Karen M. and Rodney F. rented a house together. The couple decided to end their affair and just be friends in July of 1992. Unfortunately, at that time, Karen M. was already pregnant. In September of 1992, Karen M. told her husband about the affair and informed him that she was pregnant. A few days later, she also told Robert F. about her condition. In response, Robert F. indicated that he did not care that Karen M. might be carrying his child. After the baby was born in March of 1993, Karen M. and her husband acted as parents to the child. Initially, Robert F. did not have any contact with the child.

When the baby was less than a month old, however, Robert F. filed a paternity action. He requested joint legal and physical custody of the child. Karen M. answered Robert F.'s petition by alleging that he was not the biological father of her child and asserting that her husband should be presumed to be the child's legal father. Robert F. filed a motion asking the court to order blood tests to prove his paternity and to give him visitation rights. In opposition to the motion, Karen M. argued that Robert F. was not the presumed father of the child, so he was not entitled to have blood tests conducted. The trial court ordered that blood tests be performed on Robert F. and the baby, but denied Robert F.'s motion for visitation. The blood tests indicated that Robert F. was the child's biological father. Afterwards, Robert F. made another motion for visitation. Relying on the marital presumption of paternity, the trial court denied Robert F.'s request for visitation. The trial court reasoned that, since Karen M. was living with her husband during the child's conception and he was not impotent or sterile, the law presumed Karen M.'s husband to be the child's legal father.

The case went to trial to determine if Robert F. had any rights with regard to the child. At trial, Karen M. testified that she never stopped living with her husband. She admitted that she and Robert F. had rented a place together. Nevertheless, Karen M. claimed that she kept ninety percent of her possessions in the house that she shared with her husband. Moreover, Karen M. told the court that, in spite of her affair with Robert F., she never stopped having sexual intercourse with her husband. According to testimony given by Karen M.'s husband, he was capable of having regular sexual relations with his wife because he was not suffering from sterility or impotency. Karen M.'s husband also stated that he did not know about his wife's affair. After hearing all of the testimony, the trial court applied the marital presumption of paternity and held that Karen M.'s husband was the legal father of her child. The appellate court affirmed the trial court's decision.

Although there was proof indicating that Robert F. was the child's biological father, the court did not permit him to establish a relationship with the child. The emphasis was not on protecting Robert F.'s parental rights, but on preserving the marriage. Karen M.'s husband overlooked her indiscretion and accepted responsibility for the child. The court refused to let Robert F. deprive the child of his or her status as a marital child. Further, in order to protect the intact marriage, the court did not permit Robert F. to interfere with that union by adjudicating him to be the child's legal father. An adjudication of paternity would have given Robert F. legal rights with regard to the child. If Robert F. had been permitted to visit the child, his doing so might have caused tension in the marriage. It would not be easy for Karen M.'s husband to forget about her infidelity if the "other man" was constantly involved in their lives. To protect the marriage, the court severed Robert F.'s only tie to the family. If the couple had chosen to get a divorce, the outcome of the case may have been different.

Some marriages cannot survive infidelity. Once one of the parties in the marriage decides to stray, the other party might be reluctant to stay. If children are born as a result of the adulterous relationship, the man may not want to establish a relationship with the child. Since one of the main purposes of the marital presumption of paternity has been defeated, courts are more likely to allow the child's biological father to be adjudicated as the child's legal father. Some courts have held that the marital presumption does not apply in situations where there is no longer an intact family or marriage to preserve. In those types of cases, the court will permit the presumption to be challenged by the husband, wife, or a third party. That is the approach that the court took in *Vargo v. Schwartz*.[25]

Victoria and Kevin Vargo had a troubled marriage. They separated several times, but remained married. Victoria gave birth to two boys and two girls. Kevin was the father of one of Victoria's sons; Hugh Johnston was the father of her other one. The paternity of the little girls was unclear. In February 2004, after blood tests proved that Richard Schwartz was the biological father of her two daughters, Victoria sued him for child support for the two little girls. Richard argued that he was not liable for child support because the girls were born during the course of Victoria's marriage to Kevin. Relying on the marital presumption of paternity, Richard claimed that, as the presumptive father, Kevin was obligated to support the children financially and that Richard himself was therefore relieved of any obligation. The court ordered Richard to pay child support while the matter was being litigated. The hearing officer determined that the presumption of paternity should not be applied to the case because Victoria and Kevin no longer had an intact marriage. Although the couple had not gotten a divorce, once he learned of Victoria's deception with regard to the paternity of the girls, Kevin left the marriage. The trial court took direction from the hearing officer, and ordered Richard to pay child support for the girls. Richard appealed the decision.

The appellate court acknowledged that the marital presumption of paternity was "one of the strongest presumptions known to the law." In addition, the court stated that if the marriage were intact and the woman's husband had established a relationship with the girls, the presumption would bar anyone from challenging his paternity. In essence, the existence of an intact marriage would make the presumption irrebuttable. On the other hand, if there was no marriage to preserve, one of the primary reasons for the presumption no longer existed. Therefore, it did not make sense for the court to apply the doctrine. At the time of the trial, the couple was separated and Victoria had filed for divorce. As a result, the trial court correctly found that the marital relationship was broken and the couple had taken steps to end the marriage. The couple gave no indication that they planned to try to mend the marriage. Consequently, the appellate court affirmed the trial court's decision not to apply the presumption. Even if the presumption applied, it could be rebutted by the woman and/or her husband. Since blood tests established that Richard was the father of the girls, the paternity could have been easily rebutted. The marriage had already been destroyed by the woman's infidelity, so there was no need for the court to attempt to save it by applying the presumption of paternity. However, some courts are more concerned about the child's welfare than the adults' relationship.

Protecting the Child

In 1989, *The War of the Roses* was a popular movie. The movie depicted a couple whose marriage had fallen apart. Instead of peacefully getting a divorce, the couple engaged in an all-out war. In some ways the movie was a case of art imitating life. Divorce is often treated as a battle. In the caption of divorce petitions, the parties are listed as opponents. For instance, the petition lists the case as "Wife vs. Husband." However, the law does not consider the couple's child to be one of the combatants in the divorce. In fact, courts take steps to insure that the relationships between parents and children remain intact. The availability of the presumption of paternity enables courts to protect established father-child relationships. In order to protect and promote the interests of children, courts prevent the adults from bastardizing children who are born during marriages. The child's status is influenced by the condition of the parent's marriage. Thus, some courts have concluded that preserving the marriage encompasses preserving the father-child relationship. As a result, even when the marriage is not intact, the court may prevent someone from challenging the presumption of paternity in order to promote the best interests of the child. A series of Utah cases illustrate this perspective. In each case, the court had to decide whether to permit an individual to challenge the presumption of paternity.

In re J. W. F. (Schoolcraft)[26] established the test used to determine when challenges would be permitted to the marital presumption of paternity. In *Schoolcraft*, the court noted the two key public policies that were promoted by making it difficult to rebut the presumption of paternity. Those policies were "preserving the stability of marriage" and "protecting children from disruptive and unnecessary attacks upon their paternity."[27] The court gave the first policy reason a broad reading. Accordingly, the marriage included the man, the woman, and the child or children born during the marriage. Hence, preserving the marriage included protecting both the relationship between the man and the woman and the relationship between the man and the child or children. When it is not necessary to protect those relationships, the courts are likely to permit the man's paternity to be challenged.[28] In *Schoolcraft*, after the mother abandoned the child, the court allowed the guardian ad litem to rebut the mother's husband's paternity because the man and the woman separated before the child was born. Further, the woman's husband did not know the child existed until the baby was nine months old, so he had not developed a relationship with the child. The woman's husband tried to use the presumption of paternity to obtain custody of the child at the abandonment hearing.[29] The court reasoned that, since the child did not have a relationship with the man, the child would not be harmed if the man's paternity was rebutted.[30]

The court took the same position in an earlier case. In *Teece v. Teece*,[31] it held that the paternity of the woman's husband could be challenged.[32] The court's decision was based on the fact that the couple was living apart at the time of the child's conception. The man was in Canada, and his wife was in the United States.[33] In addition, the man denied all responsibility for his wife's child, so there was no father-child relationship to protect. When the child was born, the wife filed suit for divorce; therefore, the marriage was beyond repair.[34] Likewise, the *Lopes v. Lopes*[35] case involved a marriage that could not be salvaged. Nonetheless, with regard to the man's paternity, the case had a different outcome because of the husband's desire to establish a relationship with the child. Shannon became pregnant with another man's child. In response, during the pregnancy, Theodore, Shannon's husband, filed for divorce.[36] Shannon requested custody of the child and asked the court to order Theodore to pay child support and to award him visitation. Theodore agreed to pay child support and asked the court to adjudicate him as the child's legal father. In response, Shannon testified that Theodore was not the child's father, refused child support, and objected to Theodore's getting visitation. Theodore asked the court to rule that Shannon's testimony with regard to his paternity was inadmissible. The court granted his request. The court reasoned that spouses should not be permitted to provide testimony that would cause children born during the marriage to be classified as illegitimate.[37] Even though the couple had decided to get a divorce, the court determined that application of the marital presumption of paternity was necessary to protect the child. Theodore wanted to have a relationship with the child born during the marriage. In order to protect that potential relationship, the court refused to admit Shannon's testimony that Theodore was not the child's father.

In *Schoolcraft* and *Teece*, the courts permitted the marital presumption to be challenged because the marriages were over and the husbands had not established relationships with the extramarital children. In each of those cases, since the children did not have relationships with their mothers' husbands, the courts concluded that they would not have been adversely impacted if the courts permitted the father-child relationships to remain severed. However, the *Lopes* court focused upon the best interests of the child and not on the relationship of the man and the woman. Thus, the court refused to permit the wife to give testimony that would make the child illegitimate and prevent the child from having a legal father.[38] As a consequence, the child's mother could not rebut her husband's paternity.[39]

The *Pearson*[40] case involved a different situation. Kimberlee and Kelly Pearson were happily married until Kimberlee had an affair with Pete Thanos. As a result of the affair, Kimberlee conceived a child, Z.P. Instead of walking away, Kelly agreed to stay in the marriage and to parent the child. He named the child and signed his birth certificate.[41] Pete had only limited contact with the child because Kelly assumed the role of the child's father. When the baby was about nine months old, the couple decided to walk away from the marriage, although Kelly did continue to act as a parent to Z.P. and N.P., his biological child with Kimberlee. With Kelly out of the picture, Pete spent time with Kimberlee and Z.P. Z.P. was fifteen months old when Kimberlee filed for divorce. Pete attempted to intervene in the matter, so that he could be adjudicated as Z.P.'s father.[42] In light of Pete's limited earlier contact with Z.P., the district court commissioner recommended that he not be permitted to intervene. The commissioner was concerned that allowing Pete to establish his paternity would interfere with the father-son relationship that existed between Kelly and Z.P. After a hearing, the district court adjudicated Pete as Z.P.'s father and awarded him joint legal custody with Kimberlee. Kelly was awarded visitation rights. The Utah Court of Appeals reversed the district court. The appellate court concluded that Pete did not have standing to contest Kelly's presumption of paternity, so Kelly was still Z.P.'s legal father. Kelly's paternity was established by his marriage to Kimberlee.[43]

The Supreme Court of Utah affirmed the court of appeal's decision. While the state supreme court acknowledged that it had permitted the marital presumption to be challenged in several cases, the court opined that the Pearsons' situation was different because the couple was still married when the child was born. Moreover, Kimberlee had allowed Kelly to establish a parent-child relationship with Z.P. The extramarital affair and the pregnancy did not end the marriage. Before the baby was born, the couple decided to stay married and to let Kelly act as a father to the child. When the child was born, the couple's commitment to their marriage did not waver. Thus, the marriage remained intact and entitled to be legally protected from a third party seeking to challenge the paternity of the woman's husband. Since the marital relationship includes the man, the woman, and the child, it warrants protection even after one party files for divorce. Moreover, the court needed to bar a challenge to Kelly's paternity in order to protect the relationship he had established with the child because that relationship survived the divorce. As a matter of fairness, a man who commits to parent an extramarital child should not have his paternity attacked after he has become attached to the child.[44]

When the couple decided to end the marriage, there appeared to be no good reason to prevent a challenge to the husband's paternity. Another man's claim of paternity would not cause tension in the marriage because the marriage was already over. However, instead of just focusing on the marital relationship, the court emphasized the existence of an intact marital unit. That unit included the child. The court decided to expand the purpose of preserving intact marriages broadly to include preserving established parent-child relationships. In this case, the parent-child relationship survived the divorce because Kelly maintained a relationship with the child after the divorce. Thus, it was necessary to prevent Pete from rebutting Kelly's paternity in order to preserve that relationship.[45] Courts have also taken that approach to promote the best interests of the child.

In some jurisdictions, courts have elevated the goal of protecting the best interests of the child over the goal of preserving intact marriages. Therefore, in deciding whether or not to permit the man's paternity to be rebutted, the court focuses upon the welfare of the child and not on the condition of the marriage.[46] The doctrine is known as the "best interests of the child" marital presumption. Under this doctrine, a person will be permitted to challenge the husband's paternity only if doing so will promote the best interests of the child.[47] Currently, the main way to rebut the husband's paternity is to present DNA evidence that the husband is not the child's biological father. This DNA evidence may be obtained through blood tests of cheek swabs. DNA tests are inexpensive and accessible, so it is relatively easy to determine if the woman's husband is not the child's biological father. Nonetheless, courts have held that, if the presumption of paternity applies, blood test results do not matter until the presumption has been rebutted. In some cases, in order to protect the best interests of the child, courts have the authority to practice judicial ignorance. If the court decides the child will be hurt by the discovery that the woman's husband is not the child's biological father, the court has the power to refuse to order blood tests. Hence, the blood test evidence is deemed inadmissible even if blood tests have been conducted.[48] In making that decision, the court will consider several factors including the relationship between the child and the woman's husband, the availability of another male figure who is willing to assume the paternal role, and the child's relationship with that man.

Trina Wilson was unhappily married, and she sought comfort in the arms of Brett Evans.[49] While Trina was having an affair with Brett, she and her husband, Harris, started trying to have a baby. When Trina discovered that she was pregnant, she celebrated with her husband. The couple made plans to welcome the baby into their home. Trina also shared the news of her pregnancy with Brett. Assuming the baby was his, Brett helped Trina gets things ready for the baby's arrival.[50] Harris was out of town when the baby was born, so Trina went through the process alone. At that time, only Trina signed the birth certificate. After he took his wife and the baby home from the hospital, Harris signed an affidavit of parentage. Trina took steps to make each man believe he was the baby's father. She sent out one set of birth announcements claiming that Harris was the father, and another set asserting that Brett was the father. Brett saw the baby only until she was six weeks old and never paid child support. However, Trina encouraged Brett's parents to establish a relationship with the child. Harris developed a father-daughter relationship with the little girl.[51]

When the child was almost a year old, Brett filed a petition seeking visitation rights. At that time, Trina informed the circuit court that Brett was not the child's father. In response, Brett asked the court to order a paternity test. Trina asserted that since the child was born during the marriage, Harris was presumed to be the child's father.[52] The judge held that in order to rebut the marital presumption of paternity, Brett had to prove that a paternity test was in the child's best interests. According to the judge, Brett failed to meet his burden because he did not present enough evidence to show that he had a relationship with the child. Brett appealed the circuit court's decision by claiming that the court erred by considering the best interests of the child. Brett claimed that the court should have ordered the paternity test. He argued that the "best interests of the child" standard was relative only to the issue of visitation and not to that of paternity. In the alternative, Brett contended that in deciding whether or not to order the paternity test, the court should have weighed his interest in being a father against Trina's interest in preserving her marriage.[53]

The court concluded that the "best interests of the child" standard was correctly applied to determine if ordering a paternity test was warranted. Applying that standard, the court opined that it would not be in the child's best interests to rebut the paternity of her mother's husband.[54] The child was a part of an intact family. Further, the child had a relationship with her mother's husband. She considered Harris to be her father and depended upon him to take care of her financial, emotional, and health needs. As a result, the court refused to let Brett interfere with the father-child relationship that had been established between the child and her mother's husband.[55] The child would not be benefited by discovering that the man she called "dad" was not her father. The marriage between Trina and Harris adjudicated him to be the child's legal father. The court refused to let the existence of a potential biological father change that status.

When a man marries a woman, he expects her to respect their marriage vows. Hence, he takes her fidelity for granted. A woman's ability to get pregnant increases the likelihood that her husband will discover that he has been cuckolded. Once a woman conceives a child with a man who is not her husband, the legal paternity of the child becomes an issue. Instead of relying on biology to adjudicate paternity, courts apply the marital presumption of paternity to conclude that the cuckolded man is the child's legal father. Even if the man objects to parenting the child, the court will not permit the presumption to be rebutted if the child would be harmed by that decision. Thus, children of passion are entitled to legal support from two parents, including a man who does not have a biological connection to the child. This is true because a woman's husband is in a better position to monitor the woman's behavior than the innocent child. The cuckolded man is clearly a victim, and in many cases, the only recourse available to him is to divorce his cheating wife. Nonetheless, the fact that the man was cuckolded does not preclude him from having to support the child who is the evidence of his wife's infidelity. In order to seek revenge or to ease his pain, the man may walk away from his wife and into the arms of another woman. As the next chapter indicates, fornicating with that woman can lead the man into a whole new set of problems.

The Fornicating Man

A man whose fornicating ways result in the conception of a child is in essence a sperm donor. The man's biological connection to the child makes him the child's legal father. Paternity is adjudicated strictly on the basis of biology. The nature of the relationship between the man and the woman is not relevant. Historically, fornication did not lead to obligation. Over the course of the years, that changed. Currently, if a man "plays," he pays. A sperm donor who delivers his sperm by having sexual intercourse with a woman is the legal father of the resulting child. A man who impregnates his long-term girlfriend is treated no differently than the man who "knocks up" a woman in a one-night stand. Paternity requires the man to provide financial support for the child. Since the man engaged in a sexual relationship with the child's mother, the law and society expect him to be responsible for providing the child with the means of getting food, clothing, and shelter. When it comes to paternal obligations, both married and unmarried men are treated equally. This chapter examines the legal journey that took the fornicating man's children from "bastards" who were treated as if they were legally fatherless to "non-marital children" who have a right to receive financial support from their fathers.

My sister refers to her son as a "chick magnet." His big brown eyes and dimples have always been pleasing to the members of the opposite sex. The little girls in his kindergarten class actually paid him twenty-five cents for the privilege of sitting next to him. His looks and love of women are a family joke. A few years ago, my niece heard rumors that a young lady claimed that my nephew was the father of her child. When my niece repeated the gossip to my sister, my sister dismissed it. She was not ready to accept the fact that her twenty-year-old son had fathered a child. My niece was curious, so she tracked down the young woman. My niece used the camera on her cellular telephone to take a picture of the little boy. The next day, my niece emailed the picture to my sister. My sister was pleasantly surprised that my niece had obtained a picture of my nephew as a baby. She replied to my niece's email by thanking her for sending her a picture of my nephew. In response, my niece sent an email stating that the picture was of the little boy alleged to be my nephew's son. My sister scrutinized the picture. She took note of the fact that the little boy had her eyes and her dimples. After recovering from her shock, my sister announced to the family that she was a grandmother. After a paternity test proved that my sister's instincts were correct, my nephew was forced to figure out how to live up to his paternal obligations. Even though he was no longer in a relationship with the child's mother, he was legally obligated to help her provide for the child.

My nephew's story is not unique. The number of young men who are becoming fathers is again on the rise. When the media reported that Bristol Palin, the unmarried daughter of then vice-presidential candidate Sarah Palin, was pregnant and unmarried, the public was shocked. An effective public relations campaign portrayed Bristol as a young woman who was willing to accept the consequences of her action. On the other hand, Levi Johnston's image was not as stellar. He joined the ranks of young men who appear to have a "King David" complex—the need to be fruitful and multiply with several different women. The world has changed dramatically since King David's time, when it was customary for a man to have as many children as he could afford to support. It did not matter if the children were conceived with several different women. The key was that the man was expected to support the children of his loins.

In recent years, the number of men having children with several different women has increased. While the existence of AIDS and HIV makes unprotected sex a life and death proposition, some men and women choose not to let condoms get in the way of pleasure. Although some may take the opportunity to get tested, it is clear that the fear of becoming infected with a sexually transmitted disease is not a deterrent to having unprotected sex. These young men are usually not mature enough to understand the demands of fatherhood. Since they are often unemployed or underemployed, they cannot provide much, if any, financial support for their children. Most of the young mothers are not as lucky as Bristol Palin. They cannot rely on family, fortune, or fame for support. Thus, they are forced to seek some type of government assistance.

These young women are seeking help in an environment that has changed dramatically. Images of "welfare queens" and "dead-beat dads" led Congress to enact welfare reform. A part of that process was to force men to be accountable for the children they helped to conceive. In response, social welfare agencies administering welfare and food stamp programs started aggressively questioning applicants about the identities of the fathers of their children. While I was practicing law, one social worker had the reputation of being especially hostile to single mothers seeking government benefits. According to local gossip, the social worker started each initial interview by stating, "Unless your name is Mary and your child's name is Jesus, you'd better write a name in the blank asking for the name of the child's father."

After the fathers are identified, the child-support enforcement agencies turn those names over to the local district attorney offices. Those offices take steps to track down the men and give them an opportunity to acknowledge or deny paternity. Once paternity is acknowledged or proven, the district attorneys usually obtain court orders to force the men to pay child support. As a result of the biological connection the man has to the child, he is recognized as the child's legal father. That status requires the man to pay money to support the child. If the man dies intestate, the child may be considered the man's legal heir. Some of the men have no relationship with the mothers of their children. Thus, they are no more than sperm donors. Nonetheless, that fact does not prevent the law from establishing their paternity.

Over the last few decades, marriage has lost some of its appeal. Even as same-sex couples fight for the right to marry, more heterosexual couples have chosen to create families without the benefit of marriage.[1] The high divorce rate and the acceptance of non-marital relationships have contributed to the decline in marriage. Today, in America, at least one out of every three babies is a non-marital child. Brad Pitt and Angelina Jolie have intentionally conceived and adopted children without the benefit of marriage. Pitt is the father of those children conceived using his sperm. Since he is not married to Angelina, Pitt is similar to a sperm donor. The only difference is the manner in which he delivered his sperm. A traditional sperm donor would deposit his sperm in a cup, and that sperm would be artificially inserted into the woman. In the case of Pitt and other men who have unprotected sex, the sperm is deposited directly into the woman. Either case may result in the conception of a child. Nevertheless, the delivery mechanism makes a difference in the legal responsibility that the man has for the child. If paternity tests show that Pitt is the father of Angelina's biological children, he is obligated to pay child support.

If a man donates sperm by having sexual intercourse with an unmarried woman, most people feel he should be financially responsible for supporting the resulting child. With regard to determining the paternity of a child born as a result of sexual intercourse, the focus is upon the biological link between the man and the child, and not on the marital status of the child's parents. Consequently, children conceived outside of marriage are treated similarly to children conceived inside of marriage. Inasmuch as the treatment is similar, however, it is not equal because the non-marital child must be the man's biological child in order for paternity to be adjudicated. As indicated in the previous chapter, a man is the presumed father of a child born to his wife during the marriage even if the child is not his biological child. Biology has not always been enough to make a man a legal father. Historically, sperm donors who delivered their sperm through sexual intercourse were not legally responsible for the children who were born as a result of their passionate encounters. Those men were permitted to sow their wild oats without consequences.

Simply Sowing Seeds

The historical treatment of non-marital children is reflected in the following quotation: "The bastard, like the prostitute, thief, and beggar, belongs to that motley crowd of disreputable social types which society has generally resented, always endured. He is a living symbol of social irregularity, an undeniable evidence of contramoral forces; in short, a problem—a problem as old and unsolved as human existence itself."[2] Since children born out of wedlock were considered to be problems, the law did not take steps to ensure that men took care of them. Non-marital children were legally fatherless and were required to fend for themselves. Under common law, the non-marital child was treated as a nonentity. As a result, men could have children without fear of the consequences. The man's paternity was not established, so he did not have an obligation to provide financial support for his non-marital child. Therefore, it was common for a wealthy man's children to end up living in an orphanage or begging in the streets. Society was not outraged by the plight of those children. That apathy continued even after the publication of books like *Oliver Twist*, a Charles Dickens novel that focused attention upon the suffering of orphans in England.

Non-marital children were believed to be living evidence of the fornication between their parents. A Christian nation was not prepared to reward the product of a sinful relationship. A woman was punished for having sexual intercourse with a man who was not her husband. As part of that punishment, she was left to struggle to rear the child alone. The art people enjoyed often imitated life. For example, in *The Scarlet Letter*, Hester Prynne was severely punished for having a child outside of wedlock. She and her daughter, Pearl, were ostracized by the other members of the community. The community leaders attempted to force Hester to reveal the name of Pearl's father. However, it is unclear what, if any, punishment the leaders would have meted out for the man. Hester was forced to work hard to provide for Pearl. The plot of this work of fiction was reflexive of the attitude towards non-marital children that existed in seventeenth-century New England.

The practice of a man having several children by several different women is not a new one. During biblical times, men routinely had children with their concubines. For example, Abraham conceived a child with Hagar, and Jacob created a child with Bilhah. Historically, English men from the upper class maintained two families. The legitimate family was the one created with a woman from the upper crust of society who came with a dowry. The second family was the one the man created with his mistress. While a biological connection was enough to establish the man's paternity, he was not obligated to support the children born as a result of sex between him and his mistress.

Eventually, society realized that the sins of the parents should not rest on the heads of the children. Thus, as early as 1576, the Elizabethan Poor Laws were adopted in England to ease the suffering of the less fortunate. Children made up a significant portion of the poor population. Consequently, bastardy statutes were included in the poor laws. Those statutes provided a way for the law to force men to support their non-marital children. The bastardy hearing was a precursor to the paternity hearing. There were criminal aspects to the procedure, which started with the arrest of the man and included a preliminary hearing before a justice of the peace. The man was tried before a jury that issued a criminal verdict and sentence. The man's paternity resulted because of his biological connection to the child. Initially, the bastardy laws were used only to help children who were receiving some type of public assistance. If the woman did not seek or was not eligible for public assistance, she was solely responsible for providing for the child. Eventually, the bastardy laws were interpreted to give relief to all non-marital children.[3]

Even after a man became obligated to provide for a child he conceived with a woman who was not his wife, the non-marital child was discriminated against when it came to inheritance. "[T]he incapacity of a bastard consists principally in this, that he cannot be heir to any one neither can he have heirs, but of his own body; for being nullius filius [the child of no one[4]], he is therefore of kin to nobody, and has no ancestor from whom any inheritance blood can be derived."[5] This statement indicates the manner in which members of society perceived non-marital children. Since non-marital children did not belong to anyone, they were not entitled to inherit from or through their biological parents. This placed non-marital children at a severe disadvantage because most of the wealth was transferred through the inheritance system.

Children born outside of marriage did not fare much better in the United States. If a woman conceived a child without a husband, her family often sent her away to have the baby. When she returned with the child, the family told members of the community that her "husband" had met some unfortunate end. The frontier was full of "widows" who had never been married. In spite of the social stigma of illegitimacy, early on, the legislatures in America took steps to make sure that children born outside of marriages received financial support from their fathers. As early as 1875, bastardy statutes existed that provided for the maintenance and support of illegitimate children. The main purposes of the statutes were to protect innocent children from poverty and to relieve the public from the burden of supporting illegitimate children. Legislators felt that a man had a moral obligation to support his offspring. However, those children were still called "bastards" and treated with disdain. For example, in 1975, a Louisiana court stated that "Upon proof of paternity, the adulterous bastard was entitled to alimony from its father."[6] The word "bastard" referred to "a child not born in wedlock, or under circumstances rendering it impossible that the husband of the mother could have been its father."[7] For years, children born out of wedlock were denied the benefits automatically received by adoptive and marital children. The key reasons given for this differential in treatment were the law's desire to protect men from false paternity claims and to discourage women from having children without the benefit of marriage. This circumstance did not change until the mid-1970s when the U.S. Supreme Court issued several decisions that required states to treat non-marital children on par with marital children.

Protecting Men from False Paternity Claims

In England, as early as 1576, in order to receive financial support for her child, an unmarried woman could file a bastardy action against the alleged father. Subsequently, the man would be arrested and held for trial. The case was tried before a jury and could result in a verdict against him. Some courts held that the man could not be found guilty solely based upon the uncorroborated testimony of the woman. The woman was treated in the same way that the law currently treats a co-conspirator in a criminal case. Courts clearly suspected her motives for bringing the action. Given the societal structure, women had reasons to lie about the parentage of their children. Women were not permitted to inherit property, and they had very little financial resources. Thus, sometimes a pregnant woman lied about the identity of her child's father in order to receive financial assistance to care for the child. This was especially true if the man with whom the woman had sexual intercourse was dead or destitute. Moreover, a woman might lie about the paternity of her child in order to secure an inheritance for the child. If a man did not have a legitimate male heir, his illegitimate child could serve in that capacity. Prior to the birth of Isaac, while lamenting his childless state, Abraham told God that he had an heir in the form of Elie'zer of Damascus, a person who was not his biological child. If a woman could establish her child as an heir, she could insure that she would be taken care of in her old age and that her child would be provided for when she died. This is not to imply that all women were motivated by greed.

Some women lied out of desperation. They sought to improve their children's station in life. Even bastard sons of noblemen were better off than legitimate sons of lower-class men. Both England and America had some type of class system in place. The persons in the upper crust fared better than those in the lower class. While the upper class lived well, the lower class struggled to make ends meet, and many could do so only by becoming servants. Their social class was especially important for female children because women in the lower class were frequently raped and abused. Some of those women were forced to become prostitutes. The women from the upper class were permitted to marry men who were financially capable of taking care of them. The plight of lower-class women was bleak. In English society in the late 1500s, men of the lower class were forced to work as servants and could never own land. In order to give their children better lives, some women falsely accused wealthy men of fathering their children. In some cases, the women lied to protect the real father of their children. For instance, in *The Scarlet Letter*, Hester refused to reveal the name of Pearl's father. Courts sought to discourage women from making false accusations by removing one of the motivations for lying. Since unmarried men were not obligated to support children they had out of wedlock, the women would not benefit from their lies.

Today, it is easy to make a paternity determination. DNA testing has given courts the tools necessary to adjudicate a man as the father of his non-marital child. After a simple blood test or cheek swab, the man's biological relationship to the child is proven or disproven. However, that was not the case a few decades ago. Courts had no way of determining paternity when an unmarried woman accused a man of fathering her child. This was especially true when the woman made her accusation after the man had passed away in order for the child to receive a share of the man's estate. In order to protect men from false paternity claims, courts held men responsible only for children they conceived in marriage or children they were found guilty of fathering in a bastardy hearing. Courts also reasoned that if a woman could not receive financial support for her non-marital children, she would be deterred from having children without the benefit of marriage.

Discouraging Sex without Marriage

In the past, society held different views about sex. Sex was linked to procreation and not pleasure. Since birth control was unreliable, sex usually resulted in pregnancy. Thus, in order to avoid bringing shame on their families, women were expected to remain virgins until they got married. Young men were permitted to "sow their wild oats" because they could not get pregnant. The non-marital child was evidence of a woman's sinful behavior. In order to dissuade women from having children without the benefit of marriage, society made it difficult for unmarried women to raise children alone. Women and their non-marital children were treated as outcasts. The women were not permitted to attend church or to go to other places frequented by "decent folks." The children were not allowed to go to school or to associate with children from "good families." Consequently, non-marital children were seldom able to "marry up" to improve their stations in life. Since women had very limited resources, those who conceived a child out of wedlock were almost guaranteed to live in poverty. Sometimes, the women had to engage in illegal activities like prostitution to provide for their children.

The law has always favored and promoted marriage for religious and social reasons. The primary purpose of marriage was for the woman to provide her husband with children. The law sought to punish women for having non-marital children by placing those children at a financial disadvantage. Therefore, men were not required to provide support to their non-marital children, and those children were not recognized as the heirs of their biological fathers. The treatment of non-marital children also served to promote marriage. If a woman wanted a good life for herself and her children, she would get married before procreating.

The harsh manner in which non-marital children were treated was also motivated by the desire to regulate sexual activities between unmarried people. Legislatures hoped that the possibility of having a child out of wedlock would act as a "cold shower" and reduce the acts of fornication. Fornication is voluntary sexual intercourse between two unmarried persons or two persons not married to each other. The act of fornication is condemned numerous times in the Bible. Further, fornication was once a crime punishable by a fine and/or imprisonment.[8] Only married couples were supposed to have sex. Fornication laws were seldom enforced, so their existence did not prevent persons from having sexual intercourse without the benefit of marriage. Legislatures enacted statutes negatively impacting non-marital children in order to promote what they considered to be legitimate family relationships. The hope was that instead of running the risk of having non-marital children, persons would limit their sexual activities to the marriage bed.

Reaping the Consequences

For years, men were able to turn blind eyes to the plight of their non-marital children. These children were punished because of the behavior of their parents. In addition, the laws were not preventing persons from having children out of wedlock. Advocates took up the cause of non-marital children and started bringing law suits to establish rights for them. Beginning in the later 1960s, the U.S. Supreme Court heard several cases involving the legal rights of non-marital children. While those cases dealt with diverse legal issues, including immigration, workers' compensation, and social security, the most important of them addressed the non-marital children's right to paternal financial support.

Lifetime Support

In the early 1970s, the U.S. Supreme Court recognized that regardless of the circumstances of their birth, children need to be financially supported. One of the cases where the Court addressed the difference in treatment between marital and non-marital children with regard to paternal support was *Gomez v. Perez*.[9] Under the common and statutory laws of the state of Texas, marital children were entitled to receive financial support from their biological fathers. However, the laws did not give non-marital children the same opportunity. The Court had to decide whether or not those laws should survive a constitutional challenge.

While a single woman, Linda Gomez engaged in a sexual relationship with Francisco Perez, and then gave birth to a girl named Zoraida. Subsequently, Gomez filed a petition seeking a court order requiring Perez to pay child support on behalf of Zoraida. After a trial on the merits, the court determined that Zoraida was Perez's biological child. The court even acknowledged that Zoraida was in financial need. Nonetheless, the court held that the child's status as a non-marital child precluded her from receiving child support because a man was legally obligated to support only his marital children. Gomez appealed the trial court's decision through the Texas court system, and attorneys representing her argued the case before the U.S. Supreme Court, alleging that the Texas laws violated the Equal Protection Clause of the Fourteenth Amendment. Their position was that the state's differential treatment of Zoraida and other non-marital children with regard to child support denied Zoraida equal protection under the law. In response, the Supreme Court held that once Texas gave one class of children the right to paternal financial support, it had to grant the same right to all classes of children, including non-marital children. As a result, Texas could not discriminate against non-marital children by declining to give them the financial benefits given to other children. The Court's finding that non-marital children had the right to receive paternal financial support to the same extent as marital children led states to attempt to treat non-marital children similarly to marital children for intestacy purposes.

A biological connection between the man and his non-marital child is enough to obligate him to provide lifetime financial support for the child. The Federal Office of Child Support Enforcement was established by Congress in 1975. The legislation that required the creation of that office also mandated that each state establish a child-support enforcement office. The states responded by putting mechanisms in place to force men to comply. To protect the integrity of the system, Congress enacted the Family Support Act of 1988. One provision of that statute set out the guidelines states had to follow when determining paternity. Once paternity is established, the states are required to make sure that the child's biological father, and not the state, financially supports the child.

The fertile man is not absolved of his obligation to support his biological child even if he makes it clear that he took steps to avoid the child's conception. That was the plight of the fertile man in *Wallis v. Smith*.[10] Prior to starting a sexual relationship, Wallis and Smith agreed that Smith would take birth control pills to avoid pregnancy. They agreed that, if Smith ever stopped taking her birth control pills, they would end their sexual relationship. Even though Wallis did not want to father a child, he did not take any precautions because he relied on Smith's promise.[11] Smith, however, unilaterally decided to stop taking birth control and did not tell Wallis. Since he did know that Smith was off the pill, Wallis continued having unprotected sex with her. After Smith became pregnant and had a baby girl, Wallis sued her for money damages. He claimed that Smith was liable for fraud, breach of contract, conversion, and other torts. He also claimed that he had suffered, and would continue to suffer, substantial economic injury as a proximate result of his unintended fatherhood because the law required him to pay child support for eighteen years. Basing its decision on prevailing public policy, the district court dismissed Wallis' complaint, and he appealed.[12]

The New Mexico Appellate Court noted that Wallis was seeking compensatory damages for the "economic injury" he would suffer because of his obligation to provide support for the child. While Wallis argued that he was not asking the court to relieve him of his child-support obligations, the court found his argument to be unpersuasive. In essence, Wallis was asking the court to reimburse him for the amount of money he anticipated paying in child support. When enacting child-support laws, the legislature had made it clear that both the father and the mother of the child had a duty to support the child financially. The court opined that it was against the public policy of the state to require Smith to indemnify Wallis for paying to support his child.[13] The court refused to enforce the agreement Smith made with regard to taking birth control pills because "children, the persons for whose benefit child-support guidelines are enacted, have the same needs regardless of whether their conception violated a promise between the parents."[14] The court was not overly sympathetic to Wallis because he could have easily taken steps to prevent the conception of a child.[15]

Moreover, the court deemed that if it entertained Wallis' contraceptive fraud case, it would be encouraging men to use creative theories to avoid supporting their non-marital children. The court stated:

> We will not re-enter the jurisprudence of illegitimacy by allowing a parent to opt out of the financial consequences of his or her sexual relationships just because they were unintended. Nor will we recognize a cause of action that trivializes one's personal responsibility in sexual relationships.[16]

In this case, a victory for Wallis would have been a defeat for non-marital children. It could have opened the floodgates for men claiming that they intended to have sex, but did not plan to become fathers. It would have unfairly placed the burden of birth control on the woman. If a woman did not take steps to avoid becoming pregnant, she would be solely responsible for supporting the resulting child. Even if the woman was willing to accept that responsibility, it would have disadvantaged children because it would have required only one person to provide financial support for them. And indeed, courts have refused to enforce contracts where women agree that men do not have to pay child support because child support is the right of the child and not the mother. An agreement not to get pregnant is similar to an agreement not to hold a man liable for child support. For his part, the fertile man was responsible for providing financial support to his non-marital children during his lifetime. However, upon his death, his duty was done. Child advocates and mothers sought to change that because the needs of the non-marital children often survive the deaths of their fathers.

Inheritance

Initially, the establishment of paternity that entitled the non-marital child to lifetime support did not extend to inheritance rights. In some circumstances, the obligation of paternal support ceased at the death of the non-marital child's legal father. This was the case even if the non-marital child was a minor and/or disabled. Inheritance was the last right that was denied to non-marital children. Finally, the U.S. Supreme Court had to step in and clarify the actions that states were required to take to ensure that non-marital children were not denied the equal protection of the law. One such step came through the case of *Trimble v. Gordon.*[17]

Deta Mona Trimble was the non-marital child of Jessie Trimble and Sherman Gordon. Paternity tests proved that Sherman was Deta's biological father. Thus, the Circuit Court of Cook County declared him to be the child's legal father and ordered him to pay child support on her behalf. Gordon did not object to the child-support order, and he freely acknowledged Deta as his daughter.[18] Jessie, Sherman, and the child lived together as a family.[19] Then, Sherman died without leaving a will. The only asset in his estate was an automobile. The probate court concluded that Deta was not Sherman's heir because of the circumstances of her birth and her mother's failure to comply with the requirements of the state's intestacy statute.[20] Under the provisions of that statute, in order for a non-marital child to inherit from his or her father, the father had to take two steps to have the child recognized as legitimate: he had to marry the child's mother and he had to acknowledge the child legally.[21]

The fact that her father failed to follow the statutory mandates prevented Deta from inheriting his whole estate. In her appeal to the Illinois Supreme Court, Trimble contended that the statute discriminated against Deta based upon her status as a non-marital child.[22] The state countered by asserting that the statutory requirements were legally necessary to encourage the creation of legitimate family relationships[23] and to protect the integrity of the probate system from fraudulent paternity claims.[24] The state supreme court upheld the probate court's decision. Then, Trimble filed an appeal with the U. S. Supreme Court,[25] which determined that the statutory requirements were not related to the state's alleged purposes.[26]

The Supreme Court acknowledged that it was important for the state to reward people for getting married before having children. Nonetheless, the Court felt that the legislature could fulfill its objectives without enacting statutes that punished non-marital children for existing. Children, including non-marital children, were unable to control their parents' actions, so the law should not disadvantage them because of those parental actions.[27] Further, the Court noted that non-marital children were powerless to force their parents to satisfy the conditions set forth in the statute. As a result, it would be unfair if non-marital children were unable to take steps to inherit from their fathers because their parents failed to marry and/or their fathers refused to acknowledge them. Consequently, the U.S. Supreme Court concluded that the statutory provisions did not promote the state's interest in encouraging specific types of family relationships.[28]

The U.S. Supreme Court determined the state's second argument with regard to protecting the probate system to be equally unpersuasive. In analyzing that argument, the Court found the statute to be overly inclusive because it disadvantaged non marital children who had definitive evidence that the deceased men were their biological fathers.[29] For instance, as a result of the application of the statute, Deta was not permitted to inherit from her father even though a competent court had issued a paternity order and a child-support order indicating that the man was her father.[30]

As a consequence of the lack of a nexus between the purposes of the statute and the conditions of the statute, the U.S. Supreme Court found the statute to be unconstitutional. The Court reasoned that a non-marital child in the jurisdiction was unduly burdened by the statutory requirements. In order to satisfy the statute so that the child could have the chance to inherit, the non-marital child or the child's mother had to show that the alleged father acknowledged the child and married the child's mother. According to the Court, that two-step requirement prevented the non-marital child from inheriting from his or her father. In Deta's case, the Court felt that it was unfair to place such a burden on the non-marital child because she could not force her parents to get married. In essence, the statute made it impossible for non-marital children to inherit from their fathers. The U.S. Supreme

Court had already condemned the practice of denying non-marital children the opportunity to inherit from their fathers. Therefore, the Court held that the statute was unconstitutional.[31] States had to put a process in place to afford non-marital children a real opportunity to inherit from their fathers. Even though states heeded the Court's mandate, the Court still had to deal with disputes involving non-marital children. An example of one such case was *Lalli v. Lalli*.[32]

Approximately a year after issuing the decision in *Trimble*, the U.S. Supreme Court heard *Lalli v. Lalli*, another case involving the inheritance rights of non-marital children. That case dealt with Robert and Maureen Lalli's quest to receive a portion of their father's estate. After Mario Lalli died without leaving a will, his widow, Rosamond, was named as the administratrix of his estate.[33] Robert and Maureen sought to be declared Mario's heirs. To prove his relationship to the deceased man, Robert submitted a notarized document in which Mario referred to Robert as his son. In addition, he filed affidavits signed by persons who swore that Mario had acknowledged Robert and Maureen as his children.[34] In response, Rosamond contended that the non-marital children were not eligible to inherit from their father because they had not fulfilled the conditions set out in the state's paternity statute. While admitting that Rosamond's statement was correct, Robert and Maureen claimed that they should not have to comply with the statute because it was unconstitutional.[35] Pointing out that the statute required non-marital children to prove paternity in a specific manner in order to inherit from their fathers, and that marital children were not required to do anything extra to be named heirs of their fathers, Robert and Maureen maintained that the statute was discriminatory. Moreover, they alleged that the evidence presented to show that Mario was their father should have been enough to satisfy the statute. Therefore, Robert and Maureen should have been allowed to inherit from their father.[36]

In order to determine the constitutionality of the statute, the Court evaluated whether the state's purpose was important and whether the statute carried out that purpose. According to the state, the statute was needed to provide for the fair and orderly distribution of probate property and to protect the probate process from persons making fraudulent claims.[37] The state's goal was to carry out the dead man's presumed intentions with regard to the division of his property. The Court concluded that the interest the statute was enacted to promote was an important one.[38]

In addition, the Court cited several reasons why the statutory procedure promoted the state's interest.[39] The Court opined that the procedure established by the statute would probably help to lessen the amount of fraudulent claims filed in the court. While the father was alive to dispute false claims, persons might be reluctant to file them. That is, persons making false paternity accusations would probably be less likely to file those claims in court if they knew they had to confront the alleged father. On the other hand, if the father was not around to defend himself from such claims, the flood gates could open and the courts would be inundated. As a result, the probate process would be even more expensive and time-consuming.[40] Moreover, the Court noted that the statute gave non-marital children more inheritance rights than existed prior to its enactment. Therefore, the legislature was trying to benefit non-marital children, not disadvantage them.[41]

The Supreme Court thought that it was important to give a man the right to present evidence showing that he was not the father of a non-marital child. The establishment of a father-child relationship places numerous legal obligations on a man. As a result, the man should be afforded the opportunity to challenge false claims of paternity. The scheme included in the challenged statute gave the man that chance by requiring that paternity disputes be resolved during his lifetime.[42] Unlike the statute at issue in *Trimble*, the statute challenged in *Lalli* represented a middle ground that the Court thought was equitable. Non-marital children were not precluded from inheriting from their fathers as long as they followed the statutory procedures.[43] In finding that the statute passed constitutional muster, the Court emphasized that the procedure set forth in the statute protected the interests of the probate courts, the non-marital children, and the alleged father.[44]

As the above cases indicate, in order for a state inheritance statute to survive a constitutional attack, it must provide non-marital children with the opportunity to inherit from their fathers. The U.S. Supreme Court has given state legislatures the discretion to establish rules governing probate matters. However, if those legislatures enact statutes expressly or implicitly preventing non-marital children from establishing a father-child relationship for inheritance purposes, the Supreme Court would probably invalidate them. In light of its decisions, it is clear that legislatures do not have to afford non-marital children exactly the same inheritance rights as marital children. Since the legal status of non-marital children is different from that of marital children, their rights with regard to inheritance may be different as long as they are given an opportunity to inherit from their fathers.

In response to the Supreme Court requirements, states have enacted laws giving non-marital children the right to prove the existence of a father-child relationship so they can inherit from their fathers. Some states focus upon the biological connection between the fornicating man and his non-marital children when deciding whether or not to recognize the children as the man's heirs. Nonetheless, in the majority of states, although biology is enough to adjudicate paternity for child-support purposes, more is needed for the non-marital child to receive a portion of his or her biological father's estate. In order for the child to be an heir under the intestacy system in most states, his or her parents must act to show the man's paternity during his lifetime.

When courts adjudicate paternity in cases dealing with children of passion, they focus upon the needs of the children instead of the actions of the men. A fornicating man runs the risk of conceiving a child when he uses sexual intercourse to donate his sperm to a woman who is not his wife because no form of birth control is one hundred percent effective when it comes to preventing pregnancy. Therefore, the man who chooses not to remain celibate should have to live with the consequences of his actions. One of those consequences is being financially responsible for his biological children who are conceived by nature. The sperm donor who conceives using scientific methods does not have to deal with that consequence.

Children of Science (Papa's Maybe)

3

The Non-Consenting Man

As the material in Part I indicates, children conceived the "old-fashioned" way have the opportunity to have a father. Under certain circumstances, the man may assume the role of "papa" by nurturing and caring for the child. However, it is not necessary for the man to have a personal connection to the child in order for the courts to recognize a legal father-child relationship. The interactions between the adults determine the legal benefits awarded to the child. State legislatures provide guidance to courts with regard to paternity adjudications. It is not surprising that the legislatures have plenty to say when it comes to allocating paternity to a man involved in the natural conception of a child. People tend to be comfortable speaking about things with which they are familiar. Conception by sexual intercourse is as old as the earth. It goes back to the time when Eve gave birth to Cain. Legislators tend to be family men and women. Thus, they have an easy time deciding that a man should be responsible for the "natural objects of his body." On the other hand, most state legislators are not scientists, and most members lack any serious level of scientific expertise. Some legislators consider assisted reproduction to be "messing with 'mother nature.'" Thus, they would like to discourage the conception of children using reproductive technology. All of this may account for the differential treatment of children of science.[1]

In most jurisdictions, when a woman conceives a child using reproductive technology, her husband is not presumed to be the legal father of the resulting child. The marital status of the couple is not enough to establish his paternity. Courts totally ignore the marital presumption of paternity and instead evaluate the man's action pre- and post-conception to determine if his actions warrant an adjudication of paternity. The emphasis is on the man's ability to make an informed decision and his intentions with regard to the child. In the cases involving children of passion, the husbands of the impregnated women have the burden of rebutting the presumption of paternity. When a child is conceived using scientific methods, the legislatures and the courts shift the burden and require the person seeking the adjudication of paternity to prove that the woman's husband agreed to the procedure that resulted in the child's conception. The husband's agreement is necessary for his paternity to be adjudicated.

According to Webster's dictionary, "consent" means to agree or to permit.[2] In tort law, one of the defenses to battery is consent.[3] An affirmative defense to a negligence case is assumption of the risk. The doctrine of assumption of risk is based upon the premise that the person implicitly consented to accept the consequences of the activity he or she undertook.[4] For example, if A voluntarily participates in a hockey game, he assumes the risk of losing his teeth. It is all about responsibility. We are all responsible for the consequences of our voluntary actions. Thus, in a medical malpractice case, the physician can avoid liability by showing that the patient consented to the procedure after being informed of the risks.[5] In this same vein, once a man consents to the insemination of his wife using the sperm of another man, he is indicating a willingness to accept the outcome of the procedure. If the procedure results in the conception of a child, it is not unreasonable for the court to acknowledge the man as the child's legal father. This reasoning has led the majority of states with artificial insemination statutes to allocate paternity to the consenting husband. However, most legislatures and courts act to protect the non-consenting man from liability. A typical statute states:

> Any child born to a married woman by means of artificial insemination shall be deemed the legitimate natural child of the woman and the woman's husband if the husband consents in writing to the artificial insemination.[6]

By mandating that the child be recognized as legitimate, the statute is recognizing the inseminated woman's husband as the child's legal father. The purpose of the statute is to ensure that the man is responsible for the child only if he plays a role in the child's conception. This is consistent with the way the law has treated paternity cases involving children of passion. In the case of a man's biological child, he is held to be legally responsible because he contributed the sperm that resulted in the child's conception. Hence, he played a very active role in the process. A married man is normally liable for the children his wife conceives during the course of their marriage. The man plays a role in the process by marrying the woman. His role begins when he says his vows establishing the contract of marriage. In this chapter, I will analyze the manner in which the law treats the non-consenting husband. Consent is the role he has to play in order to become legally responsible for the artificially conceived child. But how is that role defined?

States with Statutes Legislating Paternity

The legislatures in the majority of states and the District of Columbia have enacted statutes dealing with the artificial insemination process. The statutes apply only to situations involving artificial insemination and exclude children born using other forms of assisted reproduction. The statutes may be grouped into two broad categories. Most of them require the man's actual consent in order for the child to be identified as his legitimate child. Those statutes place the burden of proof on the person seeking the paternity adjudication. That person has to show that the woman's husband consented to her artificial insemination. A minority of states recognizes a sort of constructive consent. Statutes in those states shift the burden to the man who would like to be classified as non-consenting. In order to avoid being accountable for the child of science, the man has to convince the court that he did not consent to the procedure. Courts attribute consent to the man if he is unsuccessful in his quest to demonstrate the contrary.

The Consent Requirement

If a woman's husband fails to give written consent to her being artificially inseminated, he is not considered to be the child's legal father. The man's paternity depends upon his willingness to be a father to the child conceived using scientific methods. Different jurisdictions have different statutory writing requirements, but they all have a common purpose: to make sure that the man agreed to his wife's insemination. According to the statute in some states, a man's consent must be written, executed, and acknowledged. In other states where statutes do not specify that the man's consent must be written, courts in those jurisdictions have decided that a man may become responsible for the artificially conceived child as a consequence of his actions. This is a form of implied consent. The Arkansas legislature took a unique approach to adjudicating the paternity of the artificially inseminated woman's husband. The Arkansas statute sets forth a rebuttable presumption that the husband consented to the insemination of his wife. The husband has the burden of presenting evidence indicating that he was a non-consenting man. As a result, if the woman's husband does not submit convincing evidence proving the contrary, he is presumed to have consented to his wife's insemination.[7]

Under the provisions of the Uniform Parentage Act (UPA) and at least one state, a man may avoid responsibility for the child by withdrawing his consent. However, the man has the burden of proving that he withdrew his consent before the child was conceived.[8] In addition, if the couple divorces prior to the child's conception, the man is not legally obligated to support the child.[9] If the husband dies prior to the child of science's conception, his estate does not have a legal duty to provide support for the child. Only a few states give the posthumously conceived child the opportunity to inherit from his or her father and/or to receive government benefits as a result of his death.[10] Courts may hold the non-consenting man responsible for the artificially conceived child if his wife is able to show that he consented in some manner to her being artificially inseminated. The wife usually achieves this goal by showing that her husband was an active participant in the process. Evidence typically presented includes the fact that the man helped to choose the sperm donor and/or that the man attended his wife's medical appointments. From an evidentiary perspective, courts are often more willing to allocate paternity of a child of science to the woman's husband if there is writing involved in the case. It is clear that written consent takes precedent over other indicators of consent.

Written Consent

The artificially inseminated woman's husband who gives written consent for his wife to go through the process is the legal father of the resulting child. Thus, the issue of the child's legitimacy turns on the man's consent and not on the parents' marital status. Being born into an intact family is not sufficient to protect children of science from the stigma of illegitimacy. For instance, a statute enacted by the Minnesota legislature recognizes the inseminated woman's husband as the biological father of children his wife artificially conceives only if she obtains his written consent.[11] Since the consenting husband is deemed to be the legal father of his wife's artificially conceived child, that child is classified as legitimate. A husband who consents to his wife's insemination will be held responsible for the resulting child even if the couple does not follow the mandates of the artificial insemination statute.[12] Even when the statute clearly states that the husband of the artificially inseminated woman must consent in writing, the courts still have some discretion. Courts have used that discretion to protect the interests of both the men and the artificially conceived children. In determining whether or not the written consent requirement has been satisfied, the court may strictly interpret the artificial insemination statute or give it a broad reading.

The case of *Witbeck v. Wildhagen* provides a good example of strict compliance.[13] In November 1990, Marcia Witbeck married Eric Wildhagen.[14] After almost a year and a half of marriage, the couple went to Christie Clinic and inquired about Marcia being artificially inseminated with donor sperm. At that time, Eric told Marcia and a nurse at the clinic that he did not want Marcia to undergo the procedure. Furthermore, Eric refused to consent to the artificial insemination of Marcia.[15] According to Marcia, Eric told her that he did not care if she became pregnant with a donor's child, but he refused to be involved in the process. The couple continued to have sex. However, Eric always wore a condom, so that he would not impregnate Marcia. After the first consultation at Christie Clinic, Marcia underwent seven artificial insemination procedures without Eric's knowledge. Finally, in October 1993, Marcia became pregnant. About three months later, Marcia filed for divorce. In her divorce petition, Marcia claimed that there were no children of the marriage, but that she was pregnant. Marcia contended that she needed financial assistance for herself and her unborn child. Therefore, Marcia requested custody of the child and a court order requiring Eric to contribute money to take care of her maintenance and pregnancy-related expenses. Marcia also asked the court to order Eric to pay child support.[16]

Marcia had a little boy on July 2, 1994. Afterwards, Eric petitioned the court for blood testing. In response, Marcia's attorney sent Eric a letter telling him about the seven artificial insemination procedures. The letter speculated that the baby was conceived as the result of artificial insemination with donor sperm, and not from sexual intercourse with Eric.[17] Later, blood tests excluded Eric as the child's biological father.[18] Since Eric was a non-consenting husband, the trial court held that he was not the child's legal father. The state statute in effect at that time stated:

> If, under the supervision of a licensed physician and with the consent of her husband, a wife is inseminated artificially with semen donated by a man not her husband, her husband shall be treated in law as if he were the natural father of a child thereby conceived. The husband's consent must be in writing executed and acknowledged by both the husband and wife. The physician who is to perform the technique shall certify their signatures and the date of the insemination, and file the husband's consent in the medical record where it shall be kept confidential and held by the patient's

physician. However, the physician's failure to do so shall not affect the legal relationship between the father and child. All papers and records pertaining to the insemination, whether part of the permanent medical record held by the physician or not, are subject to inspection only upon an order of the court for good cause shown.[19]

Even though she acknowledged that Eric was not the child's father and admitted that he had not consented to her artificial insemination, Marcia asked the court to adjudicate Eric as the child's legal father. The trial court rejected Marcia's plea and determined that Eric was not the child's legal father because he did not consent to Marcia's insemination.[20] Marcia then brought the case to the appellate court, asking it to overturn the trial court's ruling.[21] The appellate court affirmed the trial court's disposition of the case. In reaching its decision, the trial court stated, "We conclude the legislature intended a husband's written consent to be a prerequisite to the establishment of the legal father-child relationship and the imposition of a support obligation."[22] In addition, the court opined that in order to satisfy the mandates of the statute, the wife had to receive the husband's written consent each time she was inseminated. In this case, Marcia did not present any evidence indicating that Eric had ever consented to the insemination in writing or by his actions.[23]

Subsequently, the appellate court concluded that it would not be fair to obligate Eric to provide financial support for the child for several reasons. First, the evidence showed that Marcia became pregnant using the sperm of another man without Eric's knowledge or consent. Second, since Marcia filed for divorce two or three months after she discovered she was pregnant, it was clear that she never intended to raise the child with Eric. Third, prior to the trial, Eric did not have any contact with the child, and Marcia legally changed the child's last name to her maiden name. Based upon these facts, the appellate court decided that there was no equitable or legal justification for recognizing a legal father-child relationship between Eric and the child. Since a father-child relationship did not exist, Eric was not responsible for taking care of the child.[24]

After the appellate court rejected her legal argument, Marcia relied upon public policy to argue that the court should order Eric to support the child. Faced with the task of balancing both a child's need to be financially supported and a man's right not to procreate,[25] the court decided that a man's reproductive rights are just as important as a woman's. As a result, a man should not be forced into fatherhood. If the man does not take part in the child's conception, the law should not obligate him to provide financial support for the child. In this case, Eric did not know that the child had been conceived by artificial insemination until after the child was born. Prior to the child's conception, Eric made it clear that he did not want to parent a child conceived by artificial insemination. He never did anything to help Marcia conceive the child, and took steps to avoid becoming a father. Consequently, the appellate court agreed with the trial court's decision that it would be against public policy both to ignore the actions the man had taken to avoid fatherhood and to adjudicate him as the legal father of a child who was not biologically related to him.[26]

Marcia responded by arguing that she was not financially able to support the child by herself. Therefore, if the child was deemed to be legally fatherless, she would have to seek assistance from the state. In essence, Marcia was asking the court to consider the best interests of the child. The court acknowledged that public policy required it to consider the child's need for financial support in order to prevent the state from having to provide that support. Nonetheless, the court determined that the child's need for support could be fulfilled by Marcia, the child's mother. Since Marcia had used deception to conceive the child alone, she was solely responsible for taking care of the child. It was against public policy to require Eric, as a non-parent, to assume the responsibility of supporting the child. The appellate court stated:

> It is the duty of the court to ensure the rights of the child are adequately protected. In this case, the trial court did so, and the balance it struck between the attendant interests of the parties was appropriate. It would be unjust to impose a support obligation on respondent where no father-child relationship exists between him and [the child] and he did not consent to the artificial insemination procedure.[27]

The man's wife became pregnant by being artificially inseminated with another man's sperm without the man's permission. Therefore, the marital status of the couple was not enough to compel the court to name him as the child's legal father. Even though the child did not have control over the manner in which he or she was conceived, the child was considered to be legally fatherless. The husband of the child's mother was not presumed to be the father because he did not consent to his wife's insemination. Thus, when adjudicating paternity of a child conceived by artificial insemination, legislatures and courts appear to consider the needs of the child to be secondary to the rights of the man. The man's actions pre- and post-conception determine whether or not the man should be recognized as the child's legal father. Under the provisions of most state statutes, if a man does not give written consent to have his wife artificially inseminated with another man's sperm, he is not the legal father of the resulting child. If the man takes an active part in the conception of the child and never objects to being classified as the child's legal father, some courts may be willing to designate him as the legal father.

The *Witbeck* case illustrates the court's reluctance to require a man to support a child who was conceived without his consent or knowledge. It appears that the non-consenting man's right to avoid forced fatherhood is more important than the child's need to be protected from the burdens that accompany a label of illegitimacy. Courts are more willing to attribute written consent to a man who expresses a desire to be the legal father of the artificially conceived child. Thus, sometimes courts will go to great lengths to conclude that the man gave written consent to his wife's artificial insemination. That is the action taken by the court deciding the *Lane* case.[28]

The *Lane* case arose because a man who took a step away from fatherhood married a woman who wanted to embrace motherhood. Since he did not want any children, Mr. Lane had a vasectomy, and his wife's desire to have a child was not enough to persuade Mr. Lane to have his vasectomy reversed. Realizing that his marriage was in trouble, he reluctantly supported Ms. Lane's decision to become pregnant using donor sperm.[29] Then, even though Mr. Lane never signed a form consenting to the procedure, he became an active participant in the process. For example, he took his wife to her medical appointments and accompanied her to birthing classes. He also took her to the hospital when she went into labor, and was present in the delivery room when the child was born.[30] The child completed the family. Afterwards, Mr. and Ms. Lane mutually agreed to keep the circumstances of the child's birth a secret. Therefore, they told their families and friends that the husband was the child's biological father. To give validity to their story, the couple had the husband listed as the father on the child's birth certificate.[31]

The birth of the child was not enough to save the marriage. When the child was still young, Mr. Lane filed a petition to have the marriage dissolved. In that petition, he claimed that the artificially conceived child was a product of the marriage. Even though she asked the court for sole legal and physical custody, Ms. Lane did not initially dispute Mr. Lane's paternity assertions.[32] Then, however, Ms. Lane had a change of heart and filed an amended answer claiming that Mr. Lane was not the child's biological father. Ms. Lane's challenge was based on the fact that the child was conceived using artificial insemination without her husband's permission. She argued that no basis existed to adjudicate Mr. Lane as the legal father of the child.[33] The lower court rejected Ms. Lane's argument and adjudicated Mr. Lane as the child's legal father. After the court granted the couple joint legal custody of the child, Ms. Lane appealed the decision,[34] arguing that under the provisions of the artificial insemination statute, Mr. Lane could be the child's legal father only if he gave written consent to Ms. Lane's artificial insemination. Accordingly, the attorney urged the court to view Mr. Lane as a non-parent who was not eligible to share custody of the child.[35]

Thus, the appellate court had to decide whether the state's statute required the husband to give written consent in order to be recognized as the legal father of the artificially conceived child. Taking into account the plain language of the statute, the court determined that the statute required the husband's written consent to his wife's artificial insemination. If that consent was missing, the husband did not have a legal connection to the resulting child.[36] However, because the court did not want to eliminate the father-child relationship that existed between Mr. Lane and the child, it went beyond the plain language of the statute and focused upon the legislature's intent. In order to do so, the court relied upon the substantial compliance doctrine and stated that

> Under that doctrine, a court should determine whether the statute has been followed sufficiently so as to carry out the intent for which the statute was adopted and accomplishes the reasonable objectives of the statute.[37]

According to the court, the writing requirement served two main purposes. One was to enable courts to resolve "he-said, she-said" situations by requiring the person arguing for a paternity adjudication to submit written evidence of the man's consent.[38] The court also determined that the written consent requirement served a cautionary purpose. Once a man is adjudicated the father of a child, he is legally responsible for supporting the child until the age of majority or beyond if the child is disabled. Thus, a man should not enter into the decision to parent an artificially conceived child lightly. The written consent requirement gives the man the opportunity to ponder the advantages and disadvantages of parenting a child conceived using the genetic material of another man. The existence of the writing requirement was meant to ensure that the husband comprehended the seriousness of the situation prior to consenting. The writing requirement permitted the man to ponder the consequences of giving written consent.[39]

In light of the important role the written consent requirement played, the court concluded that in order to satisfy the spirit of the statute, the husband had to submit proof of some type of written consent.[40] However, the court concluded that the statute did not set forth a specific time at which the man had to put his consent in writing or the information the writing had to contain in order to satisfy the statutory requirement. The lack of legislative clarity permitted the court to be flexible when it evaluated whether the man had satisfied the written consent requirement. The court concluded that a man could comply with the terms by signing an instrument acknowledging that he was aware that his wife intended to become pregnant through artificial insemination. As long as the instrument indicated that the couple agreed that the husband would be recognized as the child's legal father, it was sufficient to satisfy the written consent requirement. In addition, the court decided that the man could give his written consent at various stages of the process. Hence, in order for the written consent to be valid, it did not have to be given prior to the child's conception.[41]

In light of its established criteria, the court decided that Mr. Lane had substantially complied with the provisions of the artificial insemination statute.[42] The court reasoned that the divorce petition and related documents constituted written consent on Mr. Lane's part. In his signed petition, Mr. Lane assumed legal responsibility for the child. By recognizing the child as a product of the marriage, Mr. Lane was deemed to have consented to the child's conception. Furthermore, the court decided that by filing a signed answer without objecting to her husband's paternity, Ms. Lane acknowledged that he should be treated as the child's legal father. Moreover, the court was also influenced by Mr. Lane's willingness to maintain a relationship with the child, which indicated that Mr. Lane wanted to consent to the child's conception.

Thus, in order to carry out the parties' original intent with regard to Mr. Lane's paternity, the court applied the substantial compliance doctrine.[43] The court's broad interpretation of the written consent requirement enabled it to reach a decision that was in line with the expectations of the couple. By acting as a father to the child, Mr. Lane indicated that he had consented to the artificial insemination of his wife. Ms. Lane could not put forth any evidence showing that Mr. Lane did not want to consent to the procedure. Consequently, the court ruled that Mr. Lane did enough to satisfy the written consent requirement.[44]

While the court's broad interpretation of the written consent requirement benefited the artificially conceived child, promoting the child's best interests was not the court's objective. Rather, the court was concerned about protecting Mr. Lane's paternal rights. The benefit to the child was just a byproduct. The case could have easily been decided in a manner that adversely impacted the child of science. For instance, if Mr. Lane had denied that he consented to the artificial insemination of his wife, the court would probably have concluded that the child was not a child of the marriage. As a consequence, the child would have been adjudicated to be legally fatherless and illegitimate. The child of science may fare better in jurisdictions that accept non-written forms of consent.

Constructive Consent

In order to satisfy the statutory requirements in some states, the man's consent does not have to be in writing. Thus, a man may be recognized as the legal father of an artificially conceived child even if he does not give written consent to the child's conception. Thus, for example, a Maryland statute permits the courts to presume that a man consented to have his wife artificially inseminated with donor sperm, which, in turn, results in the child conceived in this way being recognized as the man's legitimate child. Moreover, in Utah, the man's failure to give written consent does not preclude him from being adjudicated as the legal father of his wife's artificially conceived child. If, subsequent to the birth of the child, the husband serves in the capacity of a father by openly acknowledging the child, by words or deeds, he will be classified as the legal father. Consequently, the artificially conceived child will be recognized as the man's heir. In those states where the man's consent to the artificial insemination of his wife does not have to be written, courts are given the discretion to determine the actions the man has to take to satisfy the statutory provisions to be the resulting child's legal parent. But whereas those statutes give the courts flexibility to make paternity decisions, under some statutory schemes, the courts have no discretion because the husband's consent and/or paternity are presumed by statute.

Presumption of the Husband's Paternity

In a minority of states, legislatures seem to understand that innocent children of science need protection. Those children need paternal financial support. Normally, the only man available to provide that support is the inseminated woman's husband. Some state legislatures seek to ensure that the child receives that support by making it impossible or extremely hard for the husbands to contest their paternity. It is as if the artificially conceived child is considered to be legitimate by default. In addition, under some state statutes, the man cannot rebut his paternity after he gives his consent to artificial insemination. This approach protects the child of science from being involved in protracted litigation, and it is the one that was taken by the Uniform Status of Children of Assisted Conception Act.[45] By contrast, other statutes permit the man to present evidence in order to show that he should not be legally responsible for a child his wife conceived using the sperm of another man. In other words, the presumption of paternity may be rebuttable or irrebuttable.

Irrebuttable Presumption

In Florida, if a man consents to his wife's artificial insemination with donor sperm, he is not allowed to legally challenge his paternity. Once he gives his written consent, the man is obligated to financially support the child. Under the provisions of the Florida artificial insemination statute, if a woman is artificially inseminated while she is still married and her husband gives his written consent, the law presumes that her husband is the father of the resulting child.[46] Since the presumption is irrebuttable, once the woman's establishes that her husband gave his written consent, he is not entitled to his day in court. Thus, the husband is automatically adjudicated to be the legal father of the artificially conceived child. This approach is also taken by the Georgia legislature. The child of science is presumed to be a legitimate child of the marriage, and the woman's husband is not allowed to contest that presumption.[47] Hence, the child is on par with any child of passion who was conceived during the marriage. The rationale behind this approach is consistent with the marital presumption of paternity that is applied to benefit children of passion. Hence, the child of science will be able to inherit from the estate of his or her mother's husband, and to take advantage of other benefits that are given to legitimate children of passion.

Rebuttable Presumption

On the other hand, some states have dealt with the paternity issue by giving the woman's husband the opportunity to challenge a court order adjudicating him as the artificially conceived child's legal father. Among these states, several take a unique approach to the application of the paternity presumption.

For example, the artificial insemination statute in Delaware gives the husbands of artificially inseminated women the opportunity to disprove paternity. However, the statute places restrictions on the man's actions. Therefore, according to the Delaware statute, the woman's husband cannot contest his paternity of the child unless he files the action within two years of the date he learns of the birth of the child. The man's standing to bring the action is also conditioned upon the court's determination that he failed to consent to the insemination before or after the child was born.[48] A Texas statute affords the inseminated husband a similar opportunity to contest his paternity. In order to satisfy the Texas statute, the man must file his action within four years.[49] The time constraints on the husband filing an action to dispute his paternity are vacated if he is able to prove the following: (1) his wife was artificially inseminated with donor sperm; (2) he did not live with his wife between the time she was potentially inseminated and the time he filed the action; and (3) he did not openly hold the artificially conceived child as his legal child.[50] The approach advocated by the UPA is a hybrid of the Texas and Delaware statutes.[51]

The state of Louisiana gives the inseminated woman's husband more options when it comes to challenging paternity. If the man consents to his wife's insemination, the law presumes him to be the legal father of the resulting child. As a result, he is not permitted to file an action disclaiming the child.[52] On the other hand, the law permits a man who does not consent to having his wife conceived by artificial insemination to file suit to disavow his paternity. In order to avail himself of the protections afforded by the statute, the man must file the action within one year of discovering that his wife gave birth to an artificially conceived child. The man cannot avoid the expiration of the statute of limitations by claiming lack of knowledge of the conception because the statute attributes constructive notice to the man of things he should have discovered. Thus, if the circumstances indicate that the man should have known that his wife gave birth to a child by artificial means, the law assumes that he had that knowledge.[53] However, if the husband and wife did not cohabitate during the three hundred days before the child was born, the statute of limitations for the filing of the disavowal action would not run until the husband received written notification that an interested party claimed that he was the legal father of the artificially conceived child.[54]

Under the provisions of a New Hampshire statute, a man is presumed to be the legal father of a child born under any of the following circumstances: (1) during the time the man was married to the child's mother; (2) within 300 days after the man divorced the child's mother; or (3) within 300 days after a court issued an order granting the man and the child's mother a legal separa-tion.[55] Once the man is presumed to be the child's legal father, his name is placed on the child's birth certificate.[56] In order to rebut the presumption, the man must present clear and convincing evidence to the court indicating that he should not be recognized as the child's legal father.[57] This is not an artificial insemination statute. It is meant to cover situations involving children con-ceived by sexual intercourse. Nonetheless, it is clear that the legislature con-sidered artificially conceived children when it enacted the statute. Accord-ing to the language of the statue, the man cannot rebut the presumption by proving that the child was conceived as the result of artificial insemination if he consented to his wife being artificially inseminated.[58] An unsuccessful attempt to rebut the presumption results in the man being adjudicated as the legal father of the child. The adjudication leads the court to recognize a legal father-child relationship that causes the child to be deemed legitimate.[59]

Since the New Hampshire statute makes it difficult for the inseminated woman's husband to rebut the presumption that he is the father of her artifi-cially conceived child, and the creation of a father-child relationship makes the man legally responsible for the child, the legislature was concerned about placing such a heavy burden on the man. In fact, the legislature seemed to be more concerned about protecting the rights of the husband than about pro-moting the interests of the child. To that end, the legislature included several precautionary measures in the artificial insemination statute, the main focus of which appears to be ensuring that the man gave informed consent to his wife insemination.[60] To achieve that objective, the legislature mandated that the couple undergo counseling before the wife is artificially inseminated.[61] It should be noted that this safety measure is effective only if the woman is inseminated at a medical facility. In addition, in order for the man to be adjudicated as the child's legal father, the court must be presented with more than just his written consent to the artificial insemination. The court must be shown evidence that the man agreed in writing to serve as the child's legal parent. In effect, the legislature wanted the man to take some type of affir-mative action to indicate that he was willing to accept the legal obligations of fatherhood with regard to the artificially conceived child.[62] If a married woman conceives without her husband complying with the statutory man-dates, her husband may still be legally responsible for the resulting child. In those situations, the statute requires the court to conclusively presume that the woman's husband consented to her being inseminated unless he objects in a timely manner. Under the provisions of the statute, in order to avoid being legally responsible for the child, the man has to file an action disputing his paternity thirty days from the time he discovers or should have discovered that his wife gave birth to a child using artificial insemination.[63] The different outcomes of the cases discussed above indicate that it is difficult to predict the manner in which a court will decide a case when a man's consent is not in writing. In order to protect the interests of the men and the children, states should adopt a more uniform approach. However, the attempt at uniformity has itself led to mixed results.

The Uniform Parentage Act: Linking Paternity

The Uniform Parentage Act (UPA) seeks to link a man's actions to his paternal obligations. The provision of the UPA dealing with artificial insemination references "man and woman" as opposed to "husband and wife."[64] This approach enables courts to disregard the marital status of the adults and to address the needs of the children. If a married woman becomes pregnant using artificial insemination, her husband's actions will determine if he is the legal father of the resulting child. In particular the UPA states:

> (a) Consent by a woman, and a man who intends to be a parent of a child born to the woman by assisted reproduction must be in a record signed by the woman and the man. This requirement does not apply to a donor.

> (b) Failure of a man to sign the consent required by subsection (a), before or after the birth of the child, does not preclude a finding of paternity if the woman and the man, during the first two years of the child's life, resided together in the same household with the child and openly held out the child as their own.[65]

In order to distinguish the man from a sperm donor, the UPA requires that the man express some type of intent to parent. In offering guidance on the adjudication of paternity, the UPA advocates reviewing the man's conduct before and after the artificially conceived child is born. Thus, if a woman's husband consents to the insemination prior to the birth of the child, he is the legal parent of the resulting child.[66] In most states, if the husband does not consent to the insemination, he is released from any obligations with regard to the artificially conceived child. By contrast, recognizing that sometimes actions speak louder than words, the UPA allows a man to be acknowledged as the child's legal father even if he does not consent in advance. Consequently, a man who takes steps to bond with the child during the early stages of the child's life will be recognized as his or her legal father. This approach protects the interests of the man and the child. It also prevents a third party from severing and interfering with the legal father-child relationship. The rights of the father to custody and visitation are affirmed by the UPA, and the child is allowed to maintain a relationship with the man he or she considers to be his or her paternal parent. The UPA's approach thus permits the law to recognize and respect the relationships the child forms with the adults in his or her life.

At the same time, the UPA's approach also gives the man the opportunity to change his mind with regard to his paternity after he encounters the child. For example, in a situation where the man may not have given his consent because he did not want to parent a child using the sperm of another man, and then, after meeting the child, decided that he wants to be a father to him or her, the UPA provides the man with a second chance to make a decision about parenthood. This is a positive development because it affords the child the opportunity to be raised in an intact family. Further, it ensures that the child will not lose the financial support of the man in the event he separates from or divorces the child's mother. Once he acts as a father, the UPA does not permit him to use his failure to give consent as a tool to avoid paying child support. The law seeks to protect children from being financially abandoned by parents. Just as adoptive parents do not have the legal right to return the adopted child after the adoption is final, so, too, in cases of artificial insemination, adults should not get a chance for "do-overs" when it comes to the welfare of children.

Under the UPA's approach, the man's right not to procreate is balanced against the child's right to parental financial support. According to the U.S. Supreme Court, a person has a right to procreate.[67] In order for that right to have any validity, a person must also have the right not to procreate. To ensure that a man is not forced into fatherhood, the UPA provides him with the opportunity to dispute his paternity within two years after learning of the child's birth. In order to be relieved of his paternal obligation, the man must prove that he did not consent to his wife's artificial insemination before or after the child's birth.[68] By placing a time limit on when the man can bring the action, the UPA seeks to quickly remove the uncertainty of the child's parentage, prevent the child from developing a relationship with the man, and lessen the emotional harm the child will suffer if the man's paternity is disavowed. Moreover, if the man's wife was not inseminated with his sperm, if the couple did not live together during the probable time of the woman's insemination, and if the man never openly held the child out as his child, a paternity action may be brought at any time. When he has made no attempts to embrace the child, giving the man additional time to dispute his paternity protects him from "fatherhood by deception." Since he was not involved in the conception of the child, it may take the man longer to learn of the child's conception. The provision of the statute was designed to address cases where the man is not biologically related to the child, has severed all connections with the child's mother, and has not developed a relationship with the child. Under those circumstances, the man's status as a stranger to the child justifies him being able to challenge his paternity at any time. [69]

The UPA's approach provides flexibility by addressing contingencies that are overlooked by some state statutes, including the possibility of the man changing his mind after he consents to the artificial insemination of his wife. There are various reasons why a man may decide that he does not want to parent a child conceived using another man's sperm. Since it often takes more than one attempt for a woman to become pregnant using artificial insemination, the process can be stressful. In addition, artificially inseminated women frequently suffer more than one miscarriage. After several unsuccessful attempts, the man may decide that he is not emotionally and/or financially equipped to continue using artificial insemination to become a father. Hence, he may choose to withdraw his consent. Furthermore, the couple's relationship might suffer because of the stress of the process. The relationship that the couple had at the time the man initially consented to the insemination process may no longer exist. That change of circumstance may cause the man to change his mind about raising a child with the woman. If the couple ends up on the verge of getting a divorce, the man may want to avoid a custody battle by withdrawing his consent to parent a child with the woman. Finally, during the course of the insemination process, the man may become unemployed or experience some other adversity that leaves him unable to afford to have a child. Prior to the child's conception, the man should be able to change his mind and withdraw his consent. The UPA affords him the opportunity to do so and to avoid paternity.[70] Under the UPA, change of circumstances, including divorce[71] and death[72] may relieve the man of his obligations toward the artificially conceived child.

For all of these advantages, the UPA's approach does have one major shortcoming with regard to the paternity of the inseminated woman's husband. Under the provisions of the UPA, in order to be legally liable for the child, the man must consent to his wife's insemination and express his intention to act as a father to the child. Unfortunately, this aspect of the act protects the interests of the man to the detriment of the child. It shifts the burden to the person seeking an adjudication of paternity to prove that the man intended to be the child's legal father. Since the child is usually too young to bring an action, the burden falls on the child's mother to prove her husband's intent. Once evidence of the man's consent is presented, that should be the end of the story. When a man consents to the insemination of his wife, it is not unreasonable to conclude that he wants to be recognized as the child's legal father. A man should not be permitted to avoid paying child support by claiming that he consented to the child's conception, but never intended to have his paternity acknowledged.

Litigating Paternity

Some states have not addressed the issue of paternity and artificial insemination, even as persons in those states are using reproductive technology to conceive children. Other complicated situations arise when the parties fail to comply with the statutory mandates in place and/or the courts determine that the statutes are not applicable to the particular facts of the case. In both of those instances, courts still have to deal with paternity adjudications involving children conceived using artificial insemination, and they tend to solve those cases by relying on family-law principles to allocate paternity to the husbands of inseminated women. In such cases, the courts treat the children of science as if they were conceived through natural intercourse. That is, the needs of the children are considered to be more important than the circumstances of their conception. Thus, courts take steps to ensure that the inseminated woman's husband does not escape his legal responsibility for the child. Courts commonly utilize the estoppel doctrine to hold the man financially responsible for the child. Since artificially conceived children are not given a special status in these jurisdictions, the "best interests of the child" marital presumption doctrine may also be used to adjudicate paternity in the absence of a statutory mandate.

Estoppel

Even before legislatures enacted statutes making a woman's husband liable for the support of a child she conceived by artificial insemination, some courts relied upon the estoppel doctrine to achieve that objective. As a result of Stanley's medical condition, he and Annette were unable to consummate their marriage. The couple wanted to have a child, so they consulted a medical professional about artificial insemination.[73] Stanley and Annette signed a form consenting to Annette's artificial insemination using the sperm of a third-party donor, and Stanley agreed to pay all of the expenses associated with the procedure. On September 14, 1961, Annette gave birth to the artificially conceived child, and Annette and Stanley were listed as the parents on the birth certificate.[74] However, since the marriage was never consummated, Stanley filed an action seeking an annulment. He also alleged that there were no children of the marriage.[75] After the trial court granted the annulment, the state supreme court had to determine whether the artificially conceived child was legitimate.[76]

Under the common law in place at the time, a child was considered illegitimate if his or her mother was not married to his or her father.[77] In reviewing the statutes to see if the legislature had indicated intent to change the definition of "illegitimate child," the court concluded that the legislature meant for the status of illegitimate child to be conferred on "any child whose natural father was not married to its mother irrespective of the marital status of the mother"[78] and that the statute defining illegitimacy was intended to apply to children conceived as the result of artificial insemination.[79] In addition, the court noted that the legislature had modified the concept of illegitimacy to exclude children whose parents married after they were born. Correlatively, the legislature could have easily amended the definition so that it was not applicable to children conceived as the result of artificial insemination. The fact that the legislature had not taken that action indicated that it was comfortable with artificially conceived children being deemed illegitimate.[80] Consequently, the court held that the child "which was indisputably the offspring of artificial insemination by a third-party donor with the consent of the mother's husband, is not the legitimate issue of the husband."[81]

Despite its ruling with regard to the status of the child, the court was not prepared to relieve Stanley of his obligation to support the child financially. The court opined that Stanley's actions prior to his wife's insemination created an implied promise that he would support the resulting child.[82] The key action emphasized by the court was Stanley's signing an agreement consenting to the artificial insemination. In so doing, the court reasoned, Stanley was not just going along to please Annette, but that he gave his consent based upon his own desire to have a child. Moreover, according to the court, Annette probably would not have permitted herself to be inseminated with another man's sperm if Stanley had not given his agreement. Thus, the court applied the doctrine of equitable estoppel to require Stanley to pay child support.[83] When justifying the application of the doctrine, the court stated:

Hence, it is reasonable to presume that she was induced so to act and thus changed her position to her detriment in reliance upon the husband's expressed wishes. To relieve the husband of any duty of furnishing support for the child resulting from the artificial insemination of the wife, to which she submitted in reliance on her husband's wishes, would cast a financial burden upon the wife which in equity and conscience should be borne by the husband.[84]

As the mother of the child, Annette was obligated to take care of the child because the child lived with her. The court felt that Stanley should share that responsibility. Stanley took affirmative steps to ensure that the child was conceived by consenting to the procedure and encouraging Annette to be inseminated. After Annette had the child, she could not return it. She was required to take care of the child until the child reached the age of majority. Stanley's consent to the artificial insemination did not make him the resulting child's legal father. His paternity was established on the basis of equity. Since he encouraged Annette to become pregnant, he was estopped from denying responsibility for the child. Thus, the court held that, even though he was not the child's legal father, Stanley was obligated to pay child support because his implied promise made it the equitable outcome of the case. In the interest of fairness, the court adjudicated a man who had never had sex with his wife to be the legal father of her child. Therefore, it is not surprising that a man who is capable of having sexual intercourse with his wife would be obligated to support a child conceived by artificial insemination during their marriage.

The lack of a biological connection is not enough to permit a man to ignore his legal obligation to support a child conceived by artificial insemination. The fact is illustrated by the *Levin* case.[85] Donald Levin was sterile, but his wife, Barbara, wanted to have a child. After discussing options, the couple decided to become parents using the sperm of an anonymous sperm donor. Once the child was born, Donald was listed as the father on the birth certificate. Unfortunately, when the child was young, the couple decided to get a divorce.[86]

Concluding that the child was a product of the marriage, the divorce court issued an order requiring Donald to pay child support. Later, Donald made a motion seeking to be released from this obligation. Barbara responded by asking the court to increase the amount Donald was paying for child support.[87] Donald contended that he did not have a legal duty to provide any financial support for the child because he was not biologically related to the child. Donald also cited his lack of a relationship with the child as grounds for not paying child support.[88]

After reviewing all of the facts and the law, the Indiana Appellate Court determined that Donald was estopped from seeking to have his child-support obligation removed. The Indiana Supreme Court affirmed the lower court's decision.[89] According to this court, the estoppel doctrine applied to the case because it was meant to protect persons from being induced to act in reliance on untrue statements made by others. Where Donald and Barbara were concerned, the evidence indicated that Donald persuaded Barbara to become pregnant by artificial insemination using donor sperm.

In reviewing this case, the court looked at the manner in which Donald behaved before and after the birth of the child and, after reviewing the facts, concluded that it was reasonable for Barbara to think that Donald would help her provide financial support for the child. For one thing, Donald had agreed, verbally and in writing, to Barbara's insemination before the child was conceived.[90] In addition, after the birth of the child, Donald acted as a father to the child for fifteen years. Moreover, Donald never challenged the fact that the child was determined to be a product of the marriage in the divorce decree.[91] Finding that Barbara acted in good faith when she conceived the child using artificial insemination because she expected Donald to keep his word and help support the child, the court held that Donald was estopped from filing an action to have his child-support obligations eliminated.[92] In this case, the court's objective was to make sure that the man honored his arrangement. It did not really focus upon the adverse impact that severing the father-child relationship would have had on the child. By contrast, some courts obligate the woman's husband to take care of the child because it benefits the child.

The "Best Interests of the Child" Marital Presumption

When a married woman gives birth to a child conceived as the result of artificial insemination with sperm from a man whom she knows, that man is the child's biological father. All jurisdictions give that man the right to parent his child unless there is an artificial insemination statute in place that precludes that action. In jurisdictions where such a statute does apply, the woman's husband is protected from the interference of the known sperm donor. When dealing with cases involving children conceived as the result of natural insemination, courts have made it clear that the law will not recognize two legal fathers.[93] That stance appears to benefit the artificially inseminated woman's husband and the child. Even if courts were permitted to recognize two-father parenting arrangements, the woman's husband probably would not want to share his family with another man. The presence of the fertile man might serve to remind the husband of his own infertility. As the child grew, he or she might exhibit traits of the sperm donor. Hence, watching the child and his biological father together might put a strain on the relationship between the woman's husband and the child. Eventually, the woman's husband might be made to feel like an outsider in his own family. True, some blended families support the idea that children can fare well with more than one father figure. For instance, prior to the divorce, Demi Moore's children considered both Bruce Willis and Ashton Kutcher to be their fathers. Nonetheless, situations like that one are the result of agreement and coordination between the adults. If, on the other hand, the court forces the husband to allow another man to become a part of the father-child relationship, animosity between the two men is a likely outcome. And it would not be in the child's best interests to live in such a situation.

Thus, in order to protect children, courts sometimes deny biological fathers the opportunity to establish their paternity. The rationale for that approach, which has been discussed in earlier chapters, can be further understood by reviewing the court's position in *Paternity of Adam*.[94] The circumstances of that case were that while Mary and John were living together as friends, Mary's boyfriend, Bob, moved in with them. Then, after Mary parted ways with Bob, she discovered that she was pregnant with her son, Adam, and subsequently Bob refused to have his parental rights terminated. Then, Mary married John.[95] Bob went to court to be adjudicated as Adam's legal father. The district court ordered Bob, John, and Adam to submit to blood tests. In response, Mary stipulated to the fact that Adam's biological father was Bob. Nonetheless, the court held that it was not in Adam's best interests to acknowledge Bob as his father.[96] On appeal, Bob argued that the district court erred by applying the "best interests of the child" standard in a paternity case.[97]

In order to decide if it would be in the child's best interests to have Bob recognized as his legal father, the court considered several factors, including "the parties relationships with each other, their lifestyles and incomes; testimony from the parties, testimony from Adam's guardian ad litem, and testimony from a social worker retained by Mary and John."[98] As Mary's husband, John was entitled to a presumption that he was the child's legal father. Mary rebutted that presumption when she conceded that John was not the child's biological father. That fact made the case similar to one involving a child conceived by artificial insemination using donor sperm. If the child's mother acknowledges that she conceived using sperm supplied by a man other than her husband, she is rebutting the marital presumption of paternity by admitting that her husband did not father the child. Nevertheless, according to the court deciding the *Adam* case, the woman's rebuttal of her husbands' paternity was only the beginning of the story. After the husband's paternity was rebutted, the court still had to decide whether or not it was in the child's best interest for the biological father to be declared the legal father. Subsequently, the court opined that biology was only one factor it had to consider when determining the outcome that was in the child's best interests. Other factors included:

> the existence of a home environment; the stability of the present home and family; the extent to which uncertainty of parentage already exists in the child's mind; the efforts and commitments (if any) that the putative father has taken to establish supportive and financial ties with the child; as well as any other factors which may be relevant in assessing the potential benefits or detriments to the child.[99]

The court applied the "best interests of the child" standard to make an initial parentage determination. That is, the court did not declare Bob to be the legal father, and then give him the opportunity to lose that status. In this decision, biology was not enough for a person to be adjudicated a legal parent. Although nothing in the facts indicated that he was unfit, Bob was deprived of the right to parent his child because the court concluded that the presumptive father could do a better job. To that end, the court compared the life Adam might have with Bob with the one that he had with his mother and her husband. Bob had not established a relationship with the child; he had not sought to support the child financially; and he had not indicated that he was otherwise committed to taking care of the child. By contrast, John's name was on Adam's birth certificate, and he had taken the time to create an emotional connection with the child.[100] The analysis set forth in this case illustrates why a "best interests of the child" standard may be appropriate for allocating the paternity of the woman's husband. Later in this book, I will propose a theory based upon that doctrine. Next, however, I address issues surrounding relationships between non-spousal sperm donors and children thereby conceived.

4

The Fertile Man

In 2010, sperm donation was a major theme of several movies. For example, in *The Kids Are Alright*,[1] two children tracked down the man who donated the sperm that resulted in their conception. The man was a successful co-op farmer and restaurateur, and in the course of the story, he developed a social relationship with the children. Since the man was a non-spousal sperm donor, in most jurisdictions, he could never have a legal father-child relationship with the children. Art is imitating life. More and more children conceived with donor sperm are using the Internet and other resources to try to find the men who donated the sperm used to conceive them. These children seek to find their fathers for various reasons. From a practical perspective, the donor children may want to obtain medical information. Like adopted children, they may also want a relationship with their biological father and his family. The children seldom look for the sperm donor in hopes of receiving financial support. Some sperm donors have been receptive to meeting and developing relationships with their donor children. In many instances, these men are willing to give of their time because the law protects them from child-support obligations. As non-spousal sperm donors, they can enjoy the benefits of fatherhood without the burdens. The issue of the paternity of the non-spousal sperm donor is quite complex and states have addressed it in several different ways.

According to the provisions of the UPA and the statutes enacted in most jurisdictions, non-spousal sperm donors do not have any parental rights with regard to artificially conceived children.[2] Since the men have no parental rights, they have no parental obligations. Thus, they are not required to pay child support to assist in covering the children's expenses. Approaching the matter from another perspective, the legislatures in some states have addressed the parental rights of sperm donors by disregarding their biological connections to the children. In those states, sperm donors are treated as strangers to the children. That non-parent status relieves sperm donors of all financial obligations to the children.[3] Alternatively, instead of allocating the paternity of sperm donors, some state legislatures focus upon the rights the law gives to artificially conceived children. The statutes in those jurisdictions deny artificially conceived children the opportunity to receive financial support from sperm donors.[4] Taking yet another approach, a few states do not preclude non-spousal sperm donors from being adjudicated the legal fathers of children conceived using their sperm. The statutes permit courts to evaluate the man's actions to decide whether or not he should be recognized as the legal father.[5] Finally, the legislatures in some states have not passed legislation addressing the parental status of the non-spousal sperm donor at all, with the result that courts have the flexibility to determine the paternity of the non-spousal sperm donor on a case-by-case basis.[6]

Traditionally, the man who donated the sperm to impregnate an unmarried woman was considered to be the child's legal father. The fertile man differs from the fornicating man in the method he uses to replicate himself. One man releases his sperm by ejaculating into a cup; the other rids himself of sperm by ejaculating into a vagina. The activities of both men may result in their contributing to the conception of hundreds of children. Nevertheless, the men may have different expectations with regard to their duties towards those children. The fornicating man is motivated to donate his sperm by his desire to experience sexual pleasure with a woman. Every time that man has sex with a woman, protected or unprotected, he takes the chance of becoming a father. Since no form of contraceptive is one hundred percent effective, the fornicating man understands that his sexual relations with the woman may result in his being recognized as the legal father of a child. On the other hand, the fertile man is often guaranteed that his unilateral action will not lead to parental responsibility. There are three main scenarios involving the fertile man who donates his sperm using artificial methods. The men involved in each scenario may donate the sperm for different reasons.

The first situation involves the anonymous sperm donor who has no intentions of parenting a child. At the time he donates his sperm, this fertile man usually signs an agreement waiving his parental rights. This man is truly anonymous and never has contact with the inseminated woman or the resulting child. Often motivated by money, the typical anonymous sperm donor is a young man who is in college or in graduate or professional school. He is often unmarried and does not have any children.[7] This man donates his sperm in order to be compensated, and since sperm is so plentiful, he probably does not give much thought to the consequences of donating his sperm. He probably does not think about the child(ren) who may be conceived using his sperm. His key concerns usually involve collecting the promised fee and being relieved of any financial obligations for the potential child(ren). Most sperm banks promise the donors that their identities will be kept confidential. In some cases, once the child turns eighteen, the sperm bank may be willing to facilitate an introduction if the donor agrees.[8] It should be noted, though, that some anonymous donors act out of altruism. These men donate sperm in order to help other people become parents. The money is an indirect benefit, but not the primary reason for the donation. The donor wants to bless someone else with a child; however, he does not want to share in the miracle. The intentions of the known sperm donor may be different.

The second circumstance involves the known sperm donor who wants to be a part of the child's life. This man donates sperm to a friend and retains his parental rights. Under this arrangement, the parties agree that the fertile man will be legally responsible for the child. The man may not be in a relationship, but has a desire to be a father. The woman may agree to the transaction because she wants to parent a child with her close friend. Both parties can achieve their goals of parenthood without becoming entangled in an intimate relationship. This may be a good deal for a woman who is worried about her biological clock. She may want to have a child without waiting for "Mr. Right." However, the woman may not want to take on the demands of being a single parent. Thus, having her friend agree to donate and to co-parent may be the ideal situation for her. In this context the fertile man is treated like the fornicating man with regard to his parental obligations.

In the final scenario, the known sperm donor does not want to be recognized as the child's legal father. Thus, prior to donating his sperm, the man agrees to have his parental rights legally terminated. This fertile man may donate to a family member who is struggling to conceive. For instance, a man may donate sperm to his brother's wife if the brother is unable to conceive. In that case, the child will have some biological connection to the brother. A man may also donate sperm to his sister's partner if she is in a same-sex relationship in order to ensure that the child shares his sister's DNA. Women in same-sex relationships typically accept sperm donations from fertile men they know. For instance, singer Melissa Etheridge used sperm donated by her friend and fellow-musician David Crosby in order to conceive two children with her partner, Julie Cypher. Even though Crosby played an active role in the children's lives, he signed a paper relinquishing his parental rights. The manner in which paternity is allocated can have various impacts.

Legislatures and courts have attempted to deal with the paternity of non-spousal sperm donors in ways that protect the man's procreative rights and the child's financial needs. States have taken different approaches to achieve those goals. The remainder of this chapter will explore the three main ways the issue of the paternity of non-spousal sperm donors has been resolved. The position taken by the majority of states is to declare that the sperm donor can never be recognized as the legal parent of an artificially conceived child. After the fertile man donates his sperm, the man's involvement in the child's life ends. In other states, the man may become the legal father of the artificially conceived child by agreeing to assume the role or by failing to comply with the provisions of the applicable statute. States that do not have statutes dealing with the issue determine the sperm donor's paternity on a case-by-case basis relying upon family law principles.

Legal Vasectomy (Mandating Statutory Non-Paternity)

A vasectomy prevents the release of sperm when a man ejaculates. An egg cannot be fertilized when there are no sperm in the semen. Thus, a vasectomy prevents a man from conceiving a child. The man is still able to have sexual intercourse with a woman, but he is unable to become a biological father. It has long been said that donating sperm does not make a man a father. For the most part, with regard to sperm donors, the law agrees with this statement. Legislatures perform a sort of legal vasectomy by rendering the sperm donor legally incapable of fathering a child.

In most jurisdictions, sperm donors are not given parental status. As a result, the artificially conceived child does not have the right to be supported financially by his or her biological father. The DNA connection is not enough to create a legal father-child relationship. Furthermore, legislatures in some states have passed laws stripping the sperm donor of his parental status. When the statutes treat the sperm donor as a non-parent, he does not have any parental obligations to the child. In Florida, the sperm donor has the same parental rights as other men. Nonetheless, under the state's statutory scheme, the sperm donor is required to relinquish those rights.[9]

Section 702 of the UPA addresses the paternal status of sperm donors.[10] The comment to the section states, "The donor can neither sue to establish parental rights, nor be sued and required to support the resulting child. In sum, donors are eliminated from the parental equation."[11] As the court indicated in *Steven S. v. Deborah D.*,[12] this statement is true even if the sperm donor and the inseminated woman have engaged in an intimate relationship. In that case, Steven and Deborah, an unmarried couple, agreed that Steven would donate sperm in order for Deborah to conceive a child by artificial insemination. After Deborah lost the child conceived using Steven's sperm, the couple engaged in a sexual relationship that lasted several months. After it ended, Deborah conceived a child by artificial insemination using the rest of the sperm Steven had previously donated.[13] When the child was about three years old, Steven filed an action to have his paternity adjudicated. Deborah responded by claiming that since she conceived the child by artificial insemination using Steven's sperm, he was not the child's legal father. The statute in place stated that a sperm donor should not be legally recognized as the natural father of a child conceived by artificial insemination.[14] However, instead of strictly applying the statute, the trial court concluded that it would be against public policy not to adjudicate Steven as the child's legal father.[15] While the trial court was reluctant to apply the statute because Steven was a known sperm donor and the couple was involved in a sexual relationship prior to the child's conception,[16] the appellate court determined that the trial court was in error because the legislature did not create a statutory exception for situations involving known sperm donors. The statute did not distinguish between known and unknown sperm donors.[17] Therefore, the appellate court concluded that the legislature intended for all classes of sperm donors to be denied parental status with regard to the child(ren) conceived by artificial insemination using their sperm.[18] The trial court did not have the authority to change the legislature's clear intent.

Some state legislatures have explicitly indicated that donating sperm does not make a man an instant father. The state of Wisconsin, for example, enacted the following statutory language:

> The donor of semen provided to a licensed physician for use in artificial insemination of a woman other than the donor's wife is not the natural father of child conceived, bears no liability for the support of the child and has no parental rights with regard to the child.[19]

The above language indicates that a non-spouse who donates sperm to inseminate a woman does not have a duty to take care of the artificially conceived child. That lack of responsibility is present in situations involving the insemination of married and unmarried women. A sperm donor is relieved not only of financial responsibility for the artificially conceived child; any legal relationship between the donor and the child is also eliminated. This approach honors the expectations of the adult parties. The sperm donor does not anticipate being a part of the child's life. The sperm recipient plans to rear the child without the input of the sperm donor. The fornicating man who does not want to become a father may undergo a vasectomy. Likewise, the fertile man relies upon the legislatures and courts to perform a legal vasectomy to help him avoid fatherhood.

The non-parent status of a sperm donor is important for several reasons. The most successful way to protect all of the parties involved in the artificial insemination process is to determine that the sperm donor can never be recognized as the legal father of the resulting child. Such a bright-line rule promotes judicial economy. In the absence of a clear rule, the court may be called upon to constantly adjudicate the paternity of children conceived by artificial insemination. Furthermore, this approach protects the fertility clinics by helping them to obtain donors. If young men faced the possibility of being legally responsible for the children conceived using their sperm, they might be reluctant to donate. A popular sperm donor could potentially father numerous children. Thus, legal fatherhood would place a heavy financial burden on the sperm donor.

Moreover, if young men knew that there was a chance that they may be recognized as the legal father of the artificially conceived child, they might demand more money for their sperm. This would drive up the fertility clinics' costs. The decrease in the number of sperm donors would also force the clinics to pay more for the sperm. It is a case of simple supply and demand. Giving the sperm donor the possibility of being adjudicated as the legal father of the resulting child may also reduce the number of women who are willing to purchase sperm from fertility clinics. Instead of running the risk of having to share the child with the sperm donor, more women may obtain sperm from men they know and trust. Women may be negatively impacted by a scarcity of sperm donors. The women may be forced to pay more to obtain sperm from a sperm bank if viable sperm becomes in short supply. In addition, the shortage of sperm donors may also cause a facility to overuse the sperm from one donor. As a result, numerous children living in the same area could be conceived using the sperm of the same donor. This would cause a problem if the donor's children start dating and/or marrying one another. Currently, to avoid that problem, fertility clinics limit the use of sperm from the same donor. Finally, the lack of availability of sperm donors may lead to fraud. This has occurred in a few cases where the owner of the fertility clinic wanted to avoid the cost of testing sperm for HIV and AIDS.[20]

The current system of denying parental status to sperm donors also protects the young men who donate the sperm from having to be financially responsible for children with whom they do not have a relationship. By contrast, an adjudication of paternity has several financial ramifications for the sperm donor. One is that the establishment of the father-child relationship may give the artificially conceived child the opportunity to inherit from the man. If he dies intestate, the average man would want his estate to go to children he conceived through sexual intercourse. However, if the artificially conceived child is recognized as the man's legal child, that child may have the right to inherit on par with the man's other children. Even if a man makes a will, he probably will not account for the child conceived as a result of his sperm donation. Since this child would be considered to be an omitted child, the child might have the right to take a share under the will,[21] and this would clearly go against the man's intentions. Prior to making a will, a man usually spends a great deal of time thinking about how he would like to dispose of his estate. Prior to selling his sperm to a sperm bank, though, a man probably does not spend much time thinking about the consequences, especially since he tends to be young and unmarried. By the time a child is conceived using his sperm, the man's circumstances may have changed. He may have married and had children, and so the appearance of a child seeking an adjudication of paternity could be disruptive to the man's life. That situation can be avoided by establishing a bright-line rule severing the father-child relationship. The current state of the law assures potential sperm donors that this type of thing will not occur.

Furthermore, the fact that in most jurisdictions, a sperm donor can never be the legal father of the resulting child gives comfort to the women who become pregnant using donor sperm. This is especially true of unmarried women and women in same-sex relationships. Most married women are protected because their husbands are usually willing to be recognized as the legal fathers of their children. If that is the case, the sperm donors will lose the fatherhood fight. However, unmarried women and women in same-sex relationships do not have the same protection against the sperm donor who, for whatever reason, may want to be as adjudicated as the legal father of the child. For example, the man may become infertile later in life and want to form a connection with a child whom he has fathered. Thus, the inseminated woman may find herself involved in a protracted custody and/or visitation battle. That circumstance is not good for the woman or the child.

For all of its benefits, though, the practice of stripping the sperm donor of his parental rights is not without problems. The obvious consequence of that approach is that the child may be legally fatherless if the unmarried woman does not have a spouse or significant other to help her support the child. If something happens to the woman, the child may be left without any parent. The decision to sever the father-child relationship occurs before the child is old enough to have any input. When the child is old enough to inquire about the identity of his or her father, the child may be devastated to learn that his or her father voluntarily walked away. This often occurs in situations involving adopted children. The law refuses to let a woman contract away the child's right to child support because child support is the right of the child and not the mother.[22] Following this same reasoning, one could argue that the law should not be able to contract away a child's option to have a relationship with his or her biological father. This is especially true because, by giving up his parental rights, the man is also walking away from his financial obligations to the child. It may not be fair for the legislature or the child's mother to take away the child's right to parental support. The process of making the sperm donor legally sterile may adversely impact the resulting child. The law ignores the biological connection between the child and the sperm donor, and declares that the father-child relationship can never exist. Consequently, the artificially conceived child is also denied the opportunity to have a complete medical history. Given that several chronic diseases are related to genetics, it is crucial that the child has access to this information—information that the law ends up withholding from the child.

Legislatures and courts have taken steps to make the fertile man legally incapable of reproducing. Unlike the fornicating man, the fertile man is not permitted to claim ownership of his progenies. When it comes to adjudicating the paternity of the fertile man, the law treats the man as if his fertility is linked to sexual intercourse. If there is no sexual intercourse, there is no paternity. Nonetheless, some fertile men may become legal fathers in circumstances involving sexless intercourse.

Sexless Intercourse (Recognizing Paternity by Agreement)

Some states permit fertile men to accept the label of "father." In those situations, the law allows the man and the inseminated woman to create a legal father-child relationship through the use of sexless intercourse. The parties unite to ensure the conception of a child using artificial insemination. Even though the couple does not connect sexually, they may be recognized as the legal parents of the child who results from their collaboration. In some states, the law permits the sperm donor to become the legal father of the artificially conceived child by agreement. The man's paternity is established based upon his consent and not because of his biological connection to the child. The law seeks to honor the agreement made by the parties if it is not unfair or against public policy. As a result, the sperm donor is recognized as the legal father and is required to help support the child financially.

In those states, the rule is still that a non-spousal sperm donor is not considered to be the father of a child conceived artificially using his sperm. However, the law does permit the parties to opt out of the rule in order to establish the sperm donor's paternity. For instance, the Kansas statute states:

> The donor of semen provided to a licensed physician for use in artificial insemination of a woman other than the donor's wife is treated in law as if he were not the birth father of a child thereby conceived, unless agreed to in writing by the donor and the woman.[23]

The New Jersey legislature uses slightly different language to reach the same conclusion. The statute states:

> Unless the donor of semen and the woman have entered into a written contract to the contrary, the donor of semen provided to a licensed physician for use in artificial insemination of a woman other than the donor's wife is treated in law as if he were not the father of the child thereby conceived and shall have no rights or duties stemming from the conception of a child.[24]

The two above-cited statutes focus upon the establishment of the father-child relationship between the sperm donor and the artificially conceived child. A man can choose to donate his sperm and walk away from the child. New Hampshire takes a different approach. Under the provisions of its statute, "a sperm donor may be liable for support only if he signs an agreement with the other parties to that effect."[25] By attributing support obligations to the sperm donor who agrees to assume that responsibility, the statute is indirectly indicating that the sperm donor is the legal father of the child. If the man agrees to support the child, it can be implied that he is also consenting to be recognized as the child's legal parent. It would not make sense for the man to assume the burdens of fatherhood unless he also intends to reap the benefits that come with that status.

In some jurisdictions, even if the statute makes it clear that the sperm donor is not the legal father of the artificially conceived child, courts may permit the parties to change the status of the sperm donor by agreement. For example, the Colorado statute stated that a non-spousal sperm donor was not the father of a child conceived using assisted reproduction.[26] As the following case indicates,[27] that clear statement of the law did not prevent a sperm donor from seeking to be adjudicated the father of a child conceived as the result of artificial insemination using his sperm.

In 1983, J.R. and E.C. met. At that time, they were both single.[28] A couple of years later, J.R. consented to provide some of his semen so that E.C. could conceive a child by artificial insemination. As a result, J.R. ejaculated into a container and delivered the semen to E.C., whose gynecologist inseminated her with it. Afterwards, E.C. contacted J.R. and requested a second sample. J.R. complied with E.C.'s request by taking a sample of his sperm to her gynecologist's office. After E.C. was inseminated with the second sperm sample, she conceived a son whom she named R.C.[29]

When R.C. was a year old, J.R. filed a paternity action because he wanted to be recognized as the boy's legal father. In support of his petition, J.R. listed the activities he had taken pre- and post-birth to bond with the child. According to J.R., he took an active role in preparing for the child's birth, including buying items, establishing a college trust fund, and setting up a nursery for the child in his house. J.R. also told the juvenile court that E.C. knew that he wanted to be recognized as the child's father, and that she treated him as if he was. For instance, E.C. let J.R. accompany her to birthing classes and attend baby showers as one of the guests of honor. Furthermore, J.R. contended that E.C. encouraged him to bond with the child. J.R. stated that after he helped to deliver R.C., he often fed the child at night and cared for him during the day, both with E.C.'s approval.[30]

E.C. disputed all of J.R. factual claims. Her version of the facts classified him as just a sperm donor who did not want to be financially responsible for supporting the child. Nonetheless, E.C. argued that even if such an agreement existed, it would not be enforceable because it would violate the statute. E.C. filed a motion for summary judgment relying on the plain language of the statute that stated that a non-spousal sperm donor was not entitled to parental rights. E.C. urged the juvenile court to ignore J.R.'s factual contentions with regard to their discussions pertaining to his paternity. She asked the court to limit its discussion to whether or not the parties had complied with the statute.[31] In opposition to E.C.'s motion, J.R. alleged that the statue did not apply to the unique factual situation before the court. J.R. maintained that since the parties agreed that he would be the child's legal father, they had opted out of the statute. Therefore, he sought to make a promissory estoppel argument. In order to do so, J.R. asked the court to make factual findings with regard to the actions he had taken in reliance on E.C.'s promise that he would be recognized as the child's legal father.[32] The juvenile court concluded that the only relevant facts were undisputed—J.R. was a sperm donor who donated his sperm to a medical professional, so that it might be used to inseminate a woman who was not his wife. Thus, since the statute denied parental status to a non-spousal sperm donor, the juvenile court granted E.C.'s motion for summary judgment.[33]

Not surprisingly, J.R. appealed the juvenile court's decision because he wanted a trial on the merits.[34] The Colorado Supreme Court had to decide whether or not the statute prevented the parties from agreeing that J.R. would be the child's legal parent.[35] E.C. argued that the statute contained an irrebuttable presumption that a non-spousal sperm donor could never be the father of the artificially conceived child. On the other hand, J.R. claimed that the statute included a rebuttable presumption of non-paternity, and the parties had rebutted that presumption by their agreement that J.R.'s paternity would be adjudicated.[36] In the first part of its decision, the state supreme court acknowledged that the legislature intended for children of science to be treated differently from children of passion. The difference in treatment was based upon the statutory presumptions. Noting that "The biological father is normally presumed to be the legal father of a child,"[37] the court added that the general assembly had established a different list of presumptions with regard to the paternity of artificially conceived children.[38] The court's analysis indicated that whereas biology determined the paternity of children conceived as the result of sexual intercourse, biology was not as relevant when the children were conceived through sexless intercourse.

In addition, though, the supreme court determined that the statute was unclear with regard to the rights and duties of known sperm donors and unmarried women.[39] In light of that ambiguity, the court analyzed the legislative intent and arrived at the conclusion that the purpose of the statute was

> . . . to provide a legal mechanism for married and unmarried women to obtain a supply of semen for use in artificial insemination and, in the case of married recipients, to make clear that legal rights and duties of fatherhood are borne by the recipient's husband rather than the donor.[40]

The court determined that in the case of a married woman, it made sense for the legislature to intend to establish an irrebuttable presumption that her husband was the father of any children she conceived with his consent. Thus, the statute would not permit the court to enforce an agreement between the woman and the sperm donor which established the donor as the child's legal father. Moreover, the court noted that in cases involving anonymous sperm donors, the legislature probably intended for the presumption of non-paternity to be irrebuttable because a scenario wherein an unknown sperm donor contacted the woman to make such an agreement was so unlikely.[41]

With regard to known sperm donors and unmarried women, however, the court found no logical reason for the legislature to want to make the presumption of non-paternity irrebuttable.[42] Since the statute meant for the sperm donor not to be adjudicated the parent of the child, the supreme court concluded that "the General Assembly neither considered nor intended to affect the rights of known donors who gave their semen to unmarried women for use in artificial insemination with the agreement that the donor would be the father of any child so conceived." Thus, the court held that the case involving J.R. and E.C. was beyond the scope of the statute,[43] and the case was remanded so that the juvenile court could determine if an oral agreement regarding J.R.'s paternity existed. The supreme court reasoned that if the parties had not entered into an agreement prior to the insemination, the statute applied, and J.R. could not be adjudicated as the child's legal father. On the other hand, the existence of such an agreement would make the statute inapplicable. Hence, the juvenile court would have to rely upon the agreement to determine whether or not to recognize J.R. as the child's legal father.[44]

The case discussed above raises two issues. The first is whether or not a sperm donor should be allowed to establish his paternity by agreement. The second is whether or not that agreement should be required to be in writing in order to be legally recognized.

There are several reasons to answer the first question in the affirmative. One is that allowing the inseminated woman and the sperm donor to agree that the sperm donor should be recognized as the legal father encourages co-parenting arrangements. Doing so also acknowledges that biology is still important. If the biological link creates a legal relationship between the fornicating man and his child, the same should be true of the fertile man and the child conceived using his sperm. The availability of two legal parents to provide emotional and financial support will be beneficial to the child. Second, a statutory scheme that permits a sperm donor's paternity to be established by agreement gives the man the opportunity to have a relationship with his biological child. In a society where there are so many fatherless children, it is important to encourage a man to voluntarily agree to support his child. A man who consents to become a parent may be more likely to pay his child support. Third, statutes that permit the courts to honor the agreement the sperm donor makes with regard to his paternity are in line with the law's treatment of the inseminated woman's husband. That man's consent establishes his paternity. Therefore, it is not farfetched to permit a sperm donor to establish his paternity by agreement. Finally, since the agreement is mutual and voluntary, allowing the sperm donor to become a father by agreement will not adversely affect sperm donations or discourage women from using donor sperm. And while the donor does not have a duty to support the child unless he agrees to be designated as the child's legal father, the inseminated woman has only to share parenting with the sperm donor if she agrees to recognition of his paternity.

The answer to the second question is not so clear because there are both advantages and disadvantages to requiring that a sperm donor's agreement be in writing. The court in the above case was not troubled by the fact that the agreement between the sperm donor and the inseminated woman was oral. On the contrary, it entrusted the juvenile court, as fact finder, with the task of verifying the existence and terms of the agreement. The issue may have been resolved differently if E.C. had denied the existence of the oral agreement. That would have demonstrated the need for a statute requiring a sperm donor's agreement to serve as a parent to the artificially conceived child to be in writing. The writing requirement lessens evidentiary disputes by avoiding "he-said, she-said" situations. The party seeking to establish paternity has the burden of proving that the man signed an agreement consenting to be the child's legal father. If the agreement cannot be produced, the case can be resolved on summary judgment. This may protect the child from unnecessary litigation because the existence of a written agreement may prevent one or both of the parties from denying the man's paternity.

The written agreement requirement is consistent with other procedures involving children. In the case of adoption, for instance, a man may terminate his parental rights in order to permit someone else to adopt his child. That consent must be in writing. If a written document is necessary for a man to relieve himself of parental obligations, a similar instrument should be required for him to accept parental rights. Moreover, the written agreement requirement enables courts to honor and protect the expectations of the parties. If he agrees in writing, the man must fulfill his monetary obligations towards the child. This enables the child to have the financial support of two parents. As the above case indicates, after the birth of the child, the woman may seek to remove the man from the child's life. The existence of a written agreement empowers the man to be able to go to court to enforce his parental rights. This prevents the woman from being able to convert the man's sperm into a child and then deny him the opportunity to parent the child. A man has ownership interest in his sperm, and he should not be forced to involuntarily relinquish that interest once the sperm is used to create a child.

Giving the sperm donor the opportunity to accept paternity recognizes that situations involving known sperm donors should be treated differently than those involving unknown sperm donors. Further, the written agreement requirement may discourage people from entering into these types of agreements without slowing down to think about the consequences. The benefits of the approach outweigh the drawbacks. The main shortcoming of the written agreement requirement is that it may encourage litigation because the court is called upon to evaluate the validity of the contract. From a public policy perspective, courts may be reluctant to treat children like commodities that are the subjects of contracts. The ability to contractually acquire parental rights may be seen as the other side of the coin of being able to contract away parental obligations, like child support. Courts have held those kinds of contracts to be against public policy.[45]

When the fertile man agrees to be adjudicated the father of children he helped to conceive, some courts honor that commitment and recognize him as the legal father. Since the children were conceived using his seed, it make sense for them to be recognized as the "fruits of his loins." The interaction between the fertile man and the inseminated woman that results in the conception of a child is a sort of sexless intercourse. Like other types of intercourse, sexless intercourse has the potential to result in the conception of a child. By recognizing paternity by agreement, some legislatures acknowledge that the father-child relationship can be created in different ways. A fertile man who does not intend to become a legal father may take actions that result in the conception of a child. In those cases, some courts ignore the man's intent and let him reap the consequences of his actions.

Unintended Consequences

When a fornicating man has sex with a woman and she becomes pregnant, he suffers the consequences. Those consequences include being adjudicated the legal father of the child and having to pay child support. Although the man's main purpose is to enjoy his encounter with the woman, and although most times, his intent is not to procreate, the law nonetheless holds him responsible for the consequences of his actions. If the fornicating man's conduct result in the creation of a child, his biological connection to the child makes him responsible for the child. Ironically, even though the fertile man intends to help create a child, he is generally absolved of any liability for the resulting child. While there are some circumstances in which the sperm donor does have to accept the unintended consequences of his action, a man who donates his sperm usually does not intend to act as a parent to the child. The key thing that distinguishes the fertile man from the fornicating man is his ability to become a legal father. The fornicating man is presumed to be the legal father of the child he conceives with an unmarried woman. To the contrary, the fertile man is presumed not to be the legal father of the child he conceives with an unmarried woman. The majority of jurisdictions have statutes that protect the sperm donor from all parental obligations.

In order to be treated as a fertile man instead of a fornicating man, the man must be eligible to take advantage of the statutory protections. By extension, a man who fails to comply with the statutory mandates may be adjudicated as the child's legal father. In addition, in jurisdictions that do not have an applicable statute, the courts have the discretion to determine that the sperm donor is the child's legal father. In either situation, the man has to deal with the unintended consequences of his actions. The following three factors might cause courts to determine that the sperm donor is not entitled to the statutory protections that relieve him of parental obligations: the man's status as a known sperm donor; the man's relationship with the child; and the man's failure to deliver his sperm to a licensed physician or health care provider. The cases analyzed below delve further into this last scenario.

Paternity by Non-Acquiescence

In order to receive the protection of the artificial insemination statute in most states, the sperm donor is required to deposit his sperm with a licensed physician.[46] .Some of those statutes mandate that the insemination can be performed only by a licensed physician.[47] Consequently, an arrangement involving a woman who becomes pregnant by self-insemination with donor sperm is usually considered to be outside the scope of the artificial insemination statute. Thus, the man involved in the situation is treated like a fornicating man and not a fertile man. The status of "fornicator" instead of "donor" makes the man financially responsible for his biological child. Because the process of artificial insemination is not a procedure that requires any type of medical expertise, it is not difficult to imagine a situation where a woman is inseminated at home using a turkey baster. In that circumstance, the woman will usually know the donor, and so a licensed physician will not be involved in the procedure. In almost half of the states with such statutes, since the sperm donor is the biological father and he did not comply with the statute, he may be held to be legally responsible for paying child support. The primary way in which the sperm donor fails to comply with the statute is by not delivering the sperm to a licensed physician or health care provider. As *Jhordan v. Mary K.*[48] indicates, that action may result in the donor being adjudicated the legal father of the child.

The associate justice of the California appellate court started the opinion off by making the following statement:

> By statute in California a "donor of semen *provided to a licensed Physician* for use in artificial insemination of a woman other than the donor's wife is treated in law as if he were not the natural father of a child thereby conceived." Civil Code s. 7005, sub.(b) (emphasis added). In this case we hold that where impregnation takes place by artificial insemination and the parties have failed to take advantage of this statutory basis for preclusion of paternity, the donor of semen can be determined to be the father of the child in a paternity action.[49]

As the statement indicates, in order to avoid an adjudication of paternity, the sperm donor had to comply with the statute by supplying his sperm to a licensed physician. If the donor failed to abide by the terms of the statute, he would be recognized as the child's legal father. Even though the case is over twenty years old, it has not yet been overruled. A discussion of the case illustrates how courts may analyze cases involving issues of paternity by non-compliance.

This case involves a tale of three adults and one child. All three parties cooperated to insure that the child was born and supported. Mary and Victoria were close friends. Nothing in the case indicates that the women were romantically involved. Nonetheless, the women wanted to raise a child together,[50] and Mary agreed to become pregnant by artificial insemination. The only thing the women were missing was a man to donate the sperm to help them conceive a child. Seeking an appropriate donor, Mary turned to her friends and other people she knew and identified several potential candidates. Eventually, she and Victoria selected Jhordan to serve as their sperm donor.[51]

Jhordan went to Mary's home several times to deliver samples of his sperm. The court speculated that, since Mary was a nurse, she probably inseminated herself. After Mary conceived, she and Jhordan continued to stay in touch. Jhordan made preparations for the child's birth, including buying furniture and establishing a trust fund,[52] and did so with Mary's approval.

Victoria was also involved in the pre-birth activities. For example, she drove Mary to her doctor appointments and participated in birthing classes. Further, Victoria was with Mary when the baby was born. Jhordan was not present for the birth, but his name was placed on the child's birth certificate. Later, Jhordan visited Mary and the baby, and then Mary reluctantly agreed to let Jhordan see the child on a monthly basis.[53]

When the child was only a few months old, Mary terminated Jhordan's monthly visits. In response, Jhordan threatened to hire a lawyer to protect his parental rights. Mary tried to get Jhordan to sign an agreement stating that he would not try to be declared the child's legal father. Jhordan refused Mary's request and filed a suit to be declared the child's father and to be granted visitation. In a separate action, the county received a stipulated judgment against Jhordan for reimbursement of child support. Jhordan was required to reimburse the county for the public assistance Mary had received on behalf of the child.[54] As a result of the judgment, Jhordan owed past and future child support. Since Jhordan was required to pay child support, the court issued an order giving him the right to visit the child on a weekly basis. The visits were held in Victoria's home. Mary permitted Victoria to play an active role in the child's life, and Victoria considered the child to be a part of her family. For instance, Victoria's daughter acted as a sister to the child, and her parents assumed the role of grandparents.[55]

After Jhordan sought to be adjudicated the child's legal father, Victoria filed a motion to be joined as a party to the litigation. The court granted Victoria's petition, and she asked the court to award her joint legal custody with Mary. She also wanted to be declared the child's de facto parent in order to be entitled to visitation rights. Mary testified that prior to her insemination, she had told Jhordan that she did not want the sperm donor to be involved with the resulting child. According to Jhordan's testimony, however, before he donated his sperm, Mary and he agreed that he would have an ongoing relationship with any child conceived using his sperm. In its decision, the trial court adjudicated Jhordan as the child's legal father and gave him visitation rights, and while it refused to give Victoria the status of de facto parent, the court did grant her visitation rights. Mary received sole legal and physical custody of the child, and was made the sole decision-maker with regard to the child's schooling and other important issues.[56] Nonetheless, Mary and Victoria appealed the trial court's decision with regard to Jhordan's paternity and Victoria's parental status.

On appeal, Mary and Victoria argued that as a sperm donor, Jhordan was not entitled to parental rights. The women based their argument on the artificial insemination statute in place at that time. Although the women acknowledged that they had not complied with the statute's "physician requirement," they nevertheless contended that the failure to deliver the sperm to a licensed physician should not make the donor non-paternity provision inapplicable. Instead of focusing upon the plain language of the statute, the women urged the appellate court to consider the legislative intent. In attempting to down play the importance the legislature placed upon the physician requirement, the women made two arguments. First, they claimed that the physician requirement was included in the statue only because the legislature thought that licensed physicians would be the only ones supervising artificial insemination procedures. In this regard, the women seemed to imply that if the legislature had known that some women would self-inseminate, it would not have required the process to be supervised by licensed physicians. Second, the women maintained that the legislature did not intend for the physician requirement to be a mandate; it was just a recommendation on the legislature's part.[57]

Rejecting both of the arguments the women attempted to make, the court determined that the legislature made a conscious decision to include the physician requirement in the statue. The court's conclusion was based on the fact that earlier versions of the statute did not contain the physician requirement. Indeed, the requirement was not added until after substantial legislative debate. According to the court, this suggested that the decision to include the physician requirement was a thoughtful one. In addition, the appellate court noted two legitimate reasons for the legislature to have included the physician requirement in the statute. First, the existence of the physician requirement insures that a physician is involved in the artificial insemination process. This is beneficial because the physician would be able to get the donor's complete medical history and to test him to determine if he has any genetic or communicable diseases. Second, the court felt that the physician requirement gave the doctor, an independent third party, the opportunity to create a formal document setting forth the nature of the relationship between the sperm donor and the inseminated woman and the relationship between the sperm donor and the child. Such a document would help reduce litigation of cases like this one.[58]

In its decision, the court acknowledged that there are some valid arguments against the physician requirement. First, artificial insemination is a simple procedure that can be performed without the expertise of a physician. Second, the court accepted the women's argument that the presence of a physician might "offend a woman's sense of privacy and reproductive autonomy, might result in burdensome costs to some women, and might interfere with a woman's desire to conduct the procedure in a comfortable environment such as her home or to choose the donor herself."[59] However, the court did not think that the women's argument had much merit. The physician requirement did not impact the location or the nature of the insemination. That is, the requirement would not prevent the woman from self-inseminating at her home. Rather, the physician requirement mandated only that the sperm had to be delivered to a licensed physician. Nothing in the statue prevented a man from giving his sperm sample to a licensed physician so the woman could retrieve it. In order to satisfy the statue, the physician did not have to perform the artificial insemination.[60] The court ultimately concluded that there were valid arguments for and against the physician requirement. Nonetheless, the court reasoned:

> The Legislature's apparent decision to require physician involvement in order to invoke the statue cannot be subject to judicial second-guessing and cannot be disturbed, absent constitutional infirmity.[61]

The court determined that the statute did not apply to the case because a licensed physician was not involved in the artificial insemination procedure that resulted in the child's conception. As a result, the appellate court affirmed the trial court's decision adjudicating Jhordan as the child's legal father.[62] In reaching its final decision the appellate court reasoned that by not invoking the statutory protections, Mary permitted Jhordan to maintain his status as the child's biological and legal father.[63] Instead of being treated as a sperm donor with regard to paternity, Jhordan was entitled to have his paternity acknowledged. In this instance, non-compliance with the statute benefited the man because he wanted to be recognized as the child's legal father. There may be times that a sperm donor is disadvantaged for failing to comply with the statutory mandates. After evaluating the necessity of the physician requirement, the court deferred to the legislature. Since the physician requirement has the potential to adversely impact the inseminated woman and the sperm donor, it is worth exploring the pros and cons of having such a mandate.

To Self-Inseminate or Not to Self-Inseminate

A woman who decides to conceive a child through artificial insemination must make several key choices before she becomes pregnant. The first and most important step is to select a donor. If the woman is married, she usually decides to use sperm from an anonymous donor. That is the case because using a known donor may be too awkward for her husband. Men often are reluctant to let close friends and family know that they are experiencing fertility problems. Thus, married couples do not view friends and family as good sources of donor sperm. The couples are usually more comfortable obtaining sperm from an unknown donor. In some cases, the couple uses a donor with traits similar to those of the husband, so friends and family can assume that the husband is the biological father of the artificially conceived child. On the other hand, women involved in same-sex relationships often seek out known sperm donors. One reason for this choice may be to ensure that there is a male figure in the child's life. Single women, by contrast, are typically reluctant to use sperm from men that they know. A woman who has made the decision to parent by herself may be afraid that permitting the sperm donor to have a relationship with the child may lead to a custody and/or visitation battle. Given society's preference for children to be raised in two-parent households, the single woman's fear may be well founded. Either way, selection of the sperm donor is just the first leg of the journey to parenthood.

After the woman or the couple selects a donor, the next decision to be made is how the sperm is going to be obtained. The sperm donor could go to a clinic or a doctor's office and make his donation. Then, the recipients could get the sperm from the facility. On the other hand, the sperm donor could deliver the sperm directly to the person or persons planning to use it for insemination. Regardless of how the woman gets the sperm, she still has to make an important decision—to self-inseminate or not to self-inseminate. The reasons women choose to self-inseminate are varied. The most evident one is that self-insemination is so easy to do. The various medical devices that enable a woman to monitor her ovulations make it simple for a woman to know the best time to inseminate herself. Moreover, women may choose to self-inseminate in order for the conception process to seem as natural as possible. A woman may feel more comfortable being inseminated at home in a familiar environment than in a sterile environment like a physician's office. Another reason why women may opt to self-inseminate is economic. Visits to the doctor are expensive, and health insurance providers may not cover assisted reproductive procedures. Since artificial insemination does not require any special medical expertise, the woman may decide to reduce her expenses by performing the procedure herself. With regard to married couples, self-insemination gives the man the opportunity to be a part of the process by being the one who actually does the procedure. When deciding whether or not to self-inseminate, women tend to emphasize these kinds of considerations and generally do not consider the legal ramifications. Most women just assume that the donor will not have any parental rights. They do not know that by failing to comply with the statue, they are empowering the sperm donor to exercise his parental rights. Thus, it is important to evaluate the necessity of the physician requirement.

Necessity or Nuisance

Artificial insemination is not a complicated medical procedure that needs to be done by a physician. As previously mentioned, women can self-inseminate without posing a danger to their health or the health of their babies. Thus, the physician requirement is not a medical necessity. It can, however, be a nuisance. The requirement that the process involve a physician in some way may make the artificial insemination procedure too expensive for some people. In order to cut costs, low- or moderate-income women may self-inseminate using sperm obtained from men they know. If the statute does not protect those men from being adjudicated the legal fathers of the children conceived using their sperm, they may be unwilling to contribute their sperm. As a result, women with limited resources may be denied the opportunity to become mothers. Since the use of a physician is not medically necessary, the only real justification for requiring that one be involved in the process may be evidentiary. If a disinterested party is not available to testify about the insemination process, courts may have a hard time determining if the child was conceived by artificial or natural insemination.

A fornicating man should not be permitted to avoid his parental obligations by claiming that he was just a fertile man. There are often three sides to every story—his side, her side, and the truth. To get to the truth, it may be necessary for the court to be able to obtain independent evidence from an unbiased third party like a physician. The existence of a dispassionate third party will help prevent fraud and other deceptions in paternity cases. Nevertheless, it is not necessary for that person to be a physician or a person with a medical background. Another option could be for the legislature to create a statutory presumption that if a child was conceived without the assistance of a licensed physician, the child's conception was a result of natural insemination. In order to rebut the statutory presumption and take advantage of the statutory protections, the sperm donor would have to present clear and convincing evidence that the child was conceive by artificial insemination. This approach would reduce the occurrences of fraud and make artificial insemination more affordable.

Normally, the fertile man is not deemed to be the legal father of a child conceived using his sperm. Legislatures consider him to be a non-parent. He is treated simply as a supplier of a product that is necessary to conceive a child, but only if his actions are in conformance with the statutory mandates. If he does not do the things required by the statute, he will be treated as if he is a fornicating man and held responsible for the artificially conceived child whether or not that conforms to his intentions. The fertile man may be treated in the same way if the artificial insemination takes place in a jurisdiction that does not have an artificial insemination statute.

Paternity by Discretion

The law has not kept up with the advances in reproductive technology. In the majority of states, assisted reproductive technology is not heavily regulated. Legislatures have failed to address most of the legal issues that arise because of the existence of reproductive technology. One reason for this failure may be the fact that most legislators are not scientists. This is not to say that they are not intelligent enough to comprehend the problems that can arise if the use of assisted reproduction is not controlled. However, the lack of scientific knowledge may prevent legislators from understanding the adverse impacts that the unrestrictive use of reproductive technology can cause. For example, legislators could not have anticipated the octomom situation where a single woman gave birth to eight children using artificial insemination. Artificial insemination is the oldest and most commonly used form of assisted reproduction. Therefore, most states have attempted to address the paternal obligations of the men involved in the artificial insemination process.

Nonetheless, in at least sixteen states, there are no statutes addressing parental status of sperm donors. Some of those states have statutes regulating artificial insemination in animals, mainly because artificial insemination procedures were initially permitted to be performed only on domestic animals.[64] Another reason for the lack of artificial insemination legislation is that the legislatures do not want to distinguish between children of science and children of passion. Some legislatures have not passed artificial insemination statutes because they think that new laws are unnecessary. Those persons think that the current family-law doctrines are sufficient to address the issues resulting from the use of artificial insemination. If no statute is in place, courts are given the discretion to adjudicate the paternity of the sperm donor.

In those states, courts allocate the paternity of sperm donors on a case-by-case basis. Due to the lack of an artificial insemination statutory scheme, courts are forced to rely on common law principles to resolve paternity cases. Courts also attempt to apply statutes that were enacted to deal with traditional nuclear families consisting of a man, a woman, and their children. As a result of this piecemeal approach, it is difficult to predict the outcome of a case. In jurisdictions where there are statutes in place, in order to determine the paternity of the sperm donor, all the parties have to do is to read and understand the provisions of the statute. In states where there are no statutes, the sperm donor is at risk of taking on responsibilities that he did not anticipate assuming. Once his paternity is adjudicated by discretion, he is financially responsible for the child. *Jacob v. Shultz-Jacob*[65] demonstrates that point.

Because the Pennsylvania legislature has not enacted a statute setting forth the legal rights and obligations of a non-spousal sperm donor, a Pennsylvania court had to decide if a known sperm donor was responsible for child-support payments. Since there was no legislative guidance in place, the court relied upon common law to resolve the case. The case involved a man who discovered that "no good deed goes unpunished."

Jennifer L. Schultz and Jodilynn Jacob participated in a commitment ceremony and established a civil union. Afterwards, the women decided to have a child together. In order to make their dream of parenthood come true, the women convinced Carl Frampton, one of their friends, to donate his sperm. Jodilynn was artificially inseminated with Carl's sperm and conceived two children.[66] Subsequently, the women separated. Since she was the biological mother, the court awarded Jodilynn physical custody of the children, while giving Jennifer partial physical custody. Acknowledging Carl's relationship with the children, the court also awarded him partial physical custody, so that he could have the children for one weekend each month.[67]

As the non-custodial parent, Jennifer was ordered to pay child support to Jodilynn. Jennifer must have concluded that what was good for the goose was good for the gander because she asked the court to join Carl as an indispensable party. Jennifer argued that since he was given the benefit of partial custody, Carl should have to bear the burden of paying child support.[68] The trial court, which did not find Jennifer's argument to be persuasive, refused to grant her motion to join Carl to the case. According to the court, Carl's status as a sperm donor relieved him of an obligation to pay child support. Since Carl was not responsible for financially supporting the children, he was not considered to be an indispensable party to the child-support action. Jennifer filed a timely appeal.[69]

The appellate court focused more on Carl's actions than on his status as a sperm donor. In so doing, the court thought that it would be unfair to Jennifer to ignore that fact that Carl was the children's biological father. In addition, the fact that Carl acted more like a father than an uninvolved sperm donor led the court to conclude that he should be adjudicated the children's legal father. Consequently, Carl's status as the legal father required him to pay child support.[70] In the process of making its decision, the court relied on several factors to determine if Carl should be equitably estopped from denying his paternity. First, prior to the women's separation, Carl had voluntarily provided financial support for the care of the children. Since the children had come to rely upon Carl's financial support, the court felt that it would be unfair to withdraw that support. In essence, the court formalized the informal child-support arrangement Carl had with the women.[71]

Another factor that weighed in favor of Carl's paying child support was the fact that he had a paternal relationship with the children. For example, Carl attended the birth of at least one of the children. That act indicated that the parties considered Carl to be a father and not just a sperm donor. Normally, sperm donors do not take such an active part in the birth of the artificially conceived child.[72] After the birth of the children, Carl also took steps to establish a relationship with them. For instance, Carl allowed the children to call him "Papa."[73] In light of these circumstances, it would be unfair to pretend that he was nothing more than a sperm donor. The fact that Jennifer was obligated to pay child support did not relieve Carl of his duty to help support the children. As a consequence, the court concluded that all three adults were liable to provide financial support for the two children.[74] This was one of the first published cases in which a court required a sperm donor to financially support a child conceived using his genetic material. The court noted that in reaching its decision, it was motivated more by promoting the best interests of the children than by protecting the legal rights of the parents. Nevertheless, the court stated, "We recognize this is a matter which is better addressed by the legislature rather than the courts."[75] As of the time of the publication of this book, the Pennsylvania legislature still had not enacted a statute responding to the court's concerns.

Children of passion may be created without discussion or conversation. Hormones go wild, and overactive libidos turn adults into teenagers. The end result is the unplanned conception of children. The women who choose not to exercise the abortion or adoption option no longer have to bear the financial burden of raising their children alone. A married woman can usually rely on her husband for financial support even if the child resembles the mailman or the pool boy. If the woman is unmarried, her "baby daddy" is on the hook for at least eighteen years of child support. These men have the right to walk away from the women and the children, but they might as well leave their checkbooks behind because "oops babies" need food, clothing, and shelter. Courts are going to take steps to make sure that the men involved in the situations help to provide those necessities. Ironically, children of science are not treated with the same care. Children of science are often conceived after much discussion and planning. Unlike the women who give birth to children of passion, the mothers of children of science must make arrangements to ensure that they have legal fathers before those children are even conceived. If the women fail to take the necessary steps, they are solely responsible for financially supporting the children of science. The men involved in the artificial insemination process, either by being married to the inseminated women or by being sperm donors, should not be given the option of walking away from the children of science because "designed babies" have needs too.

Redefining the Family

5

Expanding the Definition of Legal Child

Presently, the imposition of the obligation to pay child support is complicated by the rise of diverse family forms, including children conceived using assisted reproduction. It appears that the law's treatment of certain classes of children with regard to parental support is connected to the manner in which society views those children. Since paternity establishment has always been entwined with the legal obligation to pay child support, societal opinion has influenced the adjudication of paternity, and where the government has enacted laws ensuring that those classes of children considered to be worthy of support had legal fathers who were obligated to provide that support, the worthiness of the class appears to be tied to public opinion. In order for children of science to receive the consistent financial support that they need, the public has to be convinced that the manner in which they are conceived is not a practice that should be discouraged. For example, given that the government has taken steps to ban cloning of humans in response to public opinion,[1] it would be difficult to lobby the legislatures to enact statutes protecting the rights of children conceived by cloning. Even if cloning was not illegal, the government may seek to discourage it by not providing a mechanism for those children to receive financial support. The law took that approach when dealing with the inheritance rights of non-marital children.

Children of Passion

While children conceived as the result of passionate encounters have always occupied a special status in the eyes of the public and the law, it appears that a hierarchy exists among those classes of children and that the legal protections given to them correspond to the public policy promoted or violated by their means of conception. In effect, the legal treatment of children has mirrored the manner in which they were conceived. If the child's conception

| 111

resulted from an act that violated a societal norm, the child was deemed not to be entitled to legal protections. This was meant to deter others from conceiving children in the unacceptable way. In light of the reverence given to marriage, children born as the result of sexual intercourse in a marriage have always been the "favorite" class. To encourage persons to get married before they procreate, the law gives marital children preferential treatment.

Adopted children were placed in the top tier with marital children in order to reward people for doing the right thing, as well as to encourage people to adopt children who had been abandoned, abused, or orphaned. People who made the choice to adopt were engaged in an activity that society considered admirable. Moreover, in order to persuade people who could not afford to support their children to give those children up for adoption, the law ensured that the children would be supported by the adoptive parents. Children who needed to be adopted had already been conceived. Thus, the manner in which they were conceived did not impact their classification as legitimate children who were worthy of being financially supported.

The deterioration of the institution of marriage contributed to the creation of two new classes of children of passion—non-marital children and stepchildren. Both of these classes of children are second-tier children. In fact, the popular phrase "to be treated like a stepchild" is often used to refer to a person who has been neglected or mistreated. These two classes of children of passion are given second-tier treatment because their very existence implies that someone has behaved in a way that society would like to discourage. Stepchildren typically come about because of divorce. Non-marital children are the result of persons having sex outside of marriage. These classes of children are the evidence of two activities that are condemned by most major religions—divorce and fornication. In order to deter people from participating in one or both of those activities, the law did not give the resulting children the legal protections enjoyed by marital and adopted children.

Children of Marriage

Originally, the acceptable way to conceive children was through sexual intercourse in a marriage. From biblical times, it was understood that the main purpose of marriage was procreation. In modern society, both parents have had a duty to support the child during the marriage. The dissolution of the marriage did not absolve either party of the obligation to provide financial support for the child. The mother usually received custody of the child. Therefore, courts ordered the man to continue to live up to his support obligation. In cases involving marital children, paternity became an issue only if the man claimed to have no biological connection to the child. In light of the special status given to marital children, the public would have been outraged if the courts failed to make sure that those children were financially supported. As a result, the man's paternity was presumed so that the marital child did not have to suffer the indignity of proving paternity. Those children were also given preference under the intestacy system, and so, if a man did not specifically disinherit his marital children in his will, the law permitted those children to take a part of his estate.[2]

The need to promote the economic best interests of marital children motivated the government to intervene when parents were not supporting their children. The usual methods of that intervention were child-neglect adjudications and terminations of parental rights.[3] The rights of adults to be parents did not supersede the child's right to economic support. If the parents did not supply the appropriate amount of financial support to provide the child with food, clothing, and shelter, the law permitted child protection agencies to file child-neglect petitions. Furthermore, if the parents refused to live up to their financial obligations with regard to their children, they lost the right to be parents. The government terminated their parental rights in order to give someone else the opportunity to support the child through adoption or through placement in the foster care system.[4]

People realized that after a woman became pregnant, circumstances could change. For instance, a man could divorce the woman or die before the child's birth. Once a man contributes to the conception of a child, society expects him to support the child financially. That expectation does not change simply because the man terminates his relationship with the child's mother or dies prior to the birth of the child. The law recognized that posthumously born children had the same need for support as those children born during the marriage and/or prior to the man's death. In order to protect those children, legislatures enacted statutes requiring courts to treat those children like other marital children. For instance, a Louisiana statute states, "If a child is born within three hundred days from the day of the termination of a marriage and his mother has married again before his birth, the first husband is presumed to be the father."[5] The purpose of this statue is to make sure that a man is financially responsible for the unborn child's support.

In most jurisdictions, stepfathers are not obligated to support stepchildren. Thus, if the child's biological father was relieved of his duty to support the child, the child would have only one person obligated to provide financial support. Once the child was conceived, the man's support obligation was attached. The termination of the marriage was not enough to release the man from his obligation. While society has always been sympathetic to the plight of widows and fatherless children, this is especially true of situations involving pregnant widows. Thus, a man is presumed to be the father of any children his wife gives birth to within a certain period of time after his death.[6] The law treats the posthumously born marital child in the same manner as other marital children. Marital children share the top tier with a class of children that the law created to acknowledge that persons can become parents by following their hearts.

Children of the Heart

The face of the family changed when people started adopting and raising other people's children as their birth children.[7] If the adoptive parents were unable to conceive children using their genetic material, the public saw adoption as a way to help those people to become parents. Adoption was also considered to be a way to provide families for children who had been abandoned or orphaned. Adoption required the persons to take affirmative steps to receive custody of the children involved. Once the adoption was finalized, no one else was given the opportunity to provide a home for the child. Thus, it was only reasonable that the adoptive parents provide financial support for the child. The law accomplished that goal by declaring that adoptive children should be treated in the same manner as marital children for the purposes of child support and inheritance. The paternity of the man who adopted a child was adjudicated as a part of the adoption process. Adoption is based upon contract principles. In exchange for having the privilege of raising the child, the man promises to provide financial support for the child. In order to encourage persons to adopt foster children with special needs, the federal government provides a fund out of which states can pay subsidies to adoptive parents—a provision which indicates that the government wants to protect the economic interests of the most vulnerable class of adopted children.[8]

In some communities adoptions were not formalized. Some men accepted responsibility for children without the benefit of going through the legal adoption process. The law refused to permit those men to walk away once the child had become financially dependent on them. In order to protect the interests of the children, courts exercised their equitable powers to recognize informal arrangements that have the attributes of legal adoptions. These situations are referred to as equitable or virtual adoptions. The equitable adoption doctrine provides a remedy for children who expected to be legally adopted. A child claiming equitable adoption is usually seeking the right to child support, inheritance, or government benefits. The purpose of the doctrine is to protect the child from being without parental support after his or her biological parents have given up their rights and agreed to the adoption. In order to warrant being considered equitably adopted, the child or someone acting on behalf of the child must prove the following: (1) the potential adoptive parent expressly or implicitly agreed to adopt the child; (2) the child acted in reliance on that agreement; (3) the biological parents relinquished custody of the child; (4) the child lived in the home of the potential adoptive parent and acted as his or her child; and (5) the potential adoptive parent took the child into his or her home and acted as a parent to the child.[9]

At least one court has held that the doctrine of equitable adoption may be applied to impose a child-support obligation on a man.[10] That question was resolved in a case involving Madonna and Antonyo Johnson, a couple who unexpectedly became parents. Michelle Clayton, the wife of Madonna's son, asked the couple to keep Jessica, her three-month- old baby, until she got back on her feet. Michelle never returned to claim the child. For ten years, the couple raised Jessica to believe that they were her parents. She called them "Mom" and "Dad" and was listed as a dependent on their federal tax returns. Furthermore, Jessica's parents gave Madonna and Antonyo permission to adopt her. They filed adoptions petitions in New Jersey and Kentucky. However, because they were both in the military, that obligation prevented them from completing the adoption process.[11] Eventually, Jessica discovered that Madonna and Antonyo were really her grandparents. At that time, the couple told Jessica that they had adopted her.[12]

When Antonyo filed for divorce, Madonna asked the court to order him to pay child support for Jessica. Antonyo argued that he was not obligated to pay child support because he was not Jessica's biological father and he had never legally adopted her. Thus, he sought to be treated as a stranger to the child.[13] On her side, Madonna urged the court to find that Antonyo had equitably adopted Jessica. Given these claims, the court had to decide whether or not to apply the equitable adoption doctrine, as well as to determine if a child who had been equitably adopted was entitled to child support.[14] Concluding that Antonyo had equitably adopted Jessica, the court found that he was legally obligated to help financially support her. Antonyo's obligations did not end when he divorced Madonna. Like any adoptive parent, Antonyo was required to pay child support.[15]

At the height of the AIDS and crack epidemics, numerous grandparents were forced to take custody of their grandchildren. Although there are a variety of reasons for those persons not taking the steps to make such adoptions formal, the key ones were a lack of knowledge and a lack of financial resources. Even in cases where the biological parents agreed to the adoptions, many of the grandparents did not know the steps they needed to take to legally adopt the children. Since children should not be punished for the inaction or ignorance of the adults, the purpose of the equitable adoption doctrine is to provide the children with a remedy, so they can receive financial support. It also permits children to have the opportunity to inherit from the persons who neglected to adopt them. In addition, even after a legal adoption has occurred, some persons may seek to avoid being financially obligated to provide for the child. Courts have applied the doctrine of adoption by estoppel to protect the interests of the child. Doing so is appropriate to prevent the adoptive parent from denying the existence of the adoption.[16]

Children of No One

The United States was founded on strict Christian principles. Christianity makes it clear that fornication is a sin. Traditionally, society took great pains to make people pay for their sins. Since pregnancy outside of a marriage was evidence of fornication, unmarried pregnant women were often hidden from society. Subsequently, society refused to acknowledge non-marital children as persons worthy of being financially supported. The law formalized that point of view by declaring that non-marital children were the children of no one.[17] Eventually, in order to spare the government the burden of having to take care of non-marital children, the law required a man to provide financial support for his non-marital children. Nonetheless, the law did not take too many affirmative steps to make sure that the man lived up to his financial obligations. The taint of illegitimacy stayed with non-marital children for a long time. I remember when my sister got pregnant during her second year of college. My mother was terrified about what people in our small community would say. Even though this was the 1980s, the shame of getting pregnant without a husband still lingered. My sister was not permitted to have a baby shower or to appear happy about the impending birth of her child. On the contrary, she was treated as if she had contracted a contagious disease. To persons outside of our circle of family and friends, my nephew was considered to be damaged goods because of the circumstances of his conception. Since we grew up in the "Bible Belt," reaction to my sister's out-of-wedlock pregnancy was probably extreme. Nonetheless, most of society still viewed non-marital children as unfortunate mistakes. For example, in

1992, then Vice President Dan Quayle criticized the CBS television network for permitting the lead character on the sitcom *Murphy Brown* to conceive a child without being married.[18]

In addition to dealing with the social stigma that came with having a child out of wedlock, the average unmarried woman has to deal with the economic burden that accompanied that status. The only assistance the government gave an unwed mother was a small welfare check and food stamps—and in those situations, seeing an unmarried woman using public assistance to provide for her child roused public outrage for a long time. While the "deadbeat" dad got a pass, the so-called "welfare queen" was loathed. However, as more and more people, and especially public figures, started proudly having children without the benefit of marriage, society started to view those children in a manner similar to that of marital children. With the law in the majority of states slowly lining up with societal opinion, a man is now generally obligated to provide financial support for his non-marital children. At the same time, though, non-marital children are not as favored as marital children because society still prefers that children be conceived inside of a marriage. Thus, unlike marital children, non-marital children have the burden of complying with certain statutory mandates in order to get the courts to establish the paternity of their fathers.

Children of Someone Else

Historically, divorce has been condemned by most of the major religions. For example, the Catholic Church teaches that marriages cannot be dissolved because they are meant to last forever. Once the man and woman stand before God and vow to stay together until death, they are not permitted to renege on that promise. Thus, the Catholic Church will not recognize a civil divorce.[19] The law, however, does, and since the majority of people who divorce and remarry have children. The law has to deal with the existence of stepchildren. At common law, stepfathers were not financially responsible for their stepchildren.[20] The child had a biological father to provide support, and the public did not feel that the man should be released from his obligation to support his child just because his wife married another man. Nonetheless, the biological father was, and is, free to consent to the stepfather's adoption of the child. The stepfather's paternity results only because of the adoption. If he does not adopt the child, the stepfather is not the child's legal father. Regardless, the relationship of stepfather and stepchild does not impose any obligation of support.[21]

Law and society recognize that divorce and paternity are linked. For instance, a Jewish woman who receives a *Get* (divorce decree) is prohibited from marrying for ninety days to ensure that if she remarries quickly and becomes pregnant, there will be no questions about the child's paternity.[22] Elizabeth Taylor was infamous for marrying seven different men. However, the public's attitude about multiple marriages has changed, and partly as a result of popular celebrities making multiple trips down the aisle. For instance, in 2011, Kelsey Grammer got married for the fourth time; meanwhile, Donald Trump has children with three different women. The public also has a different perspective on the stepparent-stepchild relationship. Some realize that if a widow with young children remarries, the stepfather may be the only one available to provide paternal support to the child. Faced with the fact that approximately one-fourth of all children will live with a stepparent before the age of majority, many courts and legislatures have reformulated the rules affecting stepparent support obligations. While the majority of states follow the common law rule that stepparents have no obligation to support their stepchildren during the stepparent's marriage to the child's custodial parent, this general rule is subject to two exceptions. In some jurisdictions, stepparent support statutes impose a duty on stepparents.

For example, a Vermont statute states:

> A stepparent has a duty to support a stepchild if they reside in the same household and if the financial resources of the natural or adoptive parents are insufficient to provide the child with a reasonable subsistence consistent with decency and health. The duty of a stepparent to support a stepchild under this section shall be coextensive with and enforceable according to the same terms as the duty of a natural or adoptive parent to support a natural or adoptive child including any such duty of support as exists under the common law of this state, for so long as the marital bond creating the step relationship shall continue.[23]

As this statute indicates, stepchildren are still not treated on par with marital or adoption children because the child's right to support is tied to the stepfather's relationship with the child's mother. The stepfather's duty to provide support is also tied to the child's need for economic support. Some states do, however, impose a duty of support on the stepparent, based on the "in loco parentis" doctrine. This obligation applies if the stepparent has voluntarily taken the child into the home and assumed parental obligations. Hawaii, for instance, has such a statute, which states:

> A stepparent who acts in loco parentis is bound to provide, maintain, and support the stepchild during the residence of the child with the stepparent if the legal parents desert the child or are unable to support the child, thereby reducing the child to destitute and necessitous circumstances.[24]

Under the terms of this statute, the stepparent's support obligation is also linked to the child's economic needs and the actions of the other adults involved in the case. Therefore, if the biological father is required to pay child support, the stepfather is relieved of his obligation to do so.[25]

After the termination of the stepparent's marriage to the child's custodial parent, the stepparent has no legal duty to support a former stepchild.[26] Therefore, none of the stepparent support statutes continues the obligation after divorce. Moreover, even if the stepparent continues his or her relationship with the stepchild, the in loco parentis doctrine does not apply after divorce.[27] However, in limited cases, courts may impose a post-divorce duty of support on stepparents based on an expanded theory of parenthood.[28] In addition, the stepparent may agree to pay post-divorce child support, and the courts are inclined to enforce those agreements unless there is a compelling reason to not do so.[29] Children of sex are conceived in different types of relationships. Their status as "natural" children makes them eligible to receive financial support from both of their parents. Frequently, children of science are not given that same protection.

Children of Science

Advances in reproductive technologies have led to the creation of three new classes of children of science—artificially conceived children, children conceived as the result of surrogacy arrangements, and posthumously conceived children. This book deals with the paternity of artificially conceived children. Surrogacy does not directly impact paternity, so I will not discuss the needs of those children in this section. However, some of the theories of determining their parentage will be explored in chapter 6. Not all artificially conceived children are treated equally. Artificially conceived children born to adults in same-sex relationships are not as protected as those born to married or cohabiting mixed-sex couples.

Inter Vivos Children

Currently, children of science conceived during the lives of their fathers are where non-marital children were several decades ago. Members of society have not fully accepted children conceived using reproductive technology. Until assisted reproduction is considered to be just another way to create a family, the artificially conceived child may not be treated on par with other classes of children. One reason for this lack of acceptance might be ignorance. Even though the number of people using artificial insemination to conceive has increased, the average American probably does not know anyone who has used that method to get pregnant. Most people are reluctant to admit that they are having infertility problems and thus would never acknowledge that they conceived their children using artificial insemination. For married couples, it is easier to let people think that the husband fathered the child. This may be one of the reasons why married couples go to such great lengths to assure that the sperm donor resembles the husband in appearance. Married women may also be afraid that their husbands will treat the children like "stepchildren" instead of biological ones. This is not a hollow fear because once the child is conceived using donor sperm, some men cannot deal with having to raise another man's child. In the case of a divorce, a man may not want to provide financial support for a child who is not biologically related to him. The man may see the child as a reminder that he is unable to conceive a child. Unmarried women who conceived using donor sperm may also wish to conceal that fact. Preferring to have friends and family think that they became pregnant as the result of sexual intercourse, these women may feel that being perceived as fornicators is more acceptable than being seen as infertile or undesirable to a man. This is especially true in cultures where a woman is valued only for her ability to conceive a child.

Most religions have condemned the practice of artificial insemination. In particular, some aspects of the three major religions prohibit a woman from being inseminated using the sperm of a man who is not her husband. Thus, for example, under the tenets of Islam, a woman can be artificially inseminated only if her husband supplies the sperm. The woman belongs to her husband, so only his genetic material should be placed inside of her. If a woman receives sperm from a man who is not her husband through sexual intercourse, it is clearly adultery. The woman's unfaithfulness to her husband is not diminished because she receives another man's sperm artificially.[30] Normally, adultery refers to the voluntary sexual intercourse between a married person and someone other than that person's spouse. In order to view artificial insemination as adultery, persons would have to give sexual intercourse a broad meaning. Under the Islamic perspective, the condemnation appears to focus upon the birth of the child, and not on the relationship between the man and the woman. At one time, the law even considered a woman who was inseminated using the sperm of a man who was not her husband to be an adulteress.[31]

In 1987, the Sacred Congregation for the Doctrine of Faith published the Instruction on Respect for Human Life in its Origins and on the Dignity of Procreation (Donum Vitae) in order to discuss the Catholic Church's teachings with regard to the morality of assisted reproduction. The drafters of that doctrine condemn artificial insemination as morally wrong. According to the teachings of the Catholic Church, the primary purpose of sex is procreation. Furthermore, the only morally acceptable way to conceive a child is through sexual intercourse in marriage. The church condemns masturbation because it does not result in the conception of a child. Since the primary way to acquire donor sperm is through masturbation, the church teaches that artificial insemination is morally wrong. Thus, a woman who conceives a child by being artificially inseminated with sperm she obtains from a man who is not her husband is deemed to have committed adultery, a sin that is repeatedly condemned in the Bible.[32] The approach of the Catholic Church is not reflective of the position most Protestant Christians take with regard to artificial insemination. Members of those groups have taken different stances on the issue.[33] My research indicates that the artificial insemination of a woman with her husband's sperm does not violate Jewish law. However, the issue of artificial insemination by donor has been heavily debated in the Jewish faith, and there appears to be no one definitive position.[34]

Even if a woman's religion does not condemn the use of artificial insemination with donor sperm, the woman may feel that using that method to become pregnant shows a lack of faith. In particular, Christian and Jewish women have to contend with the "Sarah" story. According to the Bible and the Torah, in her desperation to have a child, Sarah failed to wait on God and took matters into her own hands. As a result of her actions, Hagar gave birth to Ishmael. After Ishmael was born, Hagar made Sarah's life miserable. Sarah realized her mistake and forced Hagar to leave the camp. The Bible indicates that had Sarah waited on the Lord for the birth of Isaac, she would have spared herself a lot of heartache and pain.[35] Consequently, some women may feel that if they conceive using artificial insemination, they are not trusting God to bless them with a child.

Until attitudes about the use of assisted reproduction change, courts and legislatures may not feel compelled to move children conceived by artificial insemination from the third to the first tier of priority. In order to combat the perception that artificial insemination is an unnatural process, some scholars have started referring to the process as "alternative insemination."[36] Subtle changes like that may impact the way that the public thinks about the process. In addition, some recent movies such as *Back-Up Plan*[37] may help to remove some of the mystery and/or stigma from the assisted reproduction process. Currently, at least sixteen states have simply ignored the paternity of men involved in the artificial insemination process. Even fewer jurisdictions have dealt with the paternity of a man who becomes a father *after* he dies.

Testamentary Children

A man's paternity is usually adjudicated during his lifetime. In fact, in order for a man to be considered the legal father of a non-marital child, the child or the child's mother must take steps to have him deemed as the father prior to his death or within a certain period of time after his death.[38] In most jurisdictions, a man cannot be posthumously adjudicated as the father of a non-marital child.[39] On the other hand, if a man's wife is pregnant with his child at the time that he dies, that posthumously born child is treated as his legal child.[40] The issue becomes more complex when a woman attempts to have her dead husband acknowledged as the father of the child she conceives with his sperm after he has already died. Currently, there is a lot of debate about whether or not posthumous reproduction should be legally permitted.[41] Nevertheless, an increasing number of women are seeking to become pregnant using their dead husband's sperm.[42] Paternity matters in those cases because the posthumously conceived child needs to be financially supported. The disputes in those cases usually arise when the child's mother applies for Social Security Survivor's benefits or tries to have the child declared as the man's heir.[43] Because death ends the marriage, at the time that she conceives the child, the woman, who has been transformed from wife to widow, is being artificially inseminated with the sperm of a man who is not her husband. Given that the woman's marital status does not survive the man's death, can the posthumously conceived child acquire the status of a marital child?

In most situations where a man's paternity is adjudicated, he has taken an active role in the process. For instance, the cuckolded man marries an unfaithful woman; the fornicating man has unprotected sex with a woman;

the non-consenting man acts in a way that indicates he wants to parent the child; and the fertile man donates his sperm. In light of those various circumstances, it is logical to conclude that in order for a dead man to be declared the father of a child conceived using his sperm, he has to be actively involved in the child's conception. This is not an outrageous statement because at least one man sought to become a father by testamentary intent.[44] Prior to his death, William Kane deposited fifteen vials of his sperm with a sperm bank. Kane made it clear that he wanted his girlfriend, Ellen, to take possession of his sperm after his death. To that end, Kane not only wrote a letter to the sperm bank giving them permission to release his sperm to Ellen,[45] but also left the sperm to Ellen in his will. In addition, the language of Kane's will made it clear that he intended for Ellen to use his sperm to conceive children after he died. And furthermore, in order to have a connection with the potential posthumously conceived children, Kane wrote a letter to all of his children, including the ones who had not yet been conceived.[46] After Kane committed suicide, his existing children fought to ensure that Ellen did not receive his sperm. They did not want any posthumously conceived siblings. In spite of their objections, the court issued an order preventing the destruction of Kane's sperm. Under the terms of the settlement agreement Ellen had with the children, she received five vials of Kane's sperm.[47] Although it is unclear whether or not Kane would have been adjudicated the father of the posthumously conceived children, the court's treatment of a case involving children actually conceived using a dead man's sperm may in itself be informative.[48]

Another relevant case developed as follows. After Warren Woodward died, his wife, Lauren, used his sperm and conceived twin girls.[49] When Lauren successfully petitioned the Massachusetts Probate and Family Court for an order requiring the clerk of the city to add Warren's name to the twins' birth certificate,[50] the court adjudicated Warren as the twins' legal father, and issued an order amending their birth certificates to reflect that fact.[51] Once the twins were recognized as Warren's legal children, Lauren reapplied for Social Security Survivor's benefits on their behalf.[52] The Social Security Agency was not convinced, though, that the twins were Warren's survivors, and so Lauren was denied benefits. After exhausting her administrative remedies, Lauren filed an appeal in the U.S. District Court for the District of Massachusetts.[53] The federal court certified the issue to the Supreme Judicial Court of Massachusetts. The judge certified the following question: "Whether posthumously conceived children had a right to inherit under the Massachusetts intestacy system."[54]

In the superior court, the parties took dramatically different positions. On the one hand, Lauren argued that posthumously conceived children should always have the right to inherit from their deceased parent as long as there is proof of a biological relationship between the child and the deceased. On the other hand, the government claimed that posthumously conceived children should never have the right to inherit from their deceased parent because they would not be in existence as of the date of the parent's death.[55] The court rejected the positions of both parties as too extreme and searched for a middle ground.[56]

In order to resolve the case, the court reviewed the state's intestacy law. Since, under that law, only a decedent's "issue" had a right to inherit his or her property, the court had to determine whether the twins were Warren's issue.[57] But because the legislature did not clearly define the term "issue," the court had to look at the legislative purpose behind the intestacy statute to decide if posthumously conceived children should be classified as "issue" for inheritance purposes.[58]

As a part of its analysis, the court discussed the three state interests that needed to be considered. The first of these was the state's interest in promoting the best interest of the children, including both posthumously conceived children and children who were alive or conceived prior to the death of the parent. The second was the state's interest in preventing fraud and insuring the orderly administration of probate estates. The third was the state's interest in protecting the reproductive rights of both genetic parents, including the one who was deceased.[59]

In addressing these considerations, the court acknowledged that children have the right to receive financial support from their parents and to petition their parents' estate for support.[60] It also determined that the opportunity to inherit should be extended to posthumously conceived children because in enacting intestacy statutes that gave preference to children, the legislature intended to promote the welfare of all children.[61] In support of its decision to place posthumously conceived children in the class of children eligible to inherit under the intestacy system, the court emphasized two key points. First, the court noted that although the legislature knew that posthumously conceived children existed, it took no action to prevent them from taking under the intestacy system. In addition, the court stressed that the legislature supported the assisted reproductive technologies that were the only means by which posthumously conceived children could come into being. Thus, once they were born, the legislature was obligated to give them the same rights as other children.[62]

Next the court addressed the state's interest in the prompt and accurate administration of probate estates. The state was obligated to provide certainty to the descendant's heirs and creditors.[63] Since posthumously conceived children could be born years after the death of their parent, permitting them to inherit would make it difficult for the state to achieve that goal. Here, instead of focusing on the need for finality, the court dealt with the state's interest in preventing fraud on the probate courts. In so doing, the court concluded that the probability of fraud would be diminished by the fact that posthumously conceived children, like other non-marital children,[64] were required to prove paternity before they could inherit.[65]

The last state interest the court discussed was that of honoring the right of persons to choose if and when to reproduce.[66] In order to assist in the promotion of that state interest, the court decided that the person claiming rights on behalf of the posthumously conceived child had to present convincing evidence that the deceased person consented to the posthumous conception and agreed to support the child who resulted from the procedure.[67] This requirement would protect the reproductive rights of the deceased and further the state's goal of fraud prevention.[68]

After balancing the competing state interests, the court held that in order to advance the best interests of posthumously conceived children, these children should be given the opportunity to inherit from their deceased parents.[69] Nonetheless, the court also recognized that some precautions were necessary to protect the integrity of the probate system and the reproductive rights of the deceased parent. Consequently, before he or she can inherit from his or her deceased parent, the posthumously conceived child, or his or her representative, must satisfy a three-part test.[70] One is the provision of evidence that the child and the deceased were related by blood. Then, there must be proof that prior to his death, the man consented to the posthumous use of his genetic material to conceive a child. Finally, it has to be shown that before he died, the man agreed to provide financial support for his posthumously conceived children.[71]

The three-part *Woodward* test provides a good example to state legislatures of the best way to protect the interests of posthumously conceived children, pre-death children, the dead man, and the state.[72] The posthumously conceived child will benefit from the court's decision by having the opportunity to inherit from his or her father. The steps the living parent of the posthumously conceived child must take to enable the child to have the right to inherit are not overly burdensome. Another important factor is that the court's decision does not disregard the needs of the man's existing heirs. The expectations of those heirs will be protected because the conditions that must be satisfied for the posthumously conceived child to inherit will limit the number of potential heirs. Hence, the inheritance of the pre-existing heirs may not be substantially reduced by the birth of numerous posthumously conceived children. In addition, the mandates included in the court's decision will promote the state's goal of quickly and accurately probating estates.

The *Woodward* court's approach has been followed in other jurisdictions, and despite the circumstances surrounding their births, once posthumously conceived children exist, the public is comfortable with the law giving them the opportunity to inherit from their fathers. Some people think of posthumously reproduction as a way to help the woman heal after the loss of her husband. The children are also viewed with sympathy because they are born fatherless. The lack of a father deprives these children of his emotional support, but that should not deprive them of the man's money and/or his government benefits. For some, posthumous reproduction may be preferable to same-sex procreation.

Children of Same-Sex Relationships

Many persons in same-sex relationships use artificial insemination to create their families. The main reason those persons rely upon assisted reproduction to become parents may be necessity. In a lot of jurisdictions, it is difficult or impossible for gay and lesbian couples to adopt children.[73] Further, persons in same-sex relationships are excluded from the protections of the artificial insemination statutes, which in most states apply only to marriages or relationships consisting of men and women. William Churchill stated, "Where does the family start? It starts with a young man falling in love with a girl—no superior alternative has yet been found." This belief about the creation of a family still persists. The passage of state statutes prohibiting same-sex marriages,[74] support for the federal Defense of Marriage Act,[75] and public approval of anti–same-sex marriage legislation are just a few of the events that indicate that society is not quite ready for the government to legally recognize same-sex relationships.[76] As a consequence of societal attitudes towards same-sex relationships, legislatures and courts have not taken sufficient steps to protect the children born into those non-traditional families. In addition, the current statutory regime pertaining to the parentage of artificially conceived children has had particular negative impact on children born to women in same-sex relationships.[77]

In some of those cases, the child has been deemed to have only one legal parent because the court has both limited the scope of the artificial insemination statute and relieved the woman who is not genetically unrelated to the child from having to pay child support. In order to protect the artificially conceived children, some courts have broadly interpreted the language of the statute.[78] The following discussion of a Massachusetts case demonstrates the harmful impact a strict interpretation of an artificial insemination statute can have on a child of science conceived by the agreement of same-sex partners.[79]

T.F. and B.L. participated in a commitment ceremony and then started functioning as a married couple, with both women combining their money and each designating the other as a beneficiary on her life insurance policy and retirement plan.[80] In addition, T.F. wanted to become a mother. B.L., however, was afraid that her history of psychological problems might prevent her from being a fit parent. Nonetheless, in order to please T.F., B.L. supported her decision to have a child,[81] and together the women decided to use donor sperm to conceive. Together, both women selected the anonymous donor, and they signed the form consenting to the procedure, as well as combining their money to pay for the procedure and the prenatal expenses.[82] After two artificial insemination procedures, T.F. conceived a child. Thereafter, though, the women parted ways before the child was born.[83]

The artificially conceived baby was born prematurely. On several occasions, B.L. visited T.F. and the baby in the hospital. B.L. helped to choose the baby's name and promised that she would help to support him financially. She also acknowledged the child as her child to her family and friends.[84] Then, because of his premature birth, the child had some medical problems, and T.F. requested money from B.L. to help pay for his medical and other expenses. While at first, B.L. promised that she would do so, she then informed T.F. that she would have no further contact with her or the child.[85] In response, T.F. filed a law suit asking the court to order B.L. to pay child support. T.F. based her case upon two key arguments. First, T.F. maintained that prior to the child's conception, B.L. had orally agreed to support the artificially conceived child. T.F. urged the court to conclude that B.L. was in breach of her oral promise to pay child support. Alternatively, T.F. asked the court to apply the equitable estoppel doctrine to prevent B.L. from avoiding her child-support obligation.[86]

In its proceedings, the court determined that by making the oral promise, B.L. had entered into an implied contract to be the parent of the child.[87] Nevertheless, the court held that the contract was void because it violated the public policy of the state.[88] Addressing both of those factors, the court decided that B.L. had not made an independent promise to pay child support, so her obligation to do so stemmed from the implied contract to parent. Since that contract was void, B.L. did not have a duty to financially support a child to whom she was not biologically related and whom she had not adopted.[89]

With regard to T.F.'s equity argument, the court admitted that it had the discretion to exercise its powers to promote the best interests of children. Nonetheless, the court concluded that it could act in equity only to enforce legal duties, not to create them. Thus, since B.L. was not legally required to pay child support, the court could not order her to do so.[90] In order for T.F. to be obligated to support the child, the court had to adjudicate her as the child's legal parent. The lack of a biological link between B.L. and the child, along with B.L.'s failure to adopt the child, negated against the establishment of a parent-child relationship.[91] The court concluded that a parent-child relationship could not have been created by the artificial insemination statute because it was not applicable to the case. The statute pertained only to situations involving a woman and her spouse. B.L. was not a spouse because the women were not married to each other.[92]

The child involved in this case was deprived of a second parent because of the status of the women's relationship. Clearly, if the case had involved a married man and a woman, the man would have been obligated to pay child support. Courts have used the estoppel doctrine to force men to provide financial support for children their wives conceive artificially with or without their consent. However, since the child was born into a family consisting of a same-sex couple, the court refused to use its equitable powers to provide a remedy for the child. Artificially conceived children born as the result of collaborations between same-sex couples are deprived of financial support because society does not approve of the relationships that lead to their conceptions.

The family is the cornerstone of any society. However, the definition of "family" is constantly changing. That is, while families still consist of adults and children, there is no limit on the number of persons that make up a family unit. The fact that the law recognizes different classes of children is relative to the allocation of paternity in situations involving artificially conceived children. The legal status those children are granted determines the amount of support the men who participate in their conception are required to provide. Then, too, composition of a legal family is also governed by the numerous ways a man can be designated as a legal father.

The Evolving Meaning of Parenthood

The number of ways to create families has increased dramatically. In 2005, a justice on the Tennessee Supreme Court remarked, "We now live in an era where a child may have as many as five different 'parents.' These include a sperm donor, an egg donor, a surrogate or gestational hosts, and two non-biologically related individuals who intend to raise the child."[1] Consequently, many legal scholars and courts have argued that the manner in which legal parenthood is adjudicated should be modified to adapt to this new reality. Some have also suggested that parentage should be redefined in order to allow the law to recognize more than two legal parents. In this chapter, I analyze a few of those proposals and how they may be relevant to the adjudication of paternity in artificial insemination cases. I use the knowledge gleaned from those theories to create my proposal for the manner in which paternity should be allocated to the inseminated woman's husband and the sperm donor. The application of different tests to determine paternity is not radical because several courts have already taken that approach with regard to maternity. Focusing on ways in which courts have adjudicated maternity in several cases, I go on to apply the lessons learned to the development of an appropriate test for paternity.

Parenthood by Biology

Paternity by biology is the oldest and most commonly accepted theory of paternity. Since biology was traditionally the default position when it came to parentage, and since maternity was usually unchallenged, parentage determinations focused on paternity. The man who contributed the genetic material used to conceive the child was typically deemed to be the child's legal father. As a result of the continuing preference for biology, the fornicating man is legally responsible for supporting the child even if he does not have a relationship with the child's mother. With regard to both children of passion and children of science, the law recognizes the man who donates the genetic material used to create the child as the child's legal father unless there is a compelling public policy reason to disregard that genetic connection. For example, the cuckolded man, not the biological father, is usually held responsible for the child because the law seeks to preserve marriages and to prevent children from being classified as illegitimate. Moreover, the fertile man's biological link to the child does not make him the legal father because the law wants to encourage men to donate sperm to help infertile persons become parents. In order to put the paternity by biology theory into perspective, it is necessary to discuss maternity.

In most circumstances, it is not difficult to identify the mother of the child. The mother is the woman who supplies the genetic material to create the child and the woman who gestates and gives birth to the child. Normally, the same woman plays both roles. However, as a result of advances in reproductive technology, the manner in which some children are conceived has changed. Under these circumstances, some courts nonetheless continue to recognize the importance of biology in determining the parentage of a child. Hence, the woman who contributes the eggs used to conceive the child is the child's legal parent regardless of the role she plays in the actual birth of the child. This approach reflects the value society and the law place on blood connections. For instance, in order for a child to be legally adopted, his or her biological mother must relinquish her parental rights and consent to the adoption. The fact that the woman may have never taken the time to develop a relationship with the child is not enough to negate the legal mother-child relationship created by the biological connection between the woman and the child.[2]

This emphasis on blood relationships may also explain the fact that in the majority of states, the intestacy statutes do not recognize stepchildren as heirs of their stepparents.[3] The justification articulated for excluding stepchildren is often the belief that a person would prefer that his or her estate be inherited by persons with whom he or she has blood ties.[4] When resolving disputes in surrogacy situations, some courts have indicated that maternity should be determined solely on the basis of biology. For those courts, the resolution of the cases is simple—the contributor of the eggs is the child's legal mother. It is not unreasonable to believe that these courts would adjudicate paternity in the same manner and thus rely on biology. From the first surrogate arrangement to the present, the woman who supplied the biological material was given preference when it came to maternity.

One of the first examples of surrogacy occurred in the Bible. Abraham's wife Sara was unable to have children. Hence, she arranged for her maid, Hagar, to conceive a child with Abraham. Although Hagar became pregnant as a result of sexual intercourse, this still resembled a surrogate arrangement. After the child was born, Sara made no attempt to establish a relationship with the child. It was clear that as the contributor of the genetic material, Hagar was the child's biological and legal mother.[5] Sara was motivated by a desire to make Abraham a father; she did not want to be a mother to Hagar's child. Since Sara did not seek to be adjudicated the child's legal mother, the case would have been easy to resolve. The biological and legal parents of the child were Abraham and Hagar. According to some courts, a wife's desire to be the mother of a child conceived with a traditional surrogate's genetic material is not enough to overcome biology. *In the Matter of Baby M*[6] illustrates that point of view.

In modern times, the first major case involving surrogacy was that of *Baby M*,[7] in which the court was asked to adjudicate the legal parents of a child born as the result of a surrogate arrangement. Since only one man was involved in the arrangement, the court was charged with the task of determining which woman to recognize as the child's legal mother. The surrogate's main claim to the child was based upon the fact that the child was created using her genetic material. The surrogate also wanted the court to note that she gestated and gave birth to the child.[8] On his side, the child's father, Mr. Stern, wanted his wife to have the opportunity to become the child's legal mother through adoption,[9] and thus urged the court to ignore the biological connection between the surrogate and the child. Mr. Stern's argument was supported by the contract the parties signed. In it, the surrogate, Ms. Whitehead, agreed that after the child was born, she would permit her parental rights to be terminated, so that Ms. Stern could adopt the child.[10] Even though Ms. Stern was not a party to the surrogacy agreement, the terms of the contract gave her sole custody of the child if Mr. Stern died.[11] In exchange for keeping her part of the bargain, the contract required Mr. Stern to pay Ms. Whitehead $10,000 after she surrendered the child to him.[12]

Once the child was born, Ms. Whitehead's maternal instincts kicked in, and she realized that it would not be easy for her to just walk away from the child. In fact, Ms. Whitehead claimed that she had started bonding with the child while she was pregnant. Although Ms. Whitehead suppressed her feelings and eventually turned the child over to the Sterns,[13] giving up the child took a toll on her, and she battled with depression caused by the loss.

Subsequently, when Ms. Whitehead went to the Sterns and informed them that she could not live without the child,[14] the Sterns had compassion for Ms. Whitehead because she helped them become parents, and believing that she might injure herself, they agreed to let her take the child home with her. Ms. Whitehead promised that she would return the child within a week. After Ms. Whitehead reneged on her promise, the authorities forcibly took the child from her custody.[15] The Sterns filed an action seeking to have the court issue an order terminating Ms. Whitehead's parental rights and giving Ms. Stern permission to adopt the child.[16]

The court, however, held that the surrogate contract was void because it violated the public policy of the state.[17] Then, the court relied upon biology to adjudicate Mr. Stern and Ms. Whitehead as the child's legal parents. Once Mr. Stern's paternity was adjudicated based upon his biological connection to the child, the court treated the situation like a typical custody case. Mr. Stern was awarded custody of the child because the court decided that it would be in the best interest of the child to so order.[18] In light of her biological link to the child, the court designated Ms. Whitehead as the child's legal mother and gave her visitations rights.[19] Ms. Whitehead was not proven to be unfit, so her parental rights were not terminated. Since Ms. Whitehead did not plan to consent to the adoption, Ms. Stern was denied the chance of being the child's legal mother.[20]

While the initial parentage determinations were made solely on the basis of biology, the court also discussed the best interests of the child in the context of determining which of the legal parents should be given physical custody of the child. Since she did not have a biological connection to the child, the court did not spend time discussing Ms. Stern's rights. In its opinion, the court repeatedly treated Ms. Whitehead, the traditional surrogate, as the child's legal mother. After it invalidated the surrogate agreement, the court acted as if Mr. Stern and Ms. Whitehead had conceived the child through sexual intercourse. If a married man has a child as the result of an extramarital affair, his wife does not have any legal responsibility for the child. In keeping with that approach, the court never addressed Ms. Stern's maternal rights. Instead, it appeared to assume that since she did not supply the genetic material to create the child, Ms. Stern should not be recognized as the child's legal mother. The court awarded custody of the child to Mr. Stern because it determined that he could provide the best home for the child.

An Ohio court took a similar approach in *Belsito v. Clark, et al.*[21] Cervical cancer caused Shelly to lose her uterus, but since her ovaries were not removed, she was still able to contribute eggs to create a child.[22] Later, when

Shelly met and married Anthony Belsito, the couple asked Shelly's sister, Carol S. Clark, to serve as their surrogate.[23] After Carol agreed, the doctors fertilized Shelly's eggs with Anthony's sperm to create two embryos. The embryos were implanted in Carol's uterus, and she conceived a child.[24] In preparation for the child's birth, Shelly asked hospital personnel about the child's birth certificate and was informed that Carol would be identified as the child's mother on the birth certificate because she was the woman who was actually giving birth to the child. Shelly was further informed that since Carol and Anthony were not married to one another, the child would be classified as illegitimate.[25] Then, Shelly and Anthony filed an action requesting the court to issue an order adjudicating them as the child's legal parents so that they would not have to adopt the child. In addition, Shelly and Anthony asked the court to order the hospital to list them as the legal parents on the birth certificate and to indicate that the child was legitimate.[26]

In order to resolve the case, the court had to determine which of the parties to designate as the legal and natural parents of the child. The court's first task was to decide the manner in which a natural parent-child relationship could be created. Ultimately, the court held that it took a biological link between the woman and the child in order for the woman to be classified as the natural mother.[27] Since evidence of the blood connection between the woman and the child could be obtained by DNA testing,[28] the court held that genetics testing was the appropriate method to use to decide which persons should be adjudicated as the natural parents of a child conceived as the result of a surrogacy arrangement.[29]

The court put forth several reasons for adopting the genetic test. First, it contended that a genetic test would promote the public policy of prohibiting a woman from selling her parental rights.[30] The court also refused to recognize the gestational surrogate as the child's natural mother because she did not have a biological connection to the child.[31] Consequently, if the surrogate relinquished the child to the intended parents, she would not be selling her parental rights. Instead, the woman would just be keeping the promise she made under the surrogate agreement. Second, the court opined that it would be easy to resolve a maternity dispute by relying on the genetic test. Since technology exists that makes it possible to determine if there is a genetic connection between a woman and a child,[32] the court would only have to order DNA testing to resolve a dispute involving the adjudication of maternity.

The court concluded that since the child was conceived using Anthony's and Shelly's genetic materials, they were the child's natural parents. According to the court, the only way for the couple to lose their status as legal parents was for their parental rights to be terminated. Since the couple's actions indicated that they had no desire to surrender their parental rights, the court recognized them as the child's legal parents.[33] In deciding the case, the court made two key observations that may be useful in determining how a paternity dispute could be settled. First, the court noted that the natural mother is the woman who is biologically connected to the child. Second, it contended that being classified as natural mother entitled the woman to be acknowledged as the child's legal mother. In order for another woman to be recognized as the child's legal mother, the biological mother would have to take steps to have her parental rights terminated and indicate her willingness to allow the other woman to be deemed the legal mother of her child.[34] Thus, the court made it clear that the woman who contributed the genetic material to create the child had superior rights over the woman who gave birth to the child.[35] And, again, in the process, the court adopted the genetics test to determine maternity in a surrogacy arrangement.

In effect, the court attempted to treat a child conceived as the result of a surrogacy arrangement in a manner similar to that of a child conceived by sexual intercourse. If a man uses his penis to fertilize a woman's eggs with his sperm, she is clearly the child's natural mother. Under the standard set out in *Belsito*, the outcome would not be different just because the child was conceived using scientific means. Thus, if a doctor fertilizes a woman's eggs with a man's sperm and inserts the embryo into another woman's body, the woman who supplied the eggs does not lose her biological connection to the child. A woman who conceives a child naturally can sever her connection to the child and put the child up for adoption, so that another woman can become the child's legal mother. The reasoning of the *Belsito* case indicates that the same option is available to a woman who contributes the genetic material in a surrogacy arrangement. That woman can voluntarily relinquish her right to the child so that the surrogate or another woman can become the child's legal mother. In either case, the law cannot force the woman to turn her biological child over to another woman. This same reasoning applies to a man who donates genetic material to conceive a child. A man decision's to give up rights to his biological child must be voluntary.

The simplest way to be classified as a parent is to be biologically related to the child. Nonetheless, that fact is changing. Biology is no longer the sole indicator of parentage. Due to medical advances, it is becoming possible to have more than two biological parents. Currently, the technology exists to combine the essence of the eggs of two women to create an embryo containing the DNA of both women. Relying on a strict application of the parenthood by biology theory will lead to the classification of both women as the child's biological mother. Confused artificial insemination is a process wherein a woman is inseminated with a mixture consisting of a combination of her husband's sperm and sperm from a donor. The resulting child will have DNA from both of the men. Technically, that makes both of the men the biological father. At the same time, however, in order to avoid conflict, the courts have been reluctant to acknowledge two men as the legal father of a child. Thus, although biology is still a strong indicator of parenthood and although biological parents typically have the right to parent their children unless they are proven unfit, the law is finally responding to the fact that the definition of parent is evolving. As a result, legislatures and courts are more willing to consider factors other than biology when adjudicating parenthood.

Parenthood by Intent

Instead of simply focusing on a person's biological connection to the child, some courts evaluate the person's intentions to determine if parentage should be adjudicated. Thus, a man's intention may cause him to be deemed a legal father regardless of whether or not the child was conceived using his biological material. Here, the focus is upon the person's behavior prior to the child's birth. Courts have taken this approach when determining maternity in surrogate cases. Where parenthood by intent is concerned, the inquiry is whether the person acted in such a way as to indicate that he or she intended to parent the child. This is consistent with the general tendency of the law to consider a person's intent to determine whether or not he or she should be found to be responsible for his or her actions. For example, in tort law and criminal law, the person's intent often determines his or her level of culpability. With regard to parentage, the person's intent can be implied from his or her actions. Thus, a man who has unprotected sex implicitly intends to father a child. The law holds him to that implied intent by making him financially responsible for the resulting child.

According to Professor Marjorie Maguire Shultz, courts should adjudicate legal parenthood by considering the parties' intentions. In particular, Professor Shultz contends, "intentions that are voluntarily chosen, deliberate, express and bargained-for ought presumptively to determine legal parenthood."[36] Professor Shultz's reference to bargained-for intent indicates that she is interested in the actions that the parties take prior to the conception of the child. She also opines that conception should not necessarily be an indicator of parenthood. Conception may be the by-product of an act of passion when two people get caught up in the moment. Since an adjudication of parenthood imposes significant responsibilities on the person, it should be the result of a deliberative process.[37] Professor Shultz believes that the law should honor the intentions of the parties involved in the transaction with regard to the parentage of the child, especially where those intentions are memorialized in a written contract. Thus, Professor Shultz is really advocating parenthood by contract. In light of the fact that her arguments focus upon intent that is explicitly expressed, it is not surprising that she would limit her theory to cases involving children conceived as the result of assisted reproduction.[38]

In cases resolving both maternity and paternity disputes, some courts have based their parentage decisions on the intentions of the parties whether or not a biological connection existed between the child and the intended parents. In the process, though, courts have limited analyses of parenthood by intent to cases involving children conceived using assisted reproduction. When a court purports to award parentage based upon intent, it appears to be just enforcing the agreement made by the parties. Thus, the approach could also be referred to as parenthood by contract. Contracts seeking to sign away parental rights and/or child-support obligations have been held to be against public policy. Thus, courts are reluctant to stress the need to enforce the contracts the parties have entered. It is more acceptable for the courts to categorize the cases as honoring the intentions of the parties.

Also a proponent of the parenthood by intent theory, Professor John Lawrence Hill argues that in some circumstances "intent" should trump "biology" when it comes to adjudicating parenthood.[39] According to Professor Hill, there are three arguments in favor of an intent-based approach to parenthood. The first is "'but for' causation."[40] The underlying basis of that argument is that "the child would not have been born but for the efforts of the intended parents."[41] Professor Hill asserts that the determining factor in adjudicating parentage should not be the biological connection between the adults and the child, but the actions that the adults took to make sure that the child was conceived. Contributing the biological materials used to conceive the child may not take much thought or effort. In the case of a child conceived using assisted reproductive technology, the real work is getting together the component parts necessary to ensure that the child is conceived. This may include obtaining egg and/or sperm, and hiring a surrogate. Since most of this pre-conception work is performed by the intended parents, Professor Hill thinks that those persons should be rewarded for their effort.

In particular, he asserts that "The efforts of the biological progenitors are instrumental to the act of procreation, but the status of 'parent' should go to the persons who constitute the 'but for' cause of the child's birth."[42] One way to understand Professor Hill's position is through a house analogy. A and B want to build their dream house. Therefore, they design the house, hire the contractors, and pay for the necessary materials. Even though they never pick up a hammer or a nail, no one would dispute that the house belongs to A and B. When that same logic is applied to a surrogacy situation, the persons who arrange for the conception of the child with the intent to be the parents should be legally recognized as the parents.

Professor Hill's second argument is based upon contract principles. A surrogate agreement is a contract that should be enforced like any other contract. The surrogate should not be permitted to ignore her promise to surrender the child to the intended couple. The parties should get the benefit of their bargain. The surrogate will not be disadvantaged if she is not permitted to retain custody of the child because she was never promised custody. If the intended parents thought that the surrogate would renege on her promise to relinquish all rights to the child, they would have chosen another woman to serve as their surrogate. In either case, the surrogate would be denied the right to parent the child.[43] The intended couple should not be penalized because they trusted the surrogate to keep her word with regard to the custody of the child. Awarding parentage by intent thus not only encourages persons to keep their promises, but also protects the intended parents from being financially and emotionally harmed. People who seek the services of surrogates are usually desperate to become parents and are willing to make the financial and emotional sacrifices necessary to ensure that the child is conceived. Once the surrogate promises to give them the child, the intended parents rely on that promise and often make lifestyle changes. If the court does not require the surrogate to honor her promise, the intended parents will not be put back in the situation they were in before they relied on the surrogate's promise. The ability to award parentage based upon intent will help the court to make the intended parents whole.[44] Since children are unique, specific performance is the appropriate remedy. By ordering specific performance, the court will ensure that the intended parents receive custody of the child.

The final argument Professor Hill gives in support of the parenthood by intent theory is that of "avoidance of uncertainty."[45] In maintaining that the identity of the child's parents should be made clear at the time of conception, his approach would treat children of science similar to children of passion.

One way to designate the child's legal parents is to rely upon the parties' initial intentions. In most cases, this means that the intended parents would be recognized as the child's legal parents without having to go through a long, drawn-out custody battle after the child is born. By not definitively resolving the parentage issue before the child is born, the law leaves open the possibility of a custody dispute. That uncertainty is not good for the child, the surrogate, or the intended parents.[46] During a custody dispute, which usually lasts a long time, the child may be bounced back and forth between the homes of the surrogate and the intended parents. We have seen this happen in cases involving children who are switched at birth. Once the final custody decision is made, the relationship the child had with the losing party is likely to be severed, and this may have a long-term impact on the child's emotional health.

A bright-line rule establishing the intended parents as the legal parents will also benefit the surrogate. If a woman knows that she will definitely have to surrender the child, she will think long and hard before agreeing to serve as a surrogate. Such a rule might also encourage the parties to have the potential surrogate undergo counseling before agreeing to serve in that role. In addition, the surrogate may take steps to avoid getting emotionally attached to the child if she knows that the child belongs to someone else and that she does not have the possibility of being the child's legal mother. Under the parenthood by intent theory, once the woman agrees to give the child to the intended parents, her decision is final. The court will not honor her change of heart after the child is born.[47] This puts the surrogate on par with the sperm donor. When a man donates his sperm, in most jurisdictions, he gives up all rights to the resulting child. Most women who agree to be surrogates have good intentions, including keeping their contractual promises. Nonetheless, as *Johnson v. Calvert*[48] indicates, intentions may change when emotions and money are involved.

In a case that got a lot of media attention, a gestational surrogate wanted to be named the legal mother of a child to whom she had no biological connection. In this instance, the court decided to take a different approach than the one used in the *Baby M* case. Thus, instead of focusing upon the biological connection between the contracting woman and the child, the court based its decision on the intentions of the parties. In light of the law in place at the time, the court was not permitted to totally disregard the link that gestation created between the surrogate and the child. Under that statutory scheme, the act of gestation gave the surrogate an interest in the child. Application of that legal principle would not have changed the outcome of the *Baby M* case because the woman was a traditional surrogate who provided the egg and gestated the embryo. However, the intent of the parties was relevant to the outcome of *Johnson v. Calvert* because the case involved a gestational surrogate.

Mark and Crispina Calvert's plans to become parents were thwarted when Crispina had to have a hysterectomy. Nonetheless, since Crispina was still capable of producing eggs, the couple decided to arrange for a surrogate to carry their child.[49] When Anna Johnson agreed to act as a surrogate for the couple, the parties signed a surrogate agreement. Under the terms of that agreement, Anna would carry a child conceived using an embryo created from Mark's sperm and Crispina's egg. Then, after the birth of the child, Anna promised to relinquish her parental rights to the child and to surrender the child to the Calverts.[50] In exchange, Mark and Crispina agreed to pay Anna $10,000 in several installments and to insure Anna's life for $200,000. After Anna became pregnant with the couple's child, relations between the parties soured. Eventually, Anna demanded that the Calverts pay the remainder of the payments she was owed[51] and threatened to keep the child if she did not receive all of the money. In response, the Calverts filed a lawsuit seeking to be legally recognized as the parents of the unborn child. Then, Anna brought an action requesting to be declared the child's legal mother. The court consolidated the cases.[52]

Blood tests showed that the Calverts were the child's genetic parents. The court had to decide the identity of the child's natural mother under California law. The trial court held that the Calverts were the child's "genetic, biological, and natural" parents and that Anna had no parental rights with regard to the child.[53] After the court of appeals affirmed the trial court's decision, Anna filed an appeal with the California Supreme Court,[54] which in turn relied on the state's version of the Uniform Parentage Act (UPA) to resolve the dispute.[55] Anna based her claim to the child on the fact that she gestated and gave birth to the child. The Calverts countered by arguing that since the child was conceived using her genetic material, Crispina was the child's legal mother.[56] When allocating maternity, the court had to decide whether to give preference to the woman having the blood connection to the child or the woman giving birth to the child. In so doing, the court determined that both women were able to produce evidence of a mother-child relationship under the provisions of the UPA. Thus, according to one section of the statute, maternity could be proven by the use of genetic evidence gathered through blood testing. Since blood tests indicated that Crispina was the child's genetic mother, she could satisfy the evidentiary requirements of the statute.[57] At the same time, another portion of the statute stated that a woman could establish the mother-child relationship by showing she gave birth to the child. In the case at bar, Anna was able to prove that fact.[58] Therefore, both women satisfied the statutory mandates to prove maternity, and so the child appeared to have two natural mothers. However, the state of California would recognize only one legal mother.[59]

In order to resolve the case, the court relied upon contract principles. Since both women had a legal right to the child, the court used the parties' intentions as the "tie-breaker" and to that end analyzed the terms of the surrogacy agreement.[60] Holding that the appropriate means for determining the identity of the legal mother of the child was the "intent" test, the court stated, "she who intended to procreate the child—that is, she who intended to bring about the birth of a child that she intended to raise as her own—is the natural mother under California law."[61] The Calverts intended to have a child from their genetic material. They carried out that intent by having an embryo created using his sperm and her egg implanted in Anna. Anna agreed to assist the Calverts in carrying out their intentions. The child would not exist if the Calverts had not acted on their intentions. Anna's intent to keep the child was not recognized because it conflicted with the original intentions of the parties.[62] Under the parenthood by intent theory, the parties' pre-conception intentions are the ones that are important to the courts. Once the child is conceived, the parties do not get the right to change their minds. In this case, the intent theory was used to honor a woman's intent to be a mother. As *In re Marriage of Buzzanca*[63] shows, the approach has also been used to force a man to take on the responsibility of fatherhood.

Four persons had the possibility of being the legal parents of little Jaycee, but only one of them wanted the job. Jaycee was conceived because Luanne and John Buzzanca decided to use assisted reproduction to become parents. The couple hired a surrogate to carry and give birth to an embryo they obtained. This embryo did not contain the genetic material of either the surrogate or Luanne or John. The biological parents were never identified or involved in the case.[64] Luanne separated from John before Jaycee was born. When John filed for divorce, he claimed that there were no children born during the marriage. In her answer, Luanne informed the court that the couple was expecting a child as the result of a surrogate arrangement. Jaycee entered the world six days after Luanne acknowledged that the surrogate was pregnant.[65] In a separate action, Luanne asked the court to recognize her as Jaycee's legal mother.[66]

Jaycee's birth did not change the fact that only one person wanted to be her legal parent. The surrogate filed a stipulation making it clear that she and her husband did not want to be acknowledged as Jaycee's legal parents because they were not her biological parents.[67] John urged the court to relieve him of all financial responsibility for the child. He did not want a relationship with Jaycee, and he did not want to provide her with any type of support.[68] Jaycee thus faced the possibility of having only one legal parent. Taking a more drastic position, the trial court ruled that Jaycee did not have any legal parents. Even though her claim to be the legal mother was unchallenged, the court concluded that Luanne could not be adjudicated as the legal mother both because she was not biologically related to the child and because she did not give birth to the child. Since neither genetics nor gestation linked Luanne to the child, the court treated her as if she were a stranger to the child.[69] Furthermore, the court accepted the surrogate's stipulation and declared that she and her husband were not Jaycee's legal parents. With regard to John, the lack of a biological connection between him and Jaycee made it easy for the court to decide that he was not the legal father, so he was not obligated to provide financial support for the child. Consequently, the trial court issued an order denying Luanne's request to be named as Jaycee's legal mother and relieving John of his child-support obligations.[70]

In essence, the trial court made Jaycee a legal orphan without designating anyone to care for the minor child. That action outraged the appellate court, which failed to see how the trial court's decision served the best interests of the child or the public. As a minor child, Jaycee needed someone to support her financially. In order to make sure that an adult had a legal duty to do so, the court had to establish a parent-child relationship. By denying the existence of such a relationship, the trial court made the tax payers responsible for supporting Jaycee,[71] creating a situation that, according to the appellate court, was against the public policy of the state.[72] Normally, taxpayers are not financially responsible for children who have living parents unless the government has intervened to protect the children from abuse or neglect.

Admonishing the trial judge for his narrow view of parentage, the appellate court stated, "He failed to consider the substantial and well-settled body of law holding that there are times when *fatherhood* can be established by conduct apart from giving birth or being genetically related to a child."[73] The court went on to use the example of a man who becomes a legal father by consenting to his wife's insemination. The court did not see a logical reason to distinguish parenthood by consent from parenthood by intent, which usually occurs in a surrogacy situation. Thus, the court opined:

Just as a husband is deemed to be the lawful father of a child unrelated to him when his wife gives birth after artificial insemination, so should a husband *and* wife be deemed the lawful parents of a child after a surrogate bears a biologically unrelated child on their behalf.[74]

If Jaycee had been conceived as the result of sexual intercourse, John would have been presumed to be the legal father even though he may have been a cuckolded man. Moreover, if Jaycee had been conceived as a consequence of artificial insemination with John's consent, John would have been recognized as the legal father. Both of these examples show that biology and birth are not the only two ways for a man to become a father. A man may become a father if he consents to assisted reproduction with the intent that a child be conceived. In most cases, it is not necessary for the man to intend to parent the child. In this case, the appellate court noted that Jaycee was conceived as the result of Luanne and John's agreement with the surrogate. The couple intended for a child to result from the implantation of the embryo that they supplied. The fact that the embryo was created without using their genetic material did not make them any less responsible for the resulting child.[75]

The outcomes of these cases are consistent. In both *Johnson v. Calvert* and *In re Marriage of Buzzanca*, the parties were made to keep their promises. In the first case, the intentions were proven by the terms of the written contract. In the second case, John tried to argue that he should not be held to his intentions because he never put them in writing. Nonetheless, he admitted that he had orally agreed to have a surrogate carry a child conceived using the embryo that he helped to acquire.[76] In either case, once the courts were able to ascertain the parties' intentions with regard to the parentage of the children, the courts ultimately awarded parenthood based upon those intentions. In addition, though, whereas the intent theory of parenthood requires courts to evaluate the parties' pre-conception intentions, a person with no biological connection to a child may still obtain parental rights based upon his or her post-conception actions.

Parenthood by Psychology

Social scientists, including psychologists, were the first to argue that the psychological link between the child and the adults in his or her life is just as important as the biological link. The earliest proponents of the psychological parent theory were Joseph Goldstein, Anna Freud, and Albert J. Solnit.[77] In a book entitled *Beyond the Best Interests of the Child*, they defined a "psychological parent" as "one who, on a continuing day-to-day basis, through interaction, companionship, interplay, and mutuality, fulfills the child's psychological needs for a parent, as well as the child's physical needs."[78] Some form of this definition has been adopted by legislatures and courts. Psychological parent theorists claimed that if a child is separated from a primary caregiver, the child will suffer severe psychological trauma. Thus, they proposed that child welfare policies and laws be changed in order to protect those psychological relationships.[79]

The psychological parent doctrine was first applied in child protection cases. Proponents of the theory argued that in determining whether or not to remove children from their homes and/or to terminate the parental rights of the adults in their lives, the courts needed to consider the psychological impact of their decisions.[80] In these situations, the psychological parent theory was used to make sure that the child maintained contact with his non-custodial biological parent. Thus, advocates of the theory urged courts to apply it to make sure that the psychological parent was given visitation rights. Recently, however, the focus of the theory has shifted to accommodate the changing composition of the family and to address situations involving third parties who are not biologically related to the child. Thus, while in the past, the theory was used to protect the rights of non-custodial parents, presently, it is being used to bestow limited parental rights on third parties who have relationships with children, especially in cases involving same-sex couples.

Currently, Professor Katharine T. Bartlett is one of the primary proponents for the recognition of a psychological parent, particularly in the context of a non-exclusive parenting situation. Contending that the responsibility of parenting children need not be left to the exclusive domain of one man and one woman, she opines that a child may have more than two adults serving as parents, including adults who are psychological parents. According to Professor Bartlett, a psychological parent is an adult who assists in the provision of physical, emotional, and/or social necessities that would typically be supplied by a child's nuclear family. In order to be recognized as a psychological parent, Professor Bartlett has suggested that the adult must satisfy three conditions. First, the adult must be in physical possession of the child for at least six months prior to seeking parental status. Second, when seeking parental status, the adult must be motivated by a desire to take care of the child, who, in turn, must consider the adult to be his or her parent. Finally, the adult seeking parental status must prove that his or her relationship with the child was the result of the legal parents' consent or a court order.[81]

While the psychological parent theory has usually come up in the context of visitation when the case involves heterosexual couples, in situations involving same-sex couples, the theory may be utilized to recognize the parental rights of persons who have no biological connection to the children. If the courts apply the psychological parent doctrine to give persons parental rights, those rights must come with reciprocal duties, including the obligation to support the child financially. A child may have the right to receive life-time support and to inherit from the psychological parent in much the same way as an equitably adopted child has the right to receive financial support from the potential adoptive parents.

Several jurisdictions have adopted a psychological approach to adjudicating parenthood. Although the standard used to determine if a person is entitled to be recognized as a psychological parent varies, most of the statutory schemes focus on the actions of the third party and the biological or adoptive parents and on the impact those actions have on the child. In most jurisdictions, the statutory definitions of the psychological parent mirror the definition put forth by the original psychological parent theorists. Thus, according to the Alaska Supreme Court, such a parent is

> [O]ne who, on a day-to-day basis, through interaction, companionship, interplay, and mutuality, fulfills the child's psychological needs for an adult. This adult becomes an essential focus of the child's life, for he is not only the source of the fulfillment of the child's psychological needs. . . . The wanted child is one who is loved, valued, appreciated, and viewed as an essential person by the adult who cares for him. . . . This relationship may exist between a child and any adult; it depends not upon the category into which the adult falls—biological, adoptive, foster, or common law—but upon the quality and mutuality of the interaction.[82]

In a similar vein, the West Virginia Supreme Court defined the nature of the relationship that supports a finding that the third party acted as a psychological parent by stating:

> A "psychological parent" who has greater protection under the law in a child-custody proceeding than would ordinarily be afforded to one who is not the biological or adoptive parent of the child, is a person who, on a continuing day-to-day basis, through interaction, companionship, inter-

play, and mutually [*sic*] fulfills a child's psychological and physical needs for a parent and provides for the child's emotional and financial support.[83]

Furthermore, the Wisconsin Supreme Court developed a four-prong test for determining whether or not a person should be classified as a psychological parent. In order to demonstrate the existence of a psychological parent-child relationship, the petitioner must show:

> (1) that the biological or adoptive parent[s] consented to, and fostered, the petitioner's formation and establishment of a parent-like relationship with the child; (2) that the petitioner and the child lived together in the same household; (3) that the petitioner assumed the obligations of parenthood by taking significant responsibility for the child's care, education, and development, including contributing towards the child's support, without expectation of financial compensation; [and] (4) that the petitioner has been in a parental role for a length of time sufficient to have established with the child a bonded, dependent relationship in nature.[84]

In *Middleton v. Johnson*,[85] the South Carolina Court of Appeals decided to adopt the test set forth by the Wisconsin Supreme Court. Elizabeth Johnson and Kenneth Middleton were involved in a long-term relationship for over twenty years.[86] After the relationship was over, the couple had a one-night stand. Shortly after that intimate encounter, Elizabeth discovered that she was pregnant. Although she told Kenneth that another man was the father of her unborn child, after the child was born, Elizabeth encouraged Kenneth to play an active part in the child's life. Then, Elizabeth led Kenneth to believe that he was the child's father, so he spent time with the child and provided financial support for him.[87] When the little boy was almost one year old, as a result of a DNA test, Kenneth discovered that he was not the child's biological father. However, since the results of the DNA test did not diminish Kenneth's love for the child, he continued to act as a father to him.[88] Elizabeth did not do anything to discourage Kenneth from having a relationship with the child. On the contrary, she agreed to a joint custody arrangement under which she took care of the child from Mondays through Wednesdays and Kenneth kept him for the rest of the week.[89]

By the time the child entered third grade, Elizabeth had a new man in her life. When the couple's relationship became serious and they moved in together, Elizabeth sought to modify Kenneth's visitation schedule with the child. Kenneth agreed to rotate days every week. Eventually, Kenneth started to suspect that Elizabeth was physically abusing the child. On one occasion, Kenneth refused to return the child to Elizabeth and reported the alleged abuse to the police. In response, Elizabeth and her new husband called the police and told them that Kenneth would not give her back her son.[90] The police returned the child to Elizabeth because she had legal custody of him.[91] Then, Elizabeth took steps to sever the relationship between Kenneth and the child, including informing school officials that Kenneth was not permitted to have contact with the child. About a year later, Elizabeth and her husband relocated with the child to Florence, South Carolina.[92]

Kenneth filed a petition asking the court to give him custody of the child, as well as to appoint a guardian ad litem to represent the child. In her answer, Elizabeth argued that since Kenneth was not biologically related to the child, he did not have standing to file the custody action. After deliberating, the trial court (1) refused to grant Elizabeth's motion; (2) assigned a guardian ad litem for the child; (3) joined the biological father to the action; and (4) refused to grant Kenneth the right to visit the child.[93] The biological father never put in an appearance. When the case went to trial, Kenneth amended his petition and sought only visitation. A court-appointed therapist recommended that Kenneth be permitted to visit the child, noting that, as a result of his loss of contact with Kenneth, the child suffered emotional trauma. Nonetheless, the trial court denied Kenneth's visitation rights, reasoning that, since the child knew that he had a living biological father, Kenneth could not be recognized as a psychological parent. Thus, Kenneth was not entitled to legal visitation rights.[94]

On appeal, the court had to decide whether or not Kenneth was a psychological parent and relied on the Wisconsin four-part test to do so. The court chose this particular test because it limited the number of persons who would be eligible to be considered psychological parents.[95] Even so, before applying the test to the facts of the case, the court examined each of the four factors. The first one, which focused upon the behavior of the biological or adoptive parent, required the court to determine whether or not this parent had encouraged the third party to form a parent-like relationship with the child. The court deemed that this factor was especially important because it helped the court to gage the parent's level of involvement in the creation of the relationship between the third party and the child. The more active the parent was in the establishment of the relationship, the less of a right that the parent had to unilaterally end that relationship without cause. The court did acknowledge that a parent has the right to decide who has contact with his or her child and that in essence, the parent is responsible for creating a zone of privacy and protection around the child. Nonetheless, the court also adopted the view that once a parent invites a third party to develop a relationship with the child and it is reasonable for the child to think of the third party as a second parent, the parent's ability to sever that relationship is limited.[96]

To decide whether the second prong of the test had been satisfied, the court had to determine if the child had lived with the third party. According to the court, by requiring a third party to satisfy this part of the test, the law narrowed the pool of persons who could seek parental rights to the child. Once this had been accomplished, the last two factors of the test involved the actions of the third party who wanted to be adjudicated as the psychological parent—and, as the court noted, these two factors were the most important because they indicated the nature of the relationship between the third party and the child. In order to the fulfill the mandates of the third prong of the test, the party seeking psychological parent status had to prove that he or she actually functioned as a parent by being actively involved in the child's life, as well as showing that he or she performed caretaking duties and formed an emotional bond with the child.[97] The final prong of the psychological parent test required the court to decide if the relationship between the third party and the child should be categorized as "parental." In evaluating the nature of that relationship, the court considered the following factors: (1) the length of time the third party had been involved in the child's life; (2) the attachment that the child had to the third party; and (3) the possibility that the child would suffer emotional harm if his or her relationship with the third party was severed.[98]

In the process of examining and applying the psychological parent doctrine, the court also pointed out two restrictions. The first is that a person who is financially compensated for taking care of a child is not eligible to assume the role of psychological parent. This limitation was necessary to prevent babysitters and nannies from claiming that they are psychological parents.[99] The second is that the psychological parent doctrine does not apply to situations where two biological parents are a part of the child's life. Under those circumstances, since the child has the support of two parents, a relationship with a third party is not necessary to fill a parental void in the child's life.[100] This restraint is consistent with the law's preference for the two-parent model.[101]

After applying the four-prong test to the facts of the *Middleton v. Johnson* case, the appellate court held that the trial court should have concluded that Kenneth was the child's psychological parent.[102] Insofar as the first part of the test was concerned, the record was full of facts indicating that Elizabeth had invited Kenneth to be a part of the child's life. For example, even though they were no longer a couple, after the child was born, Elizabeth sent Kenneth pictures of the child and led him to believe that he was the biological father. In addition, when the child was young, Elizabeth agreed not only to a joint custody arrangement that permitted the child to spend at least half of each week in Kenneth's home but also to Kenneth's paying at least half of the child's daycare costs.[103] During the first ten years of the child's life, Elizabeth encouraged him to spend a substantial amount of time with Kenneth. By turning over a considerable portion of her parental obligations to Kenneth, Elizabeth implicitly consented to the development of a father-child relationship between the pair.

Where the second prong of the test was concerned, its conditions were easily satisfied: the child spent at least half of his time at Kenneth's house, where he had his own room, clothes, and school books. Likewise, with regard to the third prong of the test, the evidence showed that Kenneth functioned as a parent by meeting the child's financial and emotional needs. For example, Kenneth presented written evidence showing that he had given Elizabeth approximately $12,000 over the years to cover the child's expenses, including $250 per month in child support. Kenneth also proved that he had set up a savings account to pay for the child's education.[104] The most compelling aspect of Kenneth's claim for psychological parent status, however, related to the final prong of the test. According to the record before the court, the child had spent most of his life thinking of Kenneth as his father. The court-appointed therapist testified that, even though two years had passed, the child still missed Kenneth. The therapist further opined that the child would be adversely impacted if the court severed the relationship between the child and Kenneth.[105]

After recognizing Kenneth as the child's psychological parent, the court addressed the issue of his visitation. Kenneth's status as a psychological parent did not place him on equal footing with the biological or adoptive parent. The court admitted that a third party, even a psychological parent, could be awarded visitation over a fit parent's objections only if the court found that compelling circumstances existed.[106] The purpose of the "compelling circumstances" requirement is to rebut the presumption that the parent's decision to prohibit visitation served the best interests of the child.[107] One example of a compelling circumstance is evidence that the child would be significantly harmed if the court did not permit the third party to visit the child.[108] Such evidence demonstrating that the child was harmed by Elizabeth's refusal to let him visit Kenneth was introduced in this trial. For example, a guidance counselor from the child's school testified that she had placed him in a support group to help him deal with the grief he was feeling because of the loss of his "dad." Elizabeth reluctantly admitted that the child missed Kenneth. In light of the testimony, the court held that Kenneth's petition for visitation should be granted.[109] Nonetheless, the court emphasized that no matter how attached the child was to a third-party psychological parent, this parent would not normally have the right to demand custody. The psychological parent has limited parental rights because the legal or adoptive parent has the right to raise his or her child. Thus, in order to get custody, the psychological parent would have the difficult task of overcoming that parental right.[110]

Like the parenthood by intent theory, the psychological theory of parenthood focuses upon the intentions of the parties. When the biological or adoptive parent takes steps to foster a relationship between a third party and his or her child, that parent intends for that relationship to be permanent. Moreover, if the biological or adoptive parent intentionally turns over some of his or her parental duties to a third party, that parent knows or should know that since the third party is bearing the burdens of parenthood, he or she may eventually want to share in the benefits of parenthood. By honoring the psychological bond that the biological or adoptive parent permits the third party to form with the child, the law indicates that, if someone acts like a parent, the law might treat him or her like one. The lack of a biological or legal connection to the child is no longer enough for the court to ignore the relationship between the child and the third party.

Parenthood by Function

The functional parent is similar to the psychological or social parent. The focus is upon the actions the person takes after the birth of the child. According to Professor Nancy Polikoff, in order for a person to be classified as a functional parent, the child's legally recognized parent must create a relationship between the child and that person. In addition, the legal parent must intend for that relationship to be parental in nature. Finally, the person must maintain a functional relationship with the child.[111] Once a person acquires parenthood by function, he or she should be bound by all of the duties of a person with that status. Thus, the functional parent may be ordered to pay child support.

The functional parenthood theory may be helpful in situations involving stepparents. A significant number of children in this country live in blended homes with stepparents. Nevertheless, the most widely disregarded parent-child relationship is that of the stepparent-stepchild.[112] The very name "stepparent" conjures up images of Cinderella and her wicked stepmother. In order to obtain rights with regard to the stepchild, the stepparent has to adopt the child. However, real life is not that simple. Most stepparents never think about adoption or are prevented from doing so by the non-custodial biological parents. I grew up in a blended household. When my father married my mother, she came with three small children from her prior relationships. My mother probably would have been insulted if my father sought to adopt my half-siblings officially. A piece of paper was not needed to formalize the relationship that my father had with those children. We all grew up together without distinctions. However, my father did not have a legal obligation to provide financial support for those children (a fact he never would have commented on in the presence of my mother). Some states give stepparents visitation rights, but we did not live in one of those states. As a result, my father was not entitled to visitation rights or any other parental benefits with regard to my half-siblings. Since my parents remained married until my half-siblings were adults, the functional parent issue did not arise.

On the other hand, my sister's ex-boyfriend is the poster child for the functional parent theory. When my sister was about five months pregnant with her second child, she met a man who swept her off of her feet. They moved in together shortly before my nephew was born, and stayed together for almost twenty-two years. My sister's boyfriend provided food, clothing, and shelter for her son. He taught the little boy to ride a bike, took him to ball games, and taught him how to drive a car. My sister always told people that she was common-law married (she wasn't). Since my sister was not legally married to her boyfriend, he was not my nephew's stepfather. One of the reasons the couple never got married was that my sister did not want to take the time to go to the courthouse to get a marriage license. She would always think of something else she would rather do. Thus, it is not surprising, that my sister's boyfriend never got around to adopting my nephew. The man is not my nephew's biological, adoptive, or stepfather. Nonetheless, that fact does not stop my nephew from calling him "Dad" and my nephew's children from calling him "Grandpa." Given the time and effort my sister's boyfriend put into raising my nephew, it does not seem fair for him to be considered a non-parent.

My nephew is an adult, so the parental status of his mother's now ex-boyfriend may not matter to him. However, it may matter to my sister's ex-boyfriend. He never had a biological son of his own, and he put a lot of "sweat equity" into raising my nephew from the time he was an infant. He has also developed a close relationship with my nephew's children and may one day need to avail himself of some of the rights available to grandparents. Moreover, my sister not only insisted on her ex-boyfriend having a parental relationship with my nephew, but also referred to him as the little boy's "common-law daddy" (sometimes my sister lives in her own world). The man took his paternal responsibility seriously and functioned as a father to my nephew.

The functional parenthood theory has not been widely adopted because the existence of other more recognized parental theories may render it unnecessary. The American Law Institute (ALI), an influential group of lawyers, law professors, and judges, completed a decade-long project to promote uniformity in family law.[113] As a result of that process, the ALI Principles of the Law of Family Dissolutions recognized two new types of parents for purposes of custody and visitation—parents by estoppel and de facto parents.

Parenthood by Estoppel

In the context of determining parentage for child-support purposes, the ALI recommended the adoption of the parent by estoppel doctrine. A parent by estoppel is an individual who, even though not a legal parent, has acted as a parent under certain specified circumstances which serve to estop the legal parent from denying the individual's status as a parent. Unlike a de facto parent, a parent by estoppel is afforded all of the privileges of a legal parent.[114] According to the ALI, a man may gain parent by estoppel status in four different ways.[115] The most obvious way for the man to prove that he is entitled to be adjudicated as a parent by estoppel is to show the court that he was required to pay child support.[116] A court may impose a child-support obligation on a non-legal parent when the court decides that the person's prior actions estop him or her from denying the obligation. The example the ALI uses in its comments involve a stepfather. Sue, a single parent of one child, marries John. During the course of the marriage, John financially supports the child and assumes all parental responsibility. After a seven-year marriage, the couple divorces. John will probably be estopped from denying his child-support obligation. Once the court orders John to pay child support, Sue is estopped from denying his parental rights. The burdens and benefits of parenthood go hand in hand.

A second way for a man to become a parent by estoppel is to show that he lived with the child and fully accepted parental responsibilities[117] for the child for at least two years[118] with the reasonable, good-faith belief that he was the child's biological father. The man's belief could be a result of his marriage to the child's mother or of other actions that the woman took to make him believe that the child was his son or daughter. One of those actions may be that he had unprotected sex with the woman during the time the child was conceived, and she let him think that the child was conceived as a result of those sexual activities.[119] This section applies only to men because a woman usually knows whether or not the child is her biological child. Since a parent by estoppel is treated on par with a legal parent, the ALI recommends limiting the pool of those potential parents to persons who have actually lived with the child. Unlike a de facto parent, the man has to do more than just function as a parent; he has to actually believe that he is the parent. If the man discovered that he was not the child's biological father, he must have made a good faith effort to continue to function in that capacity in order to retain his status as a parent by estoppel.[120]

An individual may also be deemed to be a parent by estoppel based upon the existence of a co-parenting agreement between that person and the child's legal parent or parents. The agreement creates that parental status only if the individual lived with the child from birth, held the child out as his or her child, and accepted parental obligations. Typically, courts will refuse to adjudicate a man as the child's parent by estoppel if it concludes that such a ruling would not serve the child's best interests.[121] According to the comments in this portion of the report, a man who relies on an agreement to have his paternity adjudicated by estoppel must fulfill two requirements. First, he must show that he has functioned as the child's parent. Then, he must produce an agreement proving that his actions were done with the consent of the child's biological parents. Further, courts will not adjudicate a man as a parent by estoppel unless the agreement indicates that the man was permitted to assume full parental responsibilities. As a result, the man cannot become a parent by estoppel in reliance on an agreement that gives him only visitation rights and does not obligate him to pay child support or to act as the child's caretaker. This part of the report addresses situations involving parenting arrangements made prior to the child's conception. The final way for a man to become a parent by estoppel is to present evidence that he performed all of the above-discussed actions because of an agreement he had with the child's parent or parents after the child was conceived.[122]

Some courts have adopted the ALI Principles to adjudicate persons as parents by estoppel. Other courts have relied on the common law to acknowledge the relationships children have developed with the adults in their lives and to hold men responsible for child support. In those cases, the courts based their decisions on the fact that the usual elements of equitable estoppel—representation, reliance, and detriment—were present.[123] Occasionally, an individual who is not a legal parent under state law, does not have a child-support obligation, did not have the good-faith belief that he was the child's parent, did not hold himself or herself out as the child's parent, did not have an agreement with the legal parent to serve as a co-parent, and otherwise does not meet the requirements of the parent by estoppel doctrine may nonetheless have functioned as the child's primary parent. Such an individual may be recognized as a de facto parent.

De Facto Parenthood

The purpose of the de facto parent doctrine is to prevent the biological parent from severing ties between the child and the adult whom the biological parent has permitted to act as a parent to the child. In order to qualify as a de facto parent, the person has to be acting so much like a parent that the child cannot tell the difference between that person and a biological parent. The de facto parent doctrine serves to protect the interests of the "parent" who is not biologically related to the child. Consequently, the de facto parent doctrine has been applied mostly in situations involving same-sex couples. The primary purpose has been to protect the woman who lacks a biological connection to the child from being denied contact with a child whom she has nurtured. Given the nature of the doctrine, it could very easily be applied to cases involving men and women in long-term non-marital relationships. Thus, while some jurisdictions have recognized the de facto parenthood doctrine by common law, other jurisdictions have enacted statutes codifying the doctrine. Courts usually set forth a two-step approach to an adjudication of de facto parenthood. First, a court has to decide whether or not the de facto parent doctrine should be applied to the case.[124] The de facto parentage doctrine is usually reserved for persons who have no other common law or statutory remedy. Then, the court has to decide whether or not the person has satisfied the test to be adjudicated as a de facto parent.[125] The criteria necessary to classify a person as a de facto parent are similar to the ones necessary to adjudicate a person as a psychological parent.[126] However, unlike a psychological parent, in most states, a de facto parent is entitled to all of the rights and responsibilities of a biological or adoptive parent.[127]

The state of Delaware permits a person to become a parent by default, as well as acknowledging that the legal father-child relationship can be created by default. According to the relevant statute, if a court determines that a man is a de facto parent, the law will recognize him as a legal parent.[128] In order for the family court to adjudicate the man as a de facto parent, the court must find that he has satisfied the following conditions: (1) the child's parent or parents consented to and support the man's petition to be declared the child's de facto father; (2) the child's parent or parents encouraged the man to establish a "parent-like relationship" with the child; (3) the man accepted responsibility for the child; and (4) the man performed parental duties long enough for him to establish a relationship with the child which was parental in nature.[129]

The de facto parenthood theory has also been championed by the drafters of the ALI Principles. The requirements for becoming a de facto parent are strict to avoid unnecessary and inappropriate intrusion into the relationships between legal parents and their children. Pursuant to that document, a de facto parent must satisfy the following conditions:

1. live with the child for two years or more;
2. have non-financial motives;
3. present evidence of an agreement by a legal parent or evidence of a complete lack of caretaking function by the legal parent; and
4. perform caretaking duties on a regular basis at least on par with the duties performed by the parent serving as the child's primary caretaker.[130]

The drafters of the Principles included a residency requirement to reduce the pool of persons who would have standing to seek de facto parent status. By requiring the person to have resided with the child for a certain period of time, the drafters sought to deter babysitters and non-residential relatives from filing custody actions. De facto parent status elevates a person to the level of biological or adoptive parent. Since the theory is an exception to the traditional formation of the parent-child relationship, it should be narrowly construed to apply only to those persons who are invited into the lives of children by their biological parents.

The de facto theory of parenthood recognizes that sometimes reality should trump biology. It is similar to the doctrine of equitable conversion that the law recognizes in real estate transactions. Under that doctrine, equity regards as done that which ought to be done. For instance, if A and B sign a contract for A to buy Blackacre from B, the moment that A signs the contract, A has an equitable interest in the property. Since the parties intended for A to become the owner of Blackacre, the law recognizes that intent and converts A into the equitable owner of Blackacre. Thus, a person seeking to be adjudicated as a de facto parent is not asking the court to create a new parent-child relationship. That person is simply trying to get the court to recognize the parent-child relationship that actually already exists. That relationship is not based upon the biological link between the child and the potential de facto parent; the relationship is based upon the actions of the child's biological parent. One could argue that, once the biological parent agrees, by words or deeds, that the person who is not biologically related to the child will be the child's second parent, that person obtains an equitable interest in the child. Some courts recognize that interest by acknowledging that person as the child's de facto parent. Other jurisdictions reach the same outcome by relying upon the equitable parent doctrine.

Parenthood by Equity

One of the first courts to recognize paternity by equity was the Michigan Court of Appeals. The doctrine was applied to determine paternity in *Atkinson v. Atkinson*.[131] On March 1, 1973, Terri N. and Harold J. Atkinson married. During the marriage, Terri gave birth to James. When James was almost four years old, Terri left the marital home with him. A month later, Harold filed for divorce.[132] One of the main issues disputed in the divorce case was Harold's paternity. In order to resolve the issue, the trial court ordered Harold to submit to blood tests.[133] After the blood tests proved that Harold was not James' biological father, the court gave Terri custody of James and denied Harold's petition for visitation. Harold appealed the trial court's decision on several grounds. His primary argument was that the court erred when it ordered him to submit to the blood tests because, as Terri's husband, he was presumed to be the child's father. According to Harold, by ordering the blood tests, the court wrongly permitted his paternity to be rebutted.[134]

The appellate court acknowledged the marital presumption of paternity, but noted that it was no longer considered to be irrebuttable. Thus, Terri was free to rebut the presumption of Harold's paternity using the blood test results.[135] Harold admitted that he was not James' biological father. Nonetheless, he argued that the court should adjudicate his paternity based upon other theories of parenthood. For instance, Harold contended that since Terri had permitted him to develop a father-child relationship with James, she should be estopped from denying the existence of that relationship. The appellate court rejected Harold's paternity by estoppel argument because he was unable to prove reliance. Since Terri objected to Harold's paternity so early in the proceedings, he did not have the opportunity to change his position in a detrimental way.[136]

Harold tried to convince the appellate court to recognize him as the child's equitable parent by pointing out the unfairness of severing the relationship he had established with James. The appellate court granted Harold's request and adopted the "equitable parent" doctrine. The court held that a man who was not the biological father of his wife's child might be recognized as the child's natural and legal father if the following conditions were satisfied:

1. the husband and the child mutually acknowledge a relationship as father and child, or the mother of the child has cooperated in the development of such a relationship over a period of time prior to the filing of the complaint of divorce,
2. the husband desires to have the rights afforded to a parent, and
3. the husband is willing to take on the responsibility of paying child support.[137]

The case was remanded so that the trial court could determine whether or not Harold's paternity should be adjudicated on the basis of equity.[138] The court was also ordered to reconsider the custody and visitation issues.[139] The jurisdiction's prior recognition of the equitable adoption doctrine indicated that the parent-child relationship could be created based on equity. Therefore, the appellate court was comfortable relying on the equitable parent theory to determine paternity. The court saw the equitable parent doctrine as a natural extension of the equitable adoption doctrine. In addition, the court felt that in order to protect the best interests of the child, it was necessary to adopt the equitable parent doctrine. The wife had permitted Harold to establish a relationship with James, and James was old enough to appreciate that relationship. Even after the couple separated, Terri allowed Harold to remain active in James' life. The court was concerned that disregarding the established father-child relationship would be detrimental to the child.[140]

The equitable parent doctrine is alive and well in Michigan. In a recent unpublished opinion a Michigan court stated that

[t]he purpose of the equitable parent doctrine is to permanently protect an established father-child relationship that was fostered from birth to the point of divorce, and which the father wants to continue. This preserves the stability, consistency, and bond that was [sic] created while the pre-

sumption of legitimacy governed their lives, and is [*sic*] considered a benefit to the child. So, the fact that the biological father is now in the picture does not foreclose *as a matter of law* the application of the equitable parent doctrine.[141]

Courts in other jurisdictions have also adopted the equitable parent doctrine.[142] The theory of parenthood by equity is one of the few theories that appear to consider the best interests of the child. When applying the doctrine, courts are motivated not only by the need to protect the rights of the person seeking to be declared the equitable parent. They must also make sure that adjudicating the person's parentage will benefit the child by considering the child's feelings with regard to the continuation of the relationship with the non-parent. In addition, courts strive to ensure that the person requesting equitable parent status is obligated and willing to support the child financially.

Persons putting forth the theories I have discussed in this chapter were not concerned about the impact they would have on the law. They recognized that from a societal perspective, the definition of "parent" must continue to evolve to accommodate the unique ways that people come together to form families. Persons making and interpreting laws must act in accordance to that societal change. Therefore, when adjudicating paternity, courts must consider the various ways in which a man may establish a relationship with a child. Just because a relationship is non-traditional does not mean that it is any less important to the emotional and physical well-being of the child. Allocating paternity should be about promoting the best interests of the child. Sometimes in order to achieve that goal, judges must think outside of the box. The various theories of parenthood indicate that it is time for the law to rethink what it means to be a legal father.

Rethinking Paternity Adjudication
in the Best Interests of the Child

Towards a "Best Interests of the Child" Approach to Paternity Adjudication

In this chapter, I turn to a discussion of the best interests of the child. A key role of the government is to protect the health, safety, and welfare of its citizens. Although they cannot vote, children are citizens. Thus, they are entitled to be protected from harm. Parents are deemed to be protectors of children and presumed to act in their best interests. When parents fail to protect children, the government has an obligation to step in to prevent children from being harmed. There are numerous reasons for society to be concerned about the best interests of children. The obvious one is that bad people become parents who intentionally inflict physical and emotional pain on their children. We often hear about those types of parents in the news. Children born to them are the easy ones to protect through a system created for that purpose. Fortunately, those sadistic individuals make up a small percentage of our population. Nevertheless, a system must be in place to make sure that children are safe and healthy. The majority of parents become involved with the system because of unintentional abuse and/or neglect of their children. When parents behave badly, the government must step in to protect the children.

I reluctantly admit that I have recently started watching some reality television shows. They all seem to have one thing in common—they feature adults behaving badly in front of their children. While I am not an expert in parenting, I simply do not think that this is appropriate or in the best interests of the children who participate in reality television (never mind those who watch it). However, that is just my opinion, and the government is not likely to interfere with a person's parental right because he or she is acting like an idiot. If that were the case, all of the guests of the Jerry Springer Show would be declared unfit to parent. In order for the government to act, there has to be more harm to the children, although when it comes to deciding the types of behaviors that are detrimental to children, we frequently treat children like mining canaries. Early coal mines did not feature ventilation systems, so miners would routinely bring a caged canary into new coal seams. Canaries are especially sensitive to methane and carbon monoxide, which made them ideal for detecting any dangerous gas build-ups. As long as the bird kept singing, the miners knew their air supply was safe. A dead canary signaled the need for an immediate evacuation. Likewise, when it comes to protecting children, the government is often reactive instead of proactive. Thus, an abused child signals the need for immediate governmental intervention. One purpose of the "best interests of the child" doctrine is to encourage the government to step in earlier.

How lax we are when it comes to protecting the interests of children is well illustrated by the story of my friend Teddy. From the time we first met in kindergarten until the present, Teddy has been clumsy and messy. A few years ago, Teddy and his wife, Joyce, were expecting there first child, and as the due date approached, they started making preparations. One weekend, I watched as Teddy attempted to put together the baby's crib. At first, he ignored the instruction manual and tried to assemble the crib using his "man gene." Then, after several hours, Teddy finally admitted defeat and let me read the instructions to him. Relying on the instruction manual, Teddy assembled the crib in less than an hour. Joyce went into labor late one night, and they made a mad dash to the hospital. When they were less than a mile from the hospital, a police officer stopped Teddy for speeding. The first thing the officer requested was to see Teddy's driver's license. Unfortunately, in his haste to get to the hospital, Teddy had forgotten it at home. Since Joyce was close to delivering the baby in the car, the officer let Teddy off with a warning.

The day after little Michael was born, Teddy put him in the car and took him home. At the hospital, no one checked to see whether or not Teddy and Joyce had a license to parent Michael. Moreover, the hospital did not give them a parental instruction manual. An instruction manual came with the baby's crib because it was important that the crib be correctly assembled. The manufacturer did not want the crib to collapse and injure the baby. It was also crucial for Teddy to have a license proving that he knew how to drive in order to protect him and other drivers from harm. Ironically, creating a parenting manual and/or requiring parents to pass a test to receive a license to parent would be against public policy and probably unconstitutional. In this country, interfering with parental rights violates individual privacy rights.

Paternity should be about the needs of the child and not about the marital status of the parents or the desires of the men. Children come into contact with the judicial system in several different contexts. In order to legally adopt children, adults must obtain orders from competent courts. When families are ripped apart by divorce, courts often have to step in and settle custody disputes. After receiving reports that children have been abused or neglected, courts have to determine whether or not to terminate parental rights. Whenever courts have to make decisions that impact children, they must consider the best interests of those children.[1] According to one state legislature,

> Parents have the responsibility to make decisions and perform other parental functions necessary for the care and growth of their minor children. In any proceeding between parents under this chapter, the best interests of the child shall be the standard by which the court determines and allocates the parties' parental responsibilities. The state recognizes the fundamental importance of the parent-child relationship to the welfare of the child, and that the relationship between the child and each parent should be fostered unless inconsistent with the child's best interests.[2]

Currently, every American state and the District of Columbia have statutes mandating that the "best interests of the child" standard dictate the outcome of cases involving child custody, placement, or visitation.[3] Whenever the result of a case will affect a critical life issue of a child, the court must strive to promote the best interests of the child. For example, the Arkansas statute states:

> The General Assembly recognizes that children are defenseless and that there is no greater moral obligation upon the General Assembly than to provide for the protection of our children, and our child welfare system needs to be strengthened by establishing a clear policy of the State that the best interests of the children must be paramount and shall have precedence at every stage of juvenile court proceedings.[4]

The aspect of the "best interests of the child" standard that is applied depends upon the goals the courts hope to achieve. Normally, courts do not rely upon the standard to make initial parentage decisions. A man is not recognized as a legal father because the court decides that he is up to the task. Moreover, the adjudication of a particular man as the child's legal father is not usually influenced by the impact that the paternity determination will have on the child. A man's paternity depends upon his connection to the child and/or the child's mother. Nonetheless, courts are required to consider the well being of the child when deciding whether or not to permanently sever the legal connection between the child and one or both of his or her parents. For example, a Nevada statute mandates the following:

> The legislature finds that the continuing needs of a child for proper physical, mental, and emotional growth and development are the decisive considerations in proceedings for termination of parental rights.[5]

Furthermore, in cases involving marital children, some courts consider the child's best interests when they decide whether or not to allow the marital presumption of paternity to be rebutted.[6] These courts recognize that the child's status is linked to the man's paternity. Consequently, if a man is permitted to disavow his paternity, the child may be characterized as illegitimate. That label can cause the child a lot of social, economic and legal problems. Unlike cases involving children conceived as the result of passionate encounters, cases involving children conceived by scientific methods often require courts to determine which man to recognize as the legal father. Under the current system, the artificially conceived child may be deemed legally fatherless. In order to prevent the child from suffering that plight, courts should rely on the "best interests of the child" standard. If it is appropriate for courts to apply this standard when severing a father-child relationship, it should be acceptable for them to use that same standard when establishing a father-child relationship. Hence, courts should allocate paternity in a way that promotes the best interests of the scientifically conceived child.

As noted in chapter 6, the *Johnson* case involved a custody dispute between the surrogate and the contracting couple. While the court relied upon the intent of the parties to rule in favor of the couple,[7] the dissenting judge thought that the court should have adjudicated maternity based upon the best interests of the child. This judge opined that by exclusively focusing upon the intentions of the adults, the majority reached its decision without adequately considering the needs of the child. According to the dissenting justice, in order to protect the welfare of the child, the majority should have performed a "best interests of the child" analysis. That judge further claimed that application of the intent test resulted in an outcome that was beneficial to the contracting couple. The court gave the adults what they wanted without considering the impact it would have on the child. The dissenting judge argued that the court should have assessed the households and lifestyles of both mothers to determine which placement would be in the child's best interests.[8] The majority of the court appeared to treat the child just as they would treat a subject of a contract. The contracting couple bargained for the child, so the court felt that they were entitled to the child. The analysis did not focus upon the child's needs. Even though the majority of the court rejected the "best interests of the child" approach, the dissenting judge made some compelling points that courts should consider when adjudicating paternity. Courts should not strictly enforce surrogacy contracts that treat children as though they are widgets. Custody should be all about what is best for the child. A court would not enforce a contract to adopt a child if it would be detrimental to the child. In that case, the court would disregard the intentions of the contracting parties and protect the interests of the child. Children of science should be accorded the same type of protection.

Defining the Standard

Some terms are not easily defined; others need no definition. For instance, your stating that the "sky is blue" would not require you to explain what you mean by "sky." Nonetheless, the shades of blue are as varied as the people who are asked to define the color. This is analogous to the best interests of the child. While the meaning of "child" is straightforward, when courts are directed to apply the "best interests" standard, it is unclear what they are expected to do. There is no one definition of the standard. As with obscenity, courts know situations that benefit or hurt children when the courts see them. When lawyers and judges speak of the "best interests of the child," they are typically referring to the process courts use to come up with results that promote the interests of the children involved in custody, visitation, and dependency cases. Concerned mainly with children's safety and well-being, courts have to decide what action is necessary to protect them and their interests. In so doing, courts typically consider a number of factors that impact the child's welfare.[9]

Recognizing that every case is unique, state legislatures have been reluctant to articulate a strict definition of the "best interests of the child" standard. Mandates of the pertinent statutes are meant to guide courts in making decisions that promote the best interests of the children involved in the cases before them. Most state legislatures expect courts to act in ways that protect the health and safety of the child. Some states require courts to promote the best interests of the child without giving the courts specific rules to follow.[10] Instead, the legislatures in those states have identified certain goals they wanted courts to achieve with regard to the needs of children. Courts are permitted to use their discretion to carry out the mandates of the statutes.[11] Other states have enacted statutes that enumerate the specific factors courts should consider when deciding if an action is in the best interests of the child.[12] And in still other jurisdictions, courts have to consider all factors that are relevant to the best interests of the child, including ones that are not specifically listed in the statutes.[13] This flexibility allows judges to make decisions that are right for the children involved in the specific cases that the judges are deciding. For instance, the Connecticut statute states:

> "Best interest of the child" shall include, but not be limited to, a consideration of the age of the child, the nature of the relationship of the child with his or her caretaker, the length of time the child has been in the custody of the caretaker, the nature of the relationship of the child with the birth parent, the length of time the child has been in the custody of the birth parent, any relationships that may exist between the child and siblings or other children in the caretaker's household, and the psychological and medical needs of the child.[14]

Although the statutory factors vary from state to state, some are commonly considered to be crucial. One is the consistent requirement that courts in all states must strive to protect the mental and physical health of the child. To that end, the statutes mandate that courts determine whether or not domestic violence exists in the homes of the parties involved in the custody or visitation dispute.[15] In addition, courts are required to evaluate the child's emotional ties to and relationship with the persons involved in the custody or visitation dispute.[16] To make sure that the child will be adequately taken care of, courts must also determine which person is the most capable of providing the child with food, clothing, shelter, and medical care.[17] The Michigan statute contains one of the most comprehensive attempts to define the "best interests of the child" standard. The statute states:

> As used in the act, "best interests of the child" means the sum total of the following factors to be considered, evaluated, and determined by the court:
>
> - The love, affection, and other emotional ties existing between the parties involved and the child
> - The capacity and disposition of the parties involved to give the child love, affection, and guidance and to continue the education and raising of the child in his or her religion or creed, if any

- The capacity and disposition of the parties involved to provide the child with food, clothing, medical care, or other remedial care recognized and permitted under the laws of this State in place of medical care, and other material needs
- The length of time the child has lived in a stable, satisfactory environment,
- The permanence, as a family unit, of the existing or proposed custodial home or homes
- The moral fitness of the parties involved
- The home, school, and community record of the child
- The reasonable preference of the child, if the court considers the child to be of sufficient age to express preference
- The willingness of each of the parties to facilitate and encourage a close and continuing parent-child relationship between the child and the other parent or the child and parents
- Domestic violence, regardless of whether the violence was directed against or witnessed by the child
- Any other factor considered by the court to be relevant to a particular child custody dispute.[18]

Some state statutes place limits on the factors the courts may consider when determining the child's best interests. For example, the Connecticut statute states that when applying the "best interests of the child" standard, courts must not consider the socioeconomic status of the parties.[19] This is necessary to prevent courts from acting in a biased way against low-income persons. The ability to parent a child should not be linked to the person's income because there are good and bad parents at all income levels. Similarly, according to the Delaware statute, the court should not give preference to one parent over the other because of gender,[20] thereby clearly rejecting the "tender years" doctrine that gave preference to mothers over fathers if the case involved a young child.[21] Finally, the Idaho statute prohibits discrimination against persons with disabilities.[22] This not only makes the statute consistent with federal antidiscrimination laws, but also acknowledges that a person's character and/or compassion is not impacted by his or her disability.

Applying the Standard

When applying the "best interests of the child" standard, courts evaluate the factors in the context of the unique circumstances of the cases before them. Despite the fact that their language varies, the statutes reflect the legislatures' intent that the courts focus on those factors that are relevant to parental fitness and child protection, and as a survey of court cases indicates, most courts do make their decisions accordingly. Even so, depending on whether the case involves children of passion or children of science, there are significant differences in courts' approaches and decisions.

Children of Passion

The *Price* case, in which the court had to make a decision regarding the modification of a custody arrangement, provides a good demonstration of a "best interests of the child" analysis in a situation involving a child of passion.[23] In 1972, Tom and Melinda Price got married, and then had four children. After twenty-one years of marriage, Tom filed for divorce. With Melinda's agreement, the court awarded the couple joint legal custody of the children, and Tom was given physical custody.[24] Several years later, Melinda filed a motion asking the court to modify the custody arrangement, so she could get physical custody of the children.[25] In determining whether or not to modify the custody arrangement, the court considered the following seven factors: " (1) parental fitness; (2) stability; (3) primary caretaker; (4) child's preference; (5) harmful parental conduct; (6) separation of siblings; and (7) substantial change in circumstances."[26] Only the first six factors are relevant to an initial custody determination. With regard to parental fitness, the court attempted to ascertain which parent could provide the child with the best care and thus assessed the physical and mental health of each parent, as well as evaluating each one's approach to parenting.[27] Then, in order to determine the stability of each parental home, the court examined both the nature of the parental and non-parental relationships the child had established and the level of contact the child had with the external communities of the respective parental residences.[28]

When it came to determining which parent to classify as the child's primary caretaker, the court considered the actions of the parties before and after the custody dispute. Thus, while the court stipulated that the primary caretaker might be the person who had spent the most time parenting the child prior to the hearing, in the interest of fairness, the court also recognized that the primary caretaker could be the person who would be able to spend the most time with the child after the custody determination.[29] Either way, the court gave the person deemed to be the primary caretaker a slight advantage—and reasonably so, since the child probably had a closer relationship with and was more dependent on the parent who was the primary caretaker. The child's age and maturity was also a factor. If the court determined that the child was old and mature enough, the court would give weight to the child's preference.[30] Since the harmful parental conduct factor comes into play only when the parent acts in a way that negatively impacts the child's physical and/or emotional well-being,[31] the court does not have to include this factor in its analysis of every case. Likewise for situations involving siblings—and where siblings do exist, the court's decision tends to be influenced by a desire to keep siblings together.[32] After considering all of those factors, the court held that a change in custody was not in the child's best interests.[33] Thus, while courts weigh different factors to determine the appropriate custodial arrangement for the child, they all focus upon evaluating the fitness of the parents and the needs of the child involved in the case.

Moreover, when adjudicating paternity in a case involving passionately conceived children, the focus is not upon the parental fitness of the man per se. This is not relevant because a person does not have to pass a parental fitness test to become a parent. Under the parental rights doctrine, a parent who is fit cannot be denied the right to parent his or her child simply because the court thinks the child would be better off with another person. Courts are not interested in forcing the man to develop a relationship with the child. The purpose of the paternity determination is to ensure that the man meets his financial obligations to the child. If a man helps to conceive a child by having sex with the child's mother, he has a legal duty to help provide the child with food, clothing, shelter, and medical care. It does not matter if the man takes precautions to avoid fatherhood. Once a biological link is found between the man and the child, he is legally required to help support the child. In most cases, a cuckolded husband has the same obligation. The man's marital status is typically enough for him to be identified as the legal father of his wife's child. The marital presumption is about protecting the child and not punishing the man. Thus, to protect the child's best interests, courts are reluctant to give the man's right not to procreate more weight than the child's right to be financially supported. In essence, courts apply the "best interests of the child" standard to ensure that the child conceived through passion has economic support from a father. Children conceived using scientific methods are, however, treated differently.

Children of Science

Courts called upon to allocate paternity between the men involved in the artificial insemination process are concerned about the rights of the men. The interests of the child are not enough to outweigh the man's rights. When a man donates his sperm, he is intentionally making the decision to have a child conceived using his genetic material. However, if he is an anonymous sperm donor, the man does not expect to have a relationship with the child. He certainly does not want to be held financially responsible for the child. On the other hand, in a case involving a known sperm donor, that man donates to a woman he knows so that she can achieve her goal of motherhood. The man may be willing to have a relationship with the child, but he does not want to serve in the capacity of a father. Most states have statutes requiring courts to honor the desires of the sperm donors and not to name them as the legal fathers of the children they help to conceive. Thus, the court disregards the sperm donor's biological connection to the child and holds that he is not the child's legal father. It does not matter if the decision leaves the child without a father. The child's need for financial support is supplanted by the man's right not to be a father.

If a man refuses to consent to his wife's conception of a child by artificial insemination with another man's sperm, he is protected from the responsibilities of fatherhood for that child. The marital status of the couple is not enough for the court to presume that he is the father of the artificially conceived child. Furthermore, the court will not let the child's need for a father influence its decision not to let a woman force her husband into fatherhood. The man's right not to procreate includes the right to refuse to give permission to have his wife impregnated with the sperm of another man. The court will protect the man's right to "just say no" even if it is to the detriment of the artificially conceived child. The best interest of the artificially conceived child is not the court's paramount concern.

Critiquing the Standard

Courts routinely apply the "best interests of the child" standard when making decisions that impact children. Child advocates and legal scholars support the use of the standard. The key argument in favor of its application is that doing so focuses decision-making on the needs of the child, rather than on the interests of the adults involved in the case. In other words, the court's goal is to achieve an outcome that will benefit the child, regardless of whether this outcome infringes on any rights held by the parents. From this perspective, children are no longer considered to be parental property, and adults involved can lose their right to visit or to parent their children if they act in ways that are detrimental to them. Of all of the parties involved in child-custody or visitation cases, children are the ones with the weakest voices. The "best interests of the child" standard encourages courts to speak for the children. Another positive aspect of the "best interests of the child" standard is the flexibility that it gives to courts. As indicated earlier, since the standard is not clearly defined, a court can interpret it based upon the unique facts of the case being considered. That flexibility is important because different facts may lead to different outcomes. Instead of strictly applying a rule, a court is allowed to decide the case in a manner that is beneficial to the specific child involved in the case, while being guided by a standard that promotes the health, safety, and welfare of children.

Opponents of the "best interests of the child" standard claim that it gives judges too much discretion. As a consequence, application of the standard may lead to judicial bias, judicial inefficiency, and judicial uncertainty and thus to decisions that are disadvantageous to certain persons. For instance, where judicial bias is concerned, courts may favor stay-at-home mothers over working mothers or they may link the children's well-being too strictly to economics. Either way, women can be placed at a disadvantage because they typically have fewer financial resources than men. Moreover, with regard to the termination of parental rights, judicial bias may cause courts to unfairly evaluate the parenting skills of members of some racial and ethnic groups.

The vagueness of the "best interests of the child" standard also encourages inefficient litigation. Since it gives the judges so much discretion, it may encourage parties to be more likely to take their chances in court. In addition, the lack of a clear definition of the standard has forced courts to become dependent on experts, thereby advantaging persons who can afford the best experts. This practice takes financial resources away from the children and extends the decision-making process to the disadvantage of the children. Instead of receiving an unbiased report, courts are forced to decipher competing expert opinions. Thus, although the objective of the "best interests of the child" standard is to ensure that children are protected, the standard is not defined in a manner that permits courts to achieve that goal.

In fact, the factors used to uphold the standard can focus too much on the fitness of the adults and not enough on the needs of the children. This not only encourages parents to spend time and money vilifying each other, but also negatively impacts the child. In terms of financial resources, if the parents are spending significant sums on litigation, there is less money to spend on the child. In terms of emotional well-being, hostility between the parents may be damaging to the child. Where the focus is so much on the parents, courts may never get a genuine picture of the situation with regard to the children.

An additional weakness of the "best interests of the child" standard is that it leads to unpredictable decisions. Since there is no bright-line rule, it may be difficult for attorneys to predict the outcome of a case. As a result, the parties may engage in forum shopping to find judges who they perceive will be favorable to their particular positions or to avoid ones who they think will rule against them. For example, a working woman may intentionally seek to avoid a judge who has a reputation of being hard on working women—or vice versa, she may look for a judge who she feels will be more sympathetic to her position. Regardless of the specifics, forum shopping in general is not good for the system, the parents, or the children. Instead of the case being about the children, it may turn into a procedural game. Furthermore, the "best interests of the child" standard may be especially unhelpful to children in cases involving two fit parents. Where some of the factors require courts to focus on the actions of the parents prior to the separation or divorce, this approach may be counterproductive. That is, it may be difficult to predict the future based on the facts of the past because family dynamics will be different after the divorce or separation. Despite its shortcomings, the "best interests of the child" standard may still be used to protect all children. However, the standard may have to be altered to accommodate the needs of children of science.

Modifying the Standard

The factors the courts consider when deciding the best interests of the child deal mainly with the ability of the parents to provide a safe environment for the child. While the "best interests of the child" standard should thus be utilized to ensure that children of science are treated on par with children of passion, the standard does need to be modified to address the unique concerns of children of science. The courts should strive to make sure that those children have at least two parents to provide them with financial support. I characterize this as the "economic best interests of child" standard and will set forth the components of my proposed test at the end of this chapter. First, I will analyze another proposed modification to the standard designed to address the psychological well-being of children.

Psychological Best Interests Test

When a child is being physically or sexually abused, the law has a system in place to protect the child from further danger. Tests are available to attempt to verify the accusations made by the child, and the public is outraged by stories about children who have been beaten and/or molested. The more difficult cases are those involving emotional abuse. In those, the child usually does not realize that he or she is being abused and is therefore less likely to report the abuse to a grown up.

Children are taught through public service announcements and other mechanisms that parents should not hit them. Indeed, not only has corporeal punishment been banned from schools, but most members of the public frown upon any form of spanking. Thus, when a parent physically touches the child, the child knows that he or she might be being abused. I once had an interesting conversation with a parent that illustrates the level of knowledge that even young children currently have about child abuse. According to the parent, her child was acting out, so she threatened to give the child a spanking. The child responded by threatening to call 911 on the mother. Likewise, young children are constantly told about improper touching. As a result, children who are being sexually abused know that the adult is doing something that is wrong and will probably tell someone about the abuse.

On the other hand, no one tells a child that it is not okay for a parent to call him or her "stupid" or other derogatory names. Consequently, it is rare for a child to be removed from a parent's home because of emotional or psychological abuse. The current application of the "best interests of the child" standard reflects the fact that the law appears to be mainly concerned about protecting children from physical and sexual abuse. Some commentators, academics, and child advocates think that reality should be different because a child's emotional health is just as important as a child's physical health. Studies have shown that emotional scars typically take longer to heal than physical ones, and that this is equally true for abused children as well as for abused women.

Some have suggested that the "best interests of the child" standard be modified to consider all of the needs of the child. For instance, as early as 1963, the author of a note in the *Yale Law Journal* argued that instead of just focusing on the child's financial and physical needs, courts should award custody in a manner that benefited the child's psychological well-being.[34] When describing the "psychological best interests of the child" standard that he was advocating, the author noted:

> Optimum custody goals may be further defined by concentration on the psychological well-being of the child, where "psychological well-being" is used to denote the mental and emotional health of the child—specifically, a process of personality development within the framework of patterns of normal growth as posited by the behavioral sciences.[35]

Going on to discuss the manner in which the "psychological best interests of the child" test would be applied, the author observed that the court's primary aim when evaluating a case should be to

> identify and describe the existing affection-relationship(s), chiefly from the perspective of the particular child who is the subject of the custody dispute. Such relationships might be inferred from evidence shedding light on three questions: the continuity of the relationship between child and adult in terms of proximity and duration; the love of the adult toward the child; and the affection and trust of the child toward the adult . . . [36]

The author contended that evaluating the impact the custody decision would have on the child's psychological health was crucial. Placing the child in a home where he or she would receive the maximum amount of financial support would not be in the child's best interests if the placement would adversely impact the child's emotional health.[37]

A few years after this introduction of the concept of the "psychological best interests of the child" standard, Professor Joseph Goldstein, whose training included both law and psychiatry, wrote about the importance of expanding the "best interests of the child" standard to protect the child's emotional well-being when courts make custody determinations:

> If the law student (who is also hopefully the future judge) were to study the primary sources of psychoanalysis, he would see that at most and at best a psychoanalytically informed definition of the child's best interests would assist the court or adoption agency in deciding which disposition among available alternatives is likely to provide the child, whatever his endowments, with the best available opportunity to fulfill his potential in society as a civilized being.[38]

Professor Goldstein went on to co-author a trilogy arguing that one of the main deficiencies of the traditional "best interests of the child" standard is that it was applied to protect the child's physical well-being without considering the child's psychological well-being. For instance, he claimed that

> While they make the interests of a child paramount over all other claims when his physical well-being is in jeopardy, they subordinate, often intentionally, his psychological well-being to, for example, an adult's right to

assert a biological tie. Yet both well-beings are equally important, and any sharp distinction between them is artificial.[39]

It is clear that Professor Goldstein was not advocating replacing the traditional "best interests of the child" test. Rather, he was recommending that the test be modified to include an emphasis on the psychological well-being of the child. Advancing a holistic approach to promoting the interests of the child, Professor Goldstein was arguing that courts and legislatures should seek to protect the child's physical and mental health equally.

State legislatures and courts have indeed come to recognize the importance of protecting the child's emotional health. With legislatures adopting statutes that are flexible enough to permit courts to consider all factors that impact the child's well-being, courts are mindful of the emotional needs of the child when making custody and visitation decisions. For instance, if the child has a stronger emotional attachment to one parent, that parent has a better chance of being named the custodial parent. Moreover, guardians ad litem and other persons advocating on behalf of children are called upon to work with courts to make certain that the children are placed and/or permitted to remain in homes where their physical, economic, and emotional needs will be met. Courts rely upon psychologists to determine whether or not the child has been emotionally abused in the parent's home.

It is easier to argue for a "psychological best interests of the child" test when dealing with custody, visitation, or termination of parental rights issues. Since the adults involved in those kinds of cases will have some type of relationship with the child, courts can determine which placement would best protect the child's emotional health. When adjudicating paternity, however, most courts do not base their decisions on the outcome of a "best interests of the child" analysis, mainly because it is difficult to predict whether or not someone would be the best parent for the particular child involved in the case. In contrast, a child-centered approach to parentage determinations must consider the needs of the specific child. Thus, whereas evidence may indicate that the person is capable of being a good parent in general, that evidence is not relevant if the focus is on what is best for the child instead of on the fitness of the adult. Complicating matters further is the fact that psychological abuse does not leave physical evidence. Consequently, it is hard for courts to decide if a placement would be in the child's psychological best interests. In those situations, courts tend to be more reactive than proactive. The child is usually not interviewed by a mental health professional until after the child has suffered some type of emotional abuse. Thus, courts may find it even more difficult to adjudicate paternity based upon what is in the psychological best interest of the child.

Adoption cases provide the most relevant models of courts making initial parentage determinations. Since persons who are unable to conceive by sexual intercourse frequently rely on adoption to create their families, and since infertile persons often likewise use artificial insemination to become parents, persons in both of those situations may have to have their parentage determined by courts. Since courts apply the "best interests of the child" standard to decide whether or not to approve a person's application to adopt a child,[40] it should not be a stretch for courts to use a "best interests of the child" test to adjudicate the paternity of the men involved in the artificial insemination process.

In adoption proceedings, where courts have a duty to take a child-centered approach when considering what is in the child's best interests, courts must answer the following two questions: (1) whether the person seeking the adoption is qualified to take care of the child and (2) whether the adoption will promote the child's best interests. If those questions are answered in the affirmative, the courts should not consider any other factors. *In re Adoption of* Ridenour,[41] in which foster parents filed petitions in the probate court to adopt two of their foster children, illustrates the point. In that case, the children's grandparents filed motions to intervene in the proceedings because they wanted to have the right to visit the children after they were adopted.[42] The probate court not only granted the grandparents' motions to intervene but also denied the adoption petitions. Even though the probate court determined that the foster parents would make suitable parents, it concluded that the adoption would not be in the children's best interests. The court of appeals affirmed the probate court's decision. Subsequently, the foster parents appealed to the Ohio Supreme Court,[43] which spent the majority of its opinion explaining why the adoption would be in the children's best interests.[44] The court listed several factors to that effect. First, the court noted that the social service agency consented to the adoption after working with the children and the foster parents for almost two years. Second, the court stated that if they were adopted by the foster parents, the children would have the stability and continuity they needed. The girls had been living with the foster parents since they were infants.[45]According to the court's opinion:

> If the children are adopted by the Ridenours, the patterns of daily life, the mode of discipline, and the practical and spiritual rituals to which they have grown accustomed will remain constant. The emotional bonds which

the children have formed with the members of the Ridenour family will remain intact.[46]

Third, the court determined that adoption was necessary to prevent the children from being bounced around the foster care system. The court noted that waiting to be adopted would be detrimental to the children because they were emotionally attached to their foster parents. The court also observed that other potential adoptive parents might not be willing to adopt the two girls and that it would not be in the girls' best interests to grow up in separate families.[47] Furthermore, the state supreme court determined that the probate court had abused its discretion by elevating the rights of the grandparents over the best interests of the children.[48] In effect, the probate court denied the foster parents' adoptions petitions strictly because it felt that the adoption would make it hard for the grandparents to visit the children after the adoption.[49] The supreme court, by contrast, made it clear that the main concern in adoption cases should be protecting the best interests of the children. Thus, the holding of the case indicates that courts will approve a man's adoption petition only if that decision would serve the child's best interests. Insofar as protecting the welfare of the child is the court's paramount concern, children of science are entitled to be valued in the same way as any other children. Therefore, a man should not be adjudicated as a father of an artificially conceived child unless that classification would be in the child's best interests.

The law cannot force parents, especially non-custodial parents, to develop and maintain relationships with their children. The most legislatures and courts can do is to penalize parents who fail to provide financial support for their children. Currently, courts and legislatures are not working hard enough to make sure that the financial needs of children of science are being met. Courts that consider the emotional needs of children do so from the perspective of assessing the actions of the adults, by relying on the psychological parent doctrine[50] to make custody and visitation decisions. In order to promote the best interests of the artificially conceived child, courts must focus their analysis on the economic needs of the children. As the following section demonstrates, the paternity of the man in those cases should be adjudicated based upon what is in the child's economic best interests.

Economic Best Interests Test

Ecclesiastes 10:19 indicates that "money answers all things."[51] This statement is provocative and shocking, but true. Most people focus on the biblical scripture that states that the love of money is the root of all evil[52] and are surprised that the importance of money is mentioned in the Bible. The "best interests of the child" test I am proposing is based upon two important considerations. The first one is that money matters to children. The second one is that when adjudicating paternity, the court's primary objective should be to make the man financially responsible for the child. The man's willingness to have a relationship with the child is not relevant to his obligation to pay child support.

Summing Up the Costs

Children are expensive. The United States Department of Agriculture (USDA) publishes an annual report entitled "Expenditures on Children by Families." According to the 2007 USDA Report, it cost approximately 3.2 percent more to raise a child from birth to the age of seventeen than it did in 2006. The two largest expenses are housing and food. It does not take a report to convince people that children can place a financial burden on a family. From conception to adulthood, children require financial support. When my niece Kaylan was born, my sister, who is a single parent, asked me to be the godmother. I was so excited that I decided to go on a shopping spree. My eyes almost fell out of my head when I saw the price tags on some of the cute little outfits. I wondered out loud, "How can something with so little fabric cost so much?" Over the years, helping to supply Kaylan's needs and wants has been eye opening. The older Kaylan gets, the more her expenses increase. Recently, I wrote a large check for Kaylan's braces. Before the ink could dry, Kaylan texted me to inform me that she wanted to take driver's education. I realized that the next text would probably be a request for a car. Therefore, I need to start saving. Kaylan is thinking about money for a car, and I am thinking about money for her college. She thinks she needs a car; I know that she needs a college education. I am not complaining. I think Kaylan is a gift from God. I am only pointing out that children have financial needs that have to be met.

The poverty rate of children being supported by single women is almost five times that of those receiving financial support from two parents.[53] Financial support is important to children because it gives them the opportunity to succeed in life. Children who live in poverty are severely disadvantaged. Because they often live in neighborhoods with poor school systems, those children are less likely to get a quality education and are thus unable to be competitive when it comes to getting accepted into top colleges. Indeed, even if they are lucky enough to be admitted to a good college, they have a difficult time financing their educations and often end up overburdened with student loan debt. Generous scholarships are not enough to offset the expense of an education at a top school. Moreover, children from low-income families are usually not as healthy as their wealthier counterparts. Since most low-income neighborhoods have few, if any, supermarkets, and since healthy food also typically comes with a high price tag, it is almost impossible for low-income parents to get healthy, affordable food. Hence, they end up feeding their children fast food, which puts them at risk for heart disease, diabetes, and other obesity-related conditions. To make matters worse, those children usually do not have a safe place to exercise. City parks and recreational centers in low-income neighborhoods are often overrun by criminal activity. As a result, children from low-income families are more likely to be involved in criminal activities either as victims or criminals. A child's ability to achieve in life is linked to the financial circumstances of his or her family. Thus, it is clear that money matters to children. Courts should do whatever is necessary to ensure that children of science receive sufficient financial support.

Searching for the Culprits

As a part of welfare reform, the U.S. government started aggressively going after the fathers of children who were receiving public benefits to make sure that those fathers provided financial support for the children. The reasoning was that the taxpayers should not have to take care of a man's child if that man is capable of supporting the child. Some states are so committed to the process that they imposed criminal penalties on men who refuse to pay child support. All states have created child-support enforcement departments which are tasked with taking actions to make men fulfill their financial obligations. Even men who have relationships with their children are required to make child support payments.

Courts have held that establishing paternity is a compelling state interest because it insures that someone other than the taxpayers is financially responsible for the child. As one court noted:

> The Legislature has declared its preference for assigning *individual* responsibility for the care and maintenance of children; not leaving the task to taxpayers. That is why it has gone to considerable lengths to insure that parents will live up to their support obligations.[54]

In 2010, a man categorized as the "ultra deadbeat dad" was sentenced to twenty-three months in jail for failing to pay child support. This man, Howard Veal, fathered twenty-three children by fourteen different women.

Although Veal maintained a relationship with some of the children, he did not provide financial support for any of them. When Veal accumulated over $533,000 in child-support arrears, Michigan Assistant Attorney General Mitchell Wood decided that enough was enough and wrote to the judge asking that Veal be given a sentence that was greater than the one required by the sentencing guidelines. The judge was so outraged by Veal's failure to provide financial support for his children that he agreed that Veal should get more time in jail than the six months mandated by the statute. Consequently, the judge exercised his discretion and sentenced Veal to between twenty-three and forty-eight months in jail.[55] The judge was motivated by the need to make sure that Veal lived up to his paternal obligations. After children of science are born, they deserve to receive the financial support that they need. The courts can help ease the plight of those children by awarding paternity relying on an "economic best interests of the child" standard. The law cannot give a child a father's love and emotional support. Thus, when making initial parentage decisions, courts should focus upon promoting the child's financial interests. In some cases, this may mean that the artificially inseminated woman's husband or the sperm donor has to be held financially responsible for the artificially conceived child. The court's goal should be to ensure that the child's economic needs are met. To accomplish that goal, the court should consider the resources of the inseminated woman and the resources of the men involved in the process, evaluating those factors to determine if it is in the child's economic best interests to adjudicate the inseminated woman's husband or the sperm donor as the legal father. For instance, if the evidence shows that the child would be impoverished without a legal father, courts should take steps to make sure one of the men involved in the process is financially responsible for providing for the child. This analysis should be independent of the desires of the men. It is usually in the child's economic best interests to be financially supported by at least two parents, so courts should take steps to expand the definition of "parent" to achieve that goal. The next chapter explores several parentage proposals that may be appropriate in situations involving children of science. Each theory is designed to ensure that courts adjudicate paternity in ways that promote the best interests of those children.

8

Allocating the Paternity of Husbands, Same-Sex Partners, and Sperm Donors

In chapter 5, I discussed the different classes of children in order to illustrate the reality that the manner in which children are viewed by society impacts the manner in which the law treats them. Recognizing that correlation, one court stated:

> When social mores change, governing statutes must be interpreted to allow for those changes in a manner that does not frustrate the purposes behind their enactment. To deny the children of same-sex partners, as a class, the security of a legally recognized relationship with their second parent serves no legitimate state interest . . . .
>
> As the case law from other jurisdictions illustrates, our paramount concern should be with the effect of our laws on the reality of children's lives. It is not the courts that have engendered the diverse composition of today's families. It is the advancement of reproductive technologies and society's recognition of alternative lifestyles that have produced families in which a biological, and therefore a legal, connection is no longer the sole organizing principle. But it is the courts that are required to define, declare and protect the rights of children raised in these families, usually upon their dissolution. At that point, courts are left to vindicate the public interest in the children's financial support and emotional well-being by developing theories of parenthood, so that "legal strangers" who are de facto parents may be awarded custody or visitation or reached for support.[1]

In researching and writing this book, I learned several lessons.[2] The primary lesson is that the current system needs to be changed in order to address the paternal needs of children conceived by artificial insemination. As society gets more and more comfortable with the use of assisted reproduction, people will come to demand that those children be protected and supported in a manner similar to that of other classes of children. Members of the public will be just as outraged by a news item about a man who refuses to provide financial support for the fourteen children conceived artificially using his sperm as they are by a story about a man who does not pay child support for the twenty-three children he conceived through sexual intercourse. The men involved in the conception of children should not get a pass because of the manner in which the children are conceived. Regardless of the manner of conception, once children of science are born, they have the same financial needs as children conceived through sexual intercourse.

State legislatures should modify the current statutes addressing the rights and responsibilities of the men involved in the artificial insemination process in order to bring those statutes more in line with the manner in which families are currently formed. However, legislatures cannot think of and prepare for all contingencies. Consequently, courts should have the flexibility to determine paternity relying upon various standards consistent with family-law principles derived from existing statutes and case law. The overriding objective should be to promote the best interests of the artificially conceived child.[3] It is usually in the best interests of both the child and society to have at least two adults financially responsible for the child's support.[4] This is true even if the adults have agreed not to live together. In addition, it is in the child's best interests for the court to recognize and respect the relationships that the child has established with the adults in his or her life.

Under the present system, there is a possibility that an artificially conceived child may end up legally fatherless. For example, if a husband does not consent to the artificial insemination of his wife, he is not legally recognized as the father of the resulting child.[5] Based upon the same statutory regime, the sperm donor is never classified as the legal father. Thus, in a situation involving a non-consenting man, the artificially conceived child does not have a father. Moreover, courts cannot force the adults in the relationship to stay together for the children. They can, however, take steps to ensure that children conceived using artificial insemination have at least two legal parents.

When allocating paternity, courts should have several primary objectives. The first should be to promote the economic best interests of the child by ensuring that the child's financial needs are met. The second goal should be to ensure that the child maintains the relationship with the "primary male figure" involved in his or her life. The "primary male figure" is the man who has established a paternal relationship with the child. The third goal should be to reward the man for the contributions that he made to assist in the child's conception. The final goal should be to honor the expectations of the woman and man involved in the conception arrangement. In the event that any of these goals are in conflict, the court should do a balancing test to make sure that the paternity adjudication is in the child's best interests.

In this chapter, I present three different proposals pertaining to the allocation of the paternity of the men involved in the artificial insemination process. These proposals are not without flaws. However, if they are implemented, the plight of children of science will be greatly improved. The first proposal addresses situations involving two or more men who want to be recognized as the father of the resulting child. The second proposal is offered to assist courts faced with the decision of whether or not to acknowledge the inseminated woman's husband or same-sex partner as the paternal parent[6] of the artificially conceived child. The final proposal discusses the paternal obligations of sperm donors. These proposals are based upon parental theories discussed in chapter 6. I do not seek to join the ranks of those scholars and commentators advocating for co-parenting or non-exclusive parenting arrangements.[7] My focus is upon ensuring that the artificially conceived child has two legally recognized parents. That is, I am unwilling to throw out the two-parent model of parenting.[8] Since it is often difficult for two parents to agree on decisions impacting children, if more adults are added to the mix, life may be more chaotic for the children. Nonetheless, I am willing to eliminate the gender restrictions on the two-parent model. Thus, under my proposals, the child's two parents may be of the same gender.[9]

To that end, I am proposing two primary changes to the current system. One is that paternity be defined broadly to include the woman in a same-sex relationship who may not be biologically related to the child. Another is that the definition of paternity be expanded to include persons who are not biologically linked to the child.[10] Hence, I propose that biology not be the sole indicator of paternity. Courts should apply a series of tests or standards when determining paternity. If the person's paternity can be established under one or more of those tests or standards, he or she should be recognized as the legal paternal parent of the child. As a consequence, that person would be financially obligated to support the child and be entitled to all of the benefits of the parent-child relationship. This approach is not too radical because courts have engaged in a similar analysis in order to decide maternity in cases involving children conceived as the result of surrogacy arrangements.[11] My proposal, however, is limited to situations involving children conceived by artificial insemination. In order for my proposal to apply, the insemination procedure does not have to be performed by a licensed physician or a person with a medical background.[12] Although it is clear that an independent third party should be involved in the process in order to prevent fraud, there is no compelling reason why that person has to be a licensed physician or anyone else with a medical background. In the alternative, the court could presume that if the child was conceived without the involvement of a licensed physician, the child was conceived by sexual intercourse. The person seeking the protections provided by this proposal would have the burden of proving that the child was not conceived by sexual intercourse. Thus, again, the involvement of a neutral third party is critical to my proposal.

The theories that underlie these proposals address situations that involve one adult who is biologically unrelated to the child. I am concerned about those cases where the option before the court is either to allocate parental rights to the one person seeking it or to declare the artificially conceived child to have only one legal parent. When there is only one person vying for the role of father, the court should do an "economic best interests of the child" analysis based upon the standards set forth in my proposals. Before I turn to my discussion of those types of cases, I will look briefly at the steps courts should take to resolve disputes between two men who want to be recognized as the legal father of the artificially conceived child.

Proposal I: Resolving Custody Disputes

As in situations involving children conceived by sexual intercourse, there will be times when two men seek to be named the legal father of the artificially conceived child. For instance, the biological father may challenge the husband of the child's mother for paternal rights. In those cases, I propose the use of a three-tier paternity adjudication system based upon the expectations of the parties and the best interests of the child. Under this proposal, the first tier would include the man who contributes the genetic material used to conceive the child. As a tier-one father, the biological father would be given first preference. The classification as second- or third-tier father would be based upon the pre-conception and the post-conception actions of the men involved in the case. Absent contributing biological material, the most important thing the man can do is to take steps to ensure that the child is conceived. Therefore, the man who contributed the most effort to ensure the child's conception would be placed in the second tier. Factors that would earn him the right to be placed in this tier include obtaining the genetic material used to conceive the child, assisting the child's mother before and during the pregnancy, and contributing some of the money to cover the pregnancy-related expenses. The third tier would consist of men who, although not actively involved in the children's conception, do have relationships with the children because of post-conception actions. The man in this group has done things such as developing a relationship with the child, helping to support the child financially, and/or residing in the child's home.

In situations involving two or more potential fathers, the courts should perform a "best interests of the child" analysis, the result of which will be used to move men in the tiers. If all men are deemed equally fit, the first- tier father will prevail. There should be a rebuttal presumption that the biological father is a first-tier legal father unless that would not be in the child's best interests. As a first-tier father, the biological father has the right to be recognized as the legal father, but he also has the chance of losing that status.[13] Currently, if a man abuses or abandons his child, the law can strip him of his parental rights with regard to the child. Thus, it is logical to conclude that if evidence is presented showing that placement of the child with the man would be harmful to the child, he should lose his right to be adjudicated as the child's legal parent. In an initial parentage determination, the biological father should be deemed the legal father unless another man presents compelling evidence indicating that in order to promote the child's best interest, the court should not adjudicate that man as the child's legal father. The person contesting the biological father's paternity would have the burden of proving the detriment to the child.

In cases where the biological father is not seeking to be acknowledged as the child's father, courts would designate the men involved in the case as second- or third-tier fathers. Logically, the second-tier father would prevail over the third-tier father. A man's placement in the different tiers will be based upon the contributions he makes to the child's conception and the steps he takes to bond with the child.

Proposal II: Allocating the Paternity of the Husband or Partner

In this section, I set forth theories on which courts can rely to allocate paternity to the husband or partner of the artificially inseminated woman.[14] The list of theories is not exhaustive. It is meant to suggest options courts can use to ensure that the artificially conceived child has a second parent. These types of cases usually involve one of three possible scenarios. In the first, the husband or partner does not want to be recognized as the parent of the artificially conceived child.[15] In some cases, the husband or partner attempts to disclaim responsibility for the artificially conceived child. Since he or she is not biologically related to the child, the person may feel that he or she should not have to provide financial support for the child. Those cases typically arise because the person and the mother of the artificially conceived child have separated or divorced.[16]

Scenario-two cases are litigated because the wife or partner challenges the parenthood claim of the person with no biological connection to the child.[17] The cases in which artificially inseminated women oppose their husbands or partners being declared the second legal parent of their children often involve custody and visitation issues.[18] In those types of cases, the husband or partner usually asks the court for either joint custody of the artificially conceived child or for liberal visitation.[19] The person is also usually willing to provide financial support for the child. Nonetheless, the woman would prefer that the husband or partner not be permitted to have contact with the child. In order to accomplish that objective, the woman may focus upon the fact that the person is not biologically related to the child, because the rights of a legal parent frequently supersede the rights of a person who is a legal stranger to the child.[20] Since, in most of those types of cases, the woman has permitted the person to establish a relationship with the child, the court should evaluate the nature of that relationship to determine if it is in the child's best interests to recognize it.

The possibility also exists for a third scenario in which both the artificially inseminated woman and her husband or partner agree that the husband or partner should not be recognized as the resulting child's legal parent. The court should not honor that type of agreement unless it is in the best interests of the child to do so. In deciding whether or not to designate the woman's husband or partner as the child's parent, the court should examine the parties' actions prior to and after the conception and birth of the child. If the circumstances indicate that the husband or partner anticipated being the child's parent or that he or she actually served in that capacity, the court should allocate paternal obligations to the inseminated woman's husband or partner.

The recommendations that follow apply to all three scenarios. The specific classifications below were derived from the cases, statutes, and theories set forth in chapter 6. In some instances, I have modified the definitions of certain terms; in others, I have recapped the basis of the theories. In general, when deciding those types of paternity cases, courts should look at the contributions the person made to ensure that the child was conceived, the actions the person took before the child was born and the activities of the person after the child was born.

Contributions Made

In deciding whether or not to classify the husband or partner as the child's legal paternal parent, courts should determine if he or she contributed to the child's conception by consenting to the woman's insemination. If the person consented by action or deed, he or she should be legally obligated to provide financial support for the child. The person's consent to the child's conception is enough of a contribution to establish a link between the person and the child. In cases where the biologically unrelated person wants to be recognized as the child's parent, courts will be rewarding the person for his or her contributions to the child's conception. If the person does not want to be adjudicated as the child's parent, courts will conclude that the part he or she played in the child's conception makes him or her jointly and severally liable for the child's conception. That liability includes the duty to pay child support. In the alternative, the court should presume that since the husband or partner was married to or in a committed relationship with the child's mother at the time the child was conceived, the person is the child's legal parent. When the person enters into a relationship with the child's mother by marriage, civic union, or domestic partnership, he or she is contributing to the establishment of an environment that is conducive to the conception of a child. The husband or partner's contributions to the child's conception may include nonmonetary things like emotional support.

Paternity by Consent

At a conference where I was presenting my theory, one of my colleagues asked why I chose paternity by consent as opposed to paternity by intent. Another one asked me to explain the difference between the two theories of parenthood. I felt like I was back in law school with all of the difficult questions being thrown at me. At first, I responded that "consent" was consistent with what is currently required by most of the statutes. Thus, the courts would be more willing to use it to obligate the person to support the child. The blank stares told me that my colleagues were not dazzled by my brilliance. I took a moment to think about why "consent" instead of "intent." The first logical reason I could think of was evidentiary. Intent is hard to prove because it requires the court to get into a person's head. Moreover, evidence of intent is difficult to obtain and is often unreliable. Likewise, it is hard for courts to ascertain a person's intent because it is so subjective and passive. The numerous definitions the law has for the word "intent" indicates that the concept is not very helpful when the court is seeking certainty. Another reason to reject "intent" in favor of "consent" is that intentions can change. By the time a case comes before the court, the child has usually been conceived and born. When deciding whether or not to adjudicate paternity based upon intent, courts have to consider the parties' actions from pre-conception to birth. During that period, the parties' intentions could have changed numerous times. At what step in the process is the person's intent final and binding?

Frankly, the average citizen is not impressed with "intentions," so why should the court be? The phrase "the road to hell is paved with good intentions" indicates the credit people give to intentions. How can we expect people to live up to their intentions if we are not sure of what they are? I am not comfortable permitting courts to decide something as important as paternity based upon something as uncertain as "intent." After reviewing the analyses in cases discussing parenthood by intent, I concluded that the courts were really looking at whether or not the party had consented to parent the child. The courts decided the issue of parentage based upon the fact that the intent to parent was evidenced by some type of consent. Finally, another consideration is the expectations of the parties. Courts are reluctant to enforce agreements between parties if there was not a meeting of the minds. When adjudicating paternity, it would be difficult for courts to honor the expectations of the parties if they are based on something as vague as "intent." It is hard for one party to prove that they detrimentally relied on someone else's intentions.

Thus, courts should consider consent to be a key determinant of paternity. A person who contributes to the conception of a child should be rewarded for that contribution and held accountable for helping to place another person into an overpopulated world. A person's contributions can be active and direct or passive and indirect. The sperm donor's contribution is direct because he gives a part of himself so that the child may be conceived. Nonetheless, indirect contributions to the child's conception are not any less important. These include taking part in the decision to conceive the child and taking steps to make the conception possible. Parties who engage in those types of activities are stakeholders in the enterprise of creating the child. They also have an interest in protecting the child's well-being. The woman's husband or partner makes indirect contributions to the child's conception when he or she consents to her insemination with donor sperm. Artificial insemination statutes link consent to paternity because legislators understand the important role her husband or partner's consent plays in a woman's decision to conceive a child by artificial insemination. Judges also think that people should be held accountable for any role they play in bringing more children into the world. There are several hundred thousand children languishing in the foster care system in need of homes.[21] When a woman's husband or partner forgoes adoption and encourages the woman to increase the world's population, he or she should be required to take responsibility for the child who is conceived as a result of that action. Once a court concludes that the woman's husband consented to her artificial insemination, he is treated in the same manner as a man whose wife conceives by sexual intercourse. Thus, if he fails to pay child support, he may be criminally prosecuted.[22]

If the woman's husband or partner consents to her artificial insemination, he or she is the paternal parent of the resulting child. Thus, he or she should not be permitted to deny paternity. Nor should the child's biological mother be allowed to object to the court's classification of that person as the paternal parent. In order to protect the interests of the artificially conceived child, the husband or partner of the artificially inseminated woman should be presumed to have consented to her insemination. That person's parental obligation should attach automatically, and, if there is any challenge, he or she should have to overcome the presumption of consent. As in situations involving children of passion, when adjudicating cases involving children of science, courts should determine that the existence of a relationship between the adults rather than the man's consent dictates a finding of parentage.

Where consent is a critical factor, though, consent should be broadly interpreted to include written, implied, and/or oral consent. In order for the person's consent to be legally recognized, he or she must give informed consent.[23] The person seeking to prove non-written consent must do so by submitting clear and convincing evidence of that fact. Once the husband or partner gives written consent to the artificial insemination, that consent should be effective for one year. Prior to the expiration of that time period, the husband or partner should not be permitted to unilaterally withdraw his or her consent. At the end of the one-year period, if a child has not been conceived, the woman should be required to have the written consent renewed within a reasonable period of time based upon the particular circumstances of the case. If the consent is not renewed within that time period, the husband or partner should be deemed not to have consented to the artificial insemination of the woman. Thus, that person would not be legally obligated to support a child who is conceived after the consent expired.

Paternity by Presumption

Another contribution a person can make to the conception of a child is to enter into a relationship with the child's mother prior to the child's conception. This is considered a contribution because one of the main reasons some persons marry or enter into a committed relationship is to have children. Even in this era of "free love" and "eternal engagements," some people still think that children should be conceived only in marriage or committed relationships. Thus, when a person voluntarily decides to become involved in such a relationship, that person should not be surprised when that relationship results in the conception of a child. It is often difficult for a woman to actively engage in the artificial insemination process without the knowledge of her husband or partner. In order to prevent persons from avoiding liability by burying their heads in the sand, the concept of "knowledge" should include both actual and constructive knowledge.[24]

When the law makes a presumption, the court assumes that the presumed fact is true until it is presented with evidence to the contrary. Legal presumptions are based upon inferences that the law makes. For instance, children are presumed to be their parents' intestate heirs because the court infers that parents would want their children to have most of their property.[25] In some situations, the law does not permit the court to be told the truth. The courts' ignorance is deemed necessary to benefit the greater good. I will give a brief recap of the marital presumption and then show how it is relevant to the paternity of the artificially conceived child.

For reasons stated in chapter 1, the law presumes that a man is the father of all children his wife conceives during their marriage. While the underlying principle of the doctrine has not changed, some of its purposes have become obsolete, and so courts have refined their interpretation of the doctrine. Under the traditional version of the doctrine, a husband was presumed to be the biological father of his wife's children as long as they were born in the course of the marriage. Initially, strict evidentiary requirements prevented the presumption from being rebutted because the courts wanted to preserve the sanctity of marriage and to protect children from being classified as non-marital children. Eventually, the courts permitted interested parties, including the husband, the wife, and the child(ren), to rebut the presumption of the husband's paternity. In some cases, the man claiming to be the child's biological father was permitted to successfully rebut the presumption by showing that the husband was not the biological father of the child. In light of the advances in DNA testing, it is relatively easy to prove or disprove the husband's paternity.

In cases dealing with children conceived by artificial insemination, there is no need to do DNA testing because the wife and the husband readily admit that he does not have a biological connection to the child. In response to this dilemma, some courts have adopted the "best interests marital presumption" doctrine. Under this doctrine, the woman's husband is presumed to be the father of all children conceived by her during their marriage. The main difference between the application of this doctrine and the traditional marital presumption is that the presumption can be rebutted only if it is in the child's best interests to discover that someone other than the husband is the child's biological father.

The non-consenting husband or partner of the artificially inseminated woman should be classified as the presumptive parent of the child as long as the child's conception occurs during the marriage, civil union, or domestic partnership.[26] The presumption of paternity should be permitted to be rebutted only if it is in the best interests of the child to do so. In addition, allowing the rebuttal should be considered to be in the child's best interests only if there is another adult who may legally be recognized as the paternal parent and that person is ready, willing, and able to act as a parent to the child. In deciding whether or not to permit the presumption to be rebutted, the court should also consider the child's relationship with the presumptive parent and the child's relationship with the adult who is willing to parent if the presumption of paternity is rebutted. The only persons who should be allowed to rebut the presumption of the person's paternity should be the child's biological mother, an independent representative of the child, the mother's husband or partner, or the person seeking to be recognized as the legal parent. Since the non-consenting husband or partner would not have a biological connection to the child, this presumption standard is different from that of the traditional marital presumption. As stated earlier, under that presumption, the man had only to provide proof that he was not the biological father of the child to be released from all parental obligations to the child. In cases involving artificially conceived children, in order to rebut the presumption, the husband or partner should have to present evidence indicating either that he or she did not consent to the conception of the child or that the woman knew he or she did not intend to parent the child.

Instead of the traditional marital presumption, I am advocating the use of the "best interests of the child marital presumption" test to adjudicate paternity. Under that doctrine, if disputing the paternity of the woman's husband or partner is not in the child's best interests, the presumption becomes irrebuttable. In cases dealing with children conceived by artificial insemination, the presumption can always be rebutted by blood tests. Thus, the court has to decide whether it is in the child's best interests to order the blood tests. Application of the doctrine is illustrated in *Ban v. Quigley and Frauenfield.*[27] According to Mark Frauenfield's affidavit, he and Anna Marie Ban started a sexual relationship in February 1985. At that time, while Anna was married to Ronald Ban, the couple was separated, and so Mark moved in with Anna. In November of 1985, Anna gave birth to a child. Some time in December of that year, Anna and Ronald decided to give their marriage another try. Thus, Mark left Anna's home. Ronald supported Anna's child and held the child out as his own.[28] Then, when the child was almost five years old, Mark filed an action seeking to be adjudicated as the child's legal farther. In response, Anna filed a motion to dismiss Mark's case. The trial court did so, but for procedural reasons, without ever getting to the merits of the case. After Mark amended his complaint and asked the court to order blood tests to prove that he was the father of Anna's child, Anna and Ronald successfully filed a motion to dismiss Mark's case. Mark appealed the trial court's decision.[29]

The appellate court had to decide whether the statue permitted a man to challenge the paternity of a woman's husband. Furthermore, it had to decide whether the trial court acted in error when it dismissed Mark's motion for blood tests without considering whether or not his request was in the child's best interests. Anna argued that the statute did not give Mark the right to file a paternity action because she was a married woman. Anna urged the court to interpret the statute to mean that a man could bring a paternity action only if the child's mother was unmarried. The court, however, held that Mark had standing to file the action because doing so was not limited to the woman's husband under the statute. Rather, the statute gave standing to a man who suspected that he was the father of the child regardless of the marital status of the child's mother.[30] Then, the court analyzed the "best interests of the child" issue.

According to the appellate court, the trial court had to determine "whether it would be in the best interests of the child for the case to proceed before a putative father may be permitted to seek blood tests in an attempt to rebut the presumption of the husband's paternity."[31] In resolving the issue, the court decided that before the trial court ordered the blood tests, it had to do a "best interests of the child" analysis. The court reasoned that it would be counterproductive for the trial court to decide if the paternity rebuttal was in the child's best interests after the results of the blood tests were revealed because the woman's husband would know that he was not the child's father. That knowledge might lead the woman's husband to reject the child. The court indicated that, prior to the administration of the blood tests, "ignorance would be bliss." In order to protect the father-child relationship that had been established between the child and his mother's husband, the court instructed the trial court to deny the putative father's request for blood tests to prove that he was the child's father. To justify its decision, the court reasoned:

> The present case is a vivid example of what can occur when a court, in the pursuit of judicial economy, bastardizes a child and then determines that because of bonding[,] it is in the child's best interests to continue his or her relationship with the presumed father. The court has not only bastardized the child and relieved the presumed father of all necessity of support, but it has placed the obligation to support the child on the biological father, who has never had a bonding relationship with the child. . . . Once the judge, in the interest of judicial economy, ruptures the father/child relationship, the judge cannot return the parties to the position they were in prior to the blood test, no matter how wise or great his or her judicial power. That is a fact of life.[32]

The comments regarding judicial economy arose from the fact that the trial court wanted to order blood tests before it decided if the changing of paternity would be in the child's best interests[33] so that it could avoid having to have two separate hearings. If the blood tests proved that the man was not the child's biological child, the trial court would not have to hold a hearing to decide whether the man should be able to rebut the husband's paternity. Since the blood tests would have eliminated the man as the putative father, he would not have standing to bring the action. While the appellate court recognized that the trial court's approach would promote judicial economy, the appellate court took the position that such a benefit to the judicial system would come at the child's expense. The court was concerned about cases where blood tests proved that the "outside man" was the child's father. In those types of cases, the court wanted to make sure that the man's biological connection to the child did not automatically make him the child's legal father. As a result, the court concluded that the best course of action was for the trial court to decide whether or not permitting the man to rebut the presumption would be in the child's best interests.

Moreover, the appellate court wanted the trial court to take the latter into consideration first. That is, the trial court would first decide whether or not rebutting the husband's paternity was in the child's best interests. Then, it would decide whether or not to order the blood tests. If maintaining the status quo was in the child's best interests, the trial court would not order the blood tests. Hence, it would be as if the lawsuit was never filed, and the child's life would not be disrupted. On the other hand, if permitting the man to rebut the marital presumption would not negatively impact the child, the trial court would order the blood test. In that instance, the child's position would not be made worse by the filing of the law suit. Yet, at the same time, it is clear that the approach recommended by the appellate court would be detrimental to the putative father because he would have to live with the uncertainty surrounding the child's paternity. As the child got older, he or she could hear rumors about his or her paternity, and so leaving the child's paternity unresolved could also adversely affect the child.

The traditional application of the marital presumption doctrine was meant to preserve the marriage. A man was not permitted to rebut the husband's paternity because it would cause strife in the marriage. The "best interests of the child" version of the doctrine is more concerned about protecting the child than taking care of the needs of the adults. When applying the doctrine, the court does not care about protecting the putative man's parental rights or preventing the husband from having to provide financial support for another man's child. The emphasis is on protecting the innocent party—the child. Thus, the court stated:

> The shifting of paternity from the presumed father to the biological father could easily be detrimental to the emotional and physical well-being of any child. Although someone may suffer, it should never be the child, who is totally innocent and who has no control over or conception of the environment into which he or she has been placed.[34]

Nothing in the *Ban v. Quigley and Frauenfield* case indicates that the decision should not be applicable in a situation involving an artificially conceived child. Courts should strive to protect the welfare of all children regardless of the manner of their conception. In order to promote the best interests of the child, the courts should make it difficult for the husband or partner of the artificially inseminated woman to dispute his or her paternity. Thus far, I have examined just two standards, paternity by consent and paternity by presumption, that the courts can apply to achieve this goal. The court should be just as diligent when the artificially inseminated woman tries to object to her husband or partner being adjudicated as the legal parent of her child. The contribution the husband or partner makes to the child's conception is not the only factor the court should consider when deciding whether or not to adjudicate the person's parentage. The person's actions, prior to and after the child's birth, may speak louder than his or her words.

Pre-Conception/Pre-Birth Actions

Another way for a court to decide whether or not to acknowledge the husband or partner as the legal father of the inseminated woman's child is to consider the actions that the person took to encourage the woman to conceive the child. Paternity by estoppel, which can be applicable in such cases, has been recognized by the courts and endorsed by legal scholars.[35] As indicated in chapter 3, courts have relied on estoppel to place parental responsibility on non-consenting husbands in cases involving children conceived using artificial insemination. Basically, when a husband acts in such a way as to lead his wife to believe that he is in agreement with her being artificially inseminated and that he plans to parent the child, he is estopped from claiming that he did not consent. Hence, he is the legal father of the resulting child. Application of the parent by estoppel doctrine may be triggered by the man's words or his deeds.

Paternity by Estoppel

The estoppel doctrine is based in contract law. Courts have recognized promissory estoppel, which is a legal remedy, and equitable estoppel, which is granted when the courts are led by fairness to guarantee a certain type of outcome. Both of the doctrines have been deemed applicable to determining paternity. Most of the cases involving the paternity of the husbands of inseminated women have involved the application of the equitable estoppel doctrine. This makes sense because in a case where the woman is able to show that her husband promised to act as a father to the child prior to the child's conception, the court is likely to adjudicate his paternity based upon consent. In short, the court is going to make the man live up to his promises. If the husband's promise is made in writing, the court will probably hold that the artificial insemination statute has been satisfied, so he is the child's legal father. Moreover, courts will utilize the equitable estoppel doctrine to identify the man as the legal father even if he did not make a specific promise because the wife reasonably relied upon his conduct to her detriment, so it would be unfair to let him deny his obligation to support the child. The American Law Institute (ALI) Principles discussed in chapter 6 recognize both forms of estoppel. A man may be adjudicated as a parent by estoppel based upon his actions and based upon a parenting agreement he made with the child's biological mother. Promissory estoppel is not an available remedy when the parties have entered into a written contract. However, if the parties attempt to change the contract orally and one party refuses to obey that modification, promissory estoppel may be an appropriate remedy.

I will briefly discuss both forms of estoppel and explain how I think courts should apply the doctrine to ensure that the husband or partner of the inseminated woman lives up to his or her parental duties. The main difference between promissory estoppel and equitable estoppel is the basis of the reliance and the existence of a promise. Application of the doctrine of promissory estoppel lets the person recover if he or she has relied on statements of future intent. On the other hand, equitable estoppel permits the person to recover only where the reliance was based on the misrepresentation of past or present facts.[36] Promissory estoppel is a remedy used by courts to enforce a statement that rises to the level of a gratuitous promise, but that does not meet all of the requirements of a legal contract.[37] Equitable estoppel is a defense courts permit in order to protect one party from being harmed by an action induced by the other person's conduct. It usually involves a misrepresentation on which a party is encouraged to rely.[38]

Promissory estoppel is usually viewed as a defensive theory; however, courts have also recognized it as an independent cause of action.[39] Promissory estoppel applies in a situation where there is not a valid contract. If the evidence indicates that a valid contract does exist, a cause of action for promissory estoppel cannot be made.[40] Promissory estoppel is an equitable remedy awarded by the court to permit the enforcement of a promise that would not otherwise be enforceable.[41] The elements of promissory estoppel are the following: (1) a clear and unambiguous promise exists; (2) the party to whom the promise was made has relied upon that promise; (3) the reliance was reasonable and foreseeable; and (4) the party claiming the estoppel was injured because of his or her reliance.[42] Courts have broad discretion when deciding whether or not to apply promissory estoppel.[43]

In terms of this doctrine, a person makes a promise when he or she manifests the intent to cause a certain outcome in the future.[44] The promise must involve more than mere words of support or encouragement. For example, a husband or partner who tells the inseminated woman that he or she supports that person's desire to have a child may not be promising to help parent the child. However, if the husband or partner states that he or she will do everything possible to ensure that the couple becomes parents, that statement might be sufficient to constitute a promise. At least one court has relied on the promissory estoppel doctrine to obligate a man to pay child support.[45] Kim Newman filed an action asking the court to order her boyfriend, Bruce Wright, to pay child support for her two children.[46] In response, Bruce accepted responsibility for supporting Kim's daughter, but alleged that he was not the father of her son. The results of DNA tests confirmed Bruce's allegations. However, the trial court still ordered Bruce to make child-support payments for both children. The trial court justified its decision by noting that Bruce had taken steps to establish a father-child relationship with Kim's son. The court also noted that, with his permission, Bruce's name was listed on the child's birth certificate and the child was given Bruce's surname.[47]

Bruce appealed the child-support order, arguing that since he was not the boy's biological or adoptive father, he did not have a legal duty to support the child. The appellate court acknowledged that Bruce's status as Kim's boyfriend did not make him the boy's legal father. Nonetheless, the court thought that Kim might have a remedy based upon contract law. The absence of a formal written contract requiring Bruce to pay child support did not preclude the court from holding him liable for child-support payments because the state's legislature had enacted a promissory estoppel statute that provided that

> [a] promise which the promisor should reasonably expect to induce action or forbearance on the part of the promise or a third person and which does induce such action or forbearance is binding if injustice can be avoided only by enforcement of the promise. The remedy granted for breach may be limited as justice requires.[48]

Based on the statute, the court concluded that promissory estoppel should be applied to prevent Bruce from denying his child-support obligations. For one thing, the evidence showed that Bruce promised Kim and her son that he would assume the role of the boy's father. That role required a man to support the child financially. By placing his name on the child's birth certificate and sharing his surname with the child, Bruce acknowledged his paternity and promised to pay child support.[49] At the time Bruce promised to parent the child, he knew that the boy was not his biological child. Therefore, his implied agreement to pay child support was knowingly and voluntarily given. For ten years, Bruce permitted the child to think of him as his father. Both the child and his mother detrimentally relied on Bruce to keep his promise to be a father to the child. For instance, Kim neither identified her son's biological father nor looked to him for child support. The court also noted that the child was deprived of an opportunity to have a relationship with his biological father because he relied on Bruce to always serve in that capacity. Finally, the court decided that an injustice would be perpetrated if Bruce was permitted to walk away from his financial obligations towards the child after ten years.[50]

The court reasoned that by acting as the child's father for those ten years, Bruce was promising that he would not walk away from the task. While the court could not force Bruce to continue to have a personal relationship with the child, it could make him a parent by estoppel, so that he would be required to pay child support. The key purpose of paternity adjudications is to identify the man who is responsible for providing the child with financial support. If the court can take this step when dealing with the paternity of a child of passion, there is no logical reason why the same legal principle cannot be used to deem the inseminated woman's husband or partner as the legal paternal parent. If the court cannot find evidence of a promise, it may still be able to rely on the estoppel doctrine to provide the child with a legal paternal parent.

Equitable estoppel is applicable to cases involving situations wherein, by his or her actions or inactions, one person induces another person to rely on him or her and this reliance turns out to be detrimental.[51] The approach of the court that heard *Brown v. Brown* is illustrative of the application of the doctrine of equitable estoppel.[52] In 1991, Hugh Brown married Kathy Brown.[53] Prior to the marriage, Hugh had a vasectomy. Due to a medical condition, Hugh had the vasectomy reversed. However, medical tests indicated that Hugh's sperm were all dead.[54] On several occasions, Hugh told Kathy that he did not want to have children. Nonetheless, Kathy gave birth to twins who were conceived by artificial insemination.[55] After the children were born, Hugh let his name be added to their birth certificates and permitted the children to take his last name. He also acted as a father to the children.[56] When Kathy filed for divorce, Hugh claimed that he should not be obligated to support the twins financially because he was not their biological father. He also noted that, since he did not consent to Kathy's insemination, he did not have a duty to support the children.[57] Both the trial court and the appellate court relied upon the estoppel doctrine to adjudicate Hugh as the children's legal father. That status required Hugh to pay child support.[58] According to the court,

> The elements of equitable estoppel are these: (1) the party to be estopped must know the facts; (2) he must intend that his conduct shall be acted on

or must so act that the party asserting estoppel has a right to believe the other party so intended; (3) the party asserting estoppel must be ignorant of the facts; (4) the party asserting estoppel must rely on the other's conduct to his detriment.[59]

Holding that Hugh was estopped from disclaiming his paternity with regard to the twins, the appellate court reasoned:

> (1) appellant knew the facts, i.e., he knew that appellee was having the artificial insemination procedure performed; (2) appellant acted as if he agreed to the procedure, accepted the children as his own, and showed every intention to support them, i.e., leading appellee to believe that he so intended; (3) appellee was ignorant of the facts asserted by appellant at the hearing, i.e., that he did not know she was having the procedure and did not plan to treat the children as his own; and (4) appellee relied to her detriment on appellant's conduct, i.e., she proceeded with the artificial insemination, fully expecting appellant to support the children as his own.[60]

Courts applying the estoppel doctrine should examine the actions of the non-consenting husband or partner prior to the conception and birth of the child. If the husband or partner acted in such a way that a reasonable person would conclude that he or she consented to the artificial insemination and intended to parent the resulting child, he or she should be estopped from denying paternity. Likewise, under those circumstances, the biological mother of the child should be estopped from claiming that her non-consenting husband or partner is not the paternal parent of her artificially conceived child. In all such cases, the court should apply the traditional estoppel principles of representation, reliance, and detriment. Paternity by estoppel should result if the husband or partner, through word or deed, represented the intent to parent the artificially conceived child, the woman permitted herself to be inseminated in reasonable reliance upon that representation, and the woman and or child will be harmed if the husband or partner is not adjudicated the paternal parent of the child. The person seeking to establish paternity by estoppel should have the burden of proving these elements.

Post-Conception/Post-Birth Actions

When asked to adjudicate the paternity of the artificially inseminated woman's husband or partner, the court's inquiry should not end once it has evaluated the person's pre-conception actions. The steps that the husband or partner takes after the artificially conceived child has been conceived and/ or born are just as relevant. In fact, the things that the husband or partner does after the child is born have the most direct impact on the child. Therefore, in order to award paternity in a way that promotes the best interests of the child, the court should review the evidence of the parties' actions once the child is born. If the husband or partner acted as the parent to the child with the consent of the child's mother, that person has earned the right to be treated as a parent. More importantly, it would probably be in the child's best interests to preserve the relationship the child has developed with his or her mother's husband or partner. The following two theories of paternity will permit the courts to protect the interests of the child and the person seeking to be declared the paternal parent. The two most important things that a child depends on a parent to provide are emotional and financial support. Once the child's biological parent voluntarily shares those duties with another adult, that parent creates the possibility that that adult will be given the status of legal parent. In order to promote the best interests of the artificially conceived child, the courts need to protect the emotional and economic relationships children have with the adults in their lives, especially the ones with their mothers' husbands or partners.

Paternity by Psychology

Children usually form emotional attachments to the persons who are in their lives on a regular basis. Those people may include babysitters, neighbors, and teachers. Legislatures and courts view those relationships as important, but not vital to the child's emotional well-being. Babysitters get fired and neighbors move. While the loss of those relationships may cause the children to suffer some emotional pain, it will not likely cause the children long-term emotional trauma. The loss of a parent, on the other hand, may scar a child for life.

The underlying premise of the psychological parent theory[61] is that the law should preserve the parent-like relationships that the child has developed with the adults in his or her life. In addressing the parental rights of a woman who was in a long-term relationship with the mother of an artificially conceived child, one court stated:

> At the heart of the psychological parent cases is the recognition that children have a strong interest in maintaining the ties that connect them to adults who love and provide for them. That interest, for constitutional as

well as social purposes, lies in the emotional bonds that develop between family members as a result of shared daily life.[62]

It is not the origin of the relationship, but the nature of the relationship that determines the impact the loss will have on the child's emotional health. An adoptive child feels the loss of an adoptive parent just as profoundly as a biological child feels the loss of a biological parent. It does not matter if the child developed a relationship with the adult as the result of biology, adoption, or some action on the part of his or her biological parent. The feeling of loss arises from the psychological connection the child has with the adult.

Once the parent-child relationship exists, courts should take steps to protect it. In order to accomplish that task, courts may have to give "parent" an expansive meaning. At times, it may mean placing psychology on par with biology. Thus, the biological parent will not be able to successfully exclude the psychological parent from the child's life. In addition, the psychological parent will be prevented from walking away from his or her financial responsibility to the child. One court noted:

> a psychological parent-child relationship that is voluntarily created by the legally recognized parent may not be unilaterally terminated after the relationship between the adults ends. Although the intent of the legally recognized parent is critical to the psychological parent analysis, the focus is on that party's intent during the formation and pendency of the parent-child relationship. The reason is that the ending of the relationship between the legal parent and the third party does not end the bond that the legal parent fostered and that actually developed between the child and the psychological parent.[63]

Professor Katharine T. Bartlett has been a strong proponent for the adoption of a psychological parent theory. Under Professor Bartlett's version of the doctrine, a psychological parent is defined as an adult who assists in the provision of necessities that would typically be supplied by the child's nuclear family.[64] Those needs may be physical, emotional, and/or social. Professor Bartlett has recommended the use of a three-part test to identify a potential psychological parent.[65] Under that test, in order to be classified as a psychological parent, the adult must satisfy all three conditions. First, the adult must be in physical possession of the child for at least six months prior to seeking parental status.[66] Second, when seeking parental status, the adult must be motivated by a desire to take care of the child and the child must consider that adult to be his or her parent.[67] Finally, the adult seeking parental status has the burden of proving that his or her relationship with the child was the result of the legal parent's consent or a court order.[68]

While I subscribe to a psychological parent theory and agree with many of Professor Bartlett's recommendations, I also see a need to propose several slight modifications. First, I would remove the requirement of a specific period of time that is stated in the first prong of Professor Bartlett's test. The husband or partner of an artificially inseminated woman should be classified as the psychological paternal parent of the resulting child if he or she resides with the child or has contact with the child for a reasonable period of time given the nature of the relationship that he or she maintains with the child's mother. I am reluctant to require the husband or partner to have to be in physical possession of the child for at least six months because it gives the inseminated woman too much control over the situation. If the couple separates or divorces when the child is only five months old, the husband or partner may not be able to satisfy Professor Bartlett's test. Rendering a child with no legal paternal parent because the mother successfully prevents her estranged husband or partner from having contact with the child is not in the child's best interests. Instead of time limits, the focus should be on the emotional ties between the husband or partner and the artificially conceived child.[69] If those ties are strong, the person should be determined to be the child's legal paternal parent.

In addition, I would eliminate the third condition of Professor Bartlett's test. The mother of the artificially conceived child should not have the power to dictate the conditions under which her husband or partner can have a relationship with a child that she conceives during their marriage, civil union, or domestic partnership. Professor Bartlett was envisioning that her theory would be applied outside of the context of a marriage or similar relationship. Thus, in that context, it would make sense to permit the legal parent to control the contact that other adults have with the child. With regard to situations involving the parental rights of the husband or partner of an artificially inseminated woman, the woman's wishes should not supplant the other adult's rights or the child's welfare. After the adults make a joint decision to parent the artificially conceived child, the rights of the biological parent should not be elevated above those of the psychological parent.

Paternity by Function/Socialization

When a person dies in a small southern community like the one where I grew up, the first thing the family does is grieve. Then, they get together to plan the funeral. The key things that matter are the food and the obituary. In order to avoid being the talk of the town, the family must make sure that there is enough food to accommodate everyone who attends the funeral. In addition, when preparing the obituary, the family has to be careful to avoid including any information that may be considered to be the airing of dirty laundry or that may result in a scandal. My brother died earlier this year, and my family was aware of these rules. After they took care of the food, my siblings worked on the obituary.

The main concern was how to classify my niece. When she was only a few months old, the state decided that my sister was not able to properly care for her. My oldest brother stepped in and moved my niece into his home. For over twenty-two years, my brother provided her with food, clothing, shelter, love, and all of the other things he would have given to his biological child. My brother never legally adopted my niece because my sister would not give her consent. Thus, when he died, it was difficult to define their relationship. On the one hand, it did not seem right to include her in the list with the other nieces and nephews. On the other, my brother could not be identified as my niece's father because that would have upset my sister. In the end, we listed her as his "special niece." For her part, my niece referred to him as her dad on her Facebook page. It would have been nice if the law had a category that accurately described the relationship my brother had with my niece. I would have categorized him as her functional father.

The functional parent is similar to the psychological parent.[70] The focus is upon the actions the person takes after the birth of the child.[71] In my brother's case, on the surface, he treated my niece as if she were his daughter. According to Professor Nancy Polikoff, who is a proponent of this theory, in order for a person to be classified as a functional parent, the child's legally recognized parent must create a relationship between the child and that person.[72] In addition, the legal parent must intend that relationship to be parental in nature. Finally, the person must maintain a functional parental relationship with the child.[73] Professor Polikoff's theory could easily be applied to a situation involving an artificially conceived child. The woman creates a relationship between the child and her husband or partner when she encourages that person to act as the child's second parent. Normally, the woman's intent that her husband or partner serve as the child's parent is reflected in the actions that she takes after the child is born. Those actions include putting that person's name on the child's birth certificate, permitting other people to believe that person is the child's parent, and allowing that person to develop a relationship with the child. In most cases when the husband or partner is seeking to be recognized as the child's legal parent, that person has already established a parental relationship with the child.

When evaluating paternity under this standard, courts should focus upon the husband's or partner's actions after the birth of the artificially conceived child. If the husband or partner acts as a paternal parent to the child, his paternity should be established by function. To function as a parent, the person should have to reside in the home with the child for a reasonable period of time,[74] provide financial support for the child, and hold the child out as his or her own. In essence, the husband or partner has to function as a father by establishing some type of relationship with the child. The UPA presumptive parent provision could serve as a model for this standard.[75] As long as the husband or partner functions as a parent to the child with the woman's consent, the law should legally recognize that relationship.

Paternity by Economic Dependence

The two previously discussed theories focus on protecting the emotional health of the artificially conceived child. Here, I would like to discuss the child's economic needs. Currently, when adjudicating paternity in cases involving children of passion, courts are chiefly concerned with protecting the economic interests of the child. Since courts cannot constantly monitor families, they are unable to force the non-custodial parents to maintain relationships with their children. The most courts can do is to encourage those persons to stay connected with their children by awarding them liberal visitation. However, courts do not link visitation directly to child support. Thus, a person cannot avoid paying child support by giving up visitation rights. As a consequence, the purpose of a paternity adjudication often boils down to forcing a man to live up to his child-support obligations. Hence, courts are currently in the business of protecting the economic best interests of children of passion. In order to achieve that same goal for children of science, courts need to recognize that parental relationships may be created by economic dependence.

I am thinking about cases where the inseminated woman's husband or partner has nothing but an economic relationship with the child. If that is the only connection he or she has to the child, that connection should be enough for the court to adjudicate that person as the child's legal parent. When determining whether to allocate paternity based upon economics, courts should look at the actions the artificially inseminated woman and her husband or partner took after the child was born. A person should be deemed to be an economic parent if the following events occurred after the child's birth. For each one, the person seeking to be adjudicated as the child's economic parent has the burden of proof. First, the child's biological mother voluntarily initiated and encouraged her husband or partner to help meet the child's economic needs. Second, the woman's husband or partner contributed a significant portion of the child's support. Those economic contributions could have consisted of cash or in-kind services. For example, the husband or partner who cooks, cleans, and/or handles other caretaking duties should receive credit for those contributions. Third, the woman's husband or partner did not expect to be reimbursed for their economic contributions. Fourth, the child is economically dependent on the woman's husband or partner and will suffer economic harm if the relationship between the child and the husband or partner is severed. Thus, when the person is adjudicated as the child's economic parent, his or her obligation to support the child financially should last as long as the child is under the age of majority.

In order to protect the interests of artificially conceived children, courts should seek to ensure that those children have two persons who are legally responsible for giving them emotional and financial support. In older, traditional family models, the persons serving those roles were the biological and adoptive parents. Now that families are being created in numerous ways, courts should rely on the different theories of parenthood to adjudicate the paternity of the husbands and partners involved in the artificial insemination process. Moreover, courts should take the same approach to make sure that when it is appropriate, the sperm donor has parental rights and obligations.

Proposal III: Allocating the Paternity of the Sperm Donor

My final proposal deals with the allocation of the paternity of the sperm donors. Under my proposal, the court would recognize three classes of sperm donors, and the paternity of the sperm donor would be determined by his classification. The underlying goal would be to deem the sperm donor as the child's legal father when doing so would promote the child's best interests.

Class One: The Sperm Donor (Known or Unknown) and the Married or Committed Woman

The first category of sperm donors includes the man who supplies sperm to inseminate a woman who is married or in a committed relationship.[76] When it comes to allocating paternity, the man's status as a known or unknown sperm donor should not be legally relevant. Instead, the woman's marital status should be the primary determinant of the man's paternity. If a married or committed woman is artificially inseminated with sperm supplied by a sperm donor who is not her husband, the sperm donor should not be recognized as the father of the child. The law should automatically terminate the sperm donor's parental rights the moment he donates his sperm. However, in a case involving a known sperm donor, the courts should enforce an agreement between the woman and the sperm donor providing that, if the woman's husband or partner predeceases the birth of the child, the sperm donor may be legally recognized as the father of the child. In the absence of such an agreement, the sperm donor should not be recognized as the legal father of the child. This approach would give the woman the option of making sure she has help taking care of the child.

Class Two: The Sperm Donor (Unknown) and the Unmarried or Uncommitted Woman

The second group of sperm donors consists of unknown men who give sperm to inseminate single women. To protect the single woman who wants to raise her artificially conceived child by herself, the law should not recognize the sperm donor as the legal father of the child. A secondary benefit of this approach would be to encourage men to donate sperm without being afraid that they will be forced into parenthood. To that end, the law should require the sperm donor's rights to be automatically terminated at the time he donates his sperm. In order for this provision to apply, the single woman would have to be artificially inseminated in a medical facility or by a licensed physician. Moreover, the woman would be required to appoint a guardian to serve as the parent to the child in the event that something happens to her (i.e., she dies in child birth). This requirement will ensure that the child receives support from at least one person. In addition, the single woman should have to make financial provisions for the child before she is permitted to be artificially inseminated in a medical facility or by a licensed physician. A key criticism of this requirement may be that the law does not compel single women who naturally conceive children to arrange alternate care in case of their demise. In response to this criticism, I would point out that a man who naturally conceives a child with a single woman is not relieved of his paternal duties. As a result, if the woman dies during child birth, the man is still legally required to support the child.

In exchange for having the right to exclude the biological father from the child's life, the single woman who conceives using donor sperm should be required to make the appropriate financial arrangements for the support of the child. The Nadya Suleman situation exhibits why this type of condition needs to be put in place. As a single mother, Suleman attempted to provide for fourteen children. Her financial struggles were documented in the media, which reported that Suleman faced foreclosure and was unable to financially provide for her children. Eventually, talk show host Oprah Winfrey and financial expert Suze Orman teamed up to help Suleman get her finances in order. That situation could have been avoided if Suleman was required to prove that she could support the children before she was permitted to conceive using artificial insemination. The guardian should not have any rights or responsibilities with regard to the child during the mother's lifetime. Instead, the guardian should serve as an honorary parent and act as a safety net for the child.[77] In order to obtain full legal parenthood, the guardian would have to adopt the child if the woman dies or becomes incapacitated. The guardian would not be permitted to be classified as a de facto, psychological, or functional parent.

Class Three: The Sperm Donor (Known) and the Unmarried or Uncommitted Woman

The final group includes known men who donate sperm to inseminate single women. When known sperm donors are involved, courts should be given the discretion to allocate paternity on a case-by-case basis. The theories in this section are not meant to be exhaustive; rather they are intended only to offer guidance to the courts, which should apply various appropriate standards to decide if the known donor should be treated as the child's legal father.

Paternity by Contract
When a single woman is artificially inseminated with sperm donated by a man whom she knows, the woman may permit the man to have contact with the child after he or she is born.[78] Hence, situations involving known sperm donors should be treated differently from those involving anonymous sperm donors. To that end, courts should enforce written agreements between the parties with regard to the man's paternity.[79] If the known sperm donor signs an agreement stating that he plans to parent the child, he should be recognized as the child's legal father.[80] The agreement to parent should be signed before the child is conceived, and both the artificially inseminated woman and the known sperm donor should sign it. I am aware that some courts have found contracts to parent to be unenforceable because they are against pub-

lic policy.[81] Nonetheless, children should not be disadvantaged because their parents engaged in actions that the public views as unacceptable. I agree that in order to protect children, courts should not enforce contracts that relieve a person of his or her parental obligations. At the same time, however, in situations involving artificial insemination, contracts to become parents should be treated like adoption contracts. Courts should honor the promises made by the adults if doing so would serve the best interests of the child.

Paternity by Intent

When deciding paternity cases, courts should focus on the person's behavior prior to the conception or birth of the child. Courts have taken this approach when determining maternity in surrogate cases.[82] Similarly, in paternity cases, the inquiry is whether the sperm donor acted in such a way as to indicate that he intended to parent the child.[83] Professor Marjorie Maguire Shultz states that legal parenthood should be determined by evaluating the intentions of the parties. Specifically, Professor Shultz opines, "intentions that are voluntarily chosen, deliberate, express and bargained-for ought presumptively to determine legal parenthood." [84]

If prior to the child's conception or birth, the sperm donor took affirmative steps to indicate that he intended to parent the child, his paternity should be recognized. In order to be classified as an intended parent, a man should have to do more than just donate his sperm to contribute to the child's conception. He should have to take steps that a parent would take in preparation for the conception or birth of a child. Those steps may include paying some of the costs of the artificial insemination process, taking the woman to the facility to be inseminated, and/or helping to choose the baby's name. Moreover, if a reasonable person would interpret the donor's actions as those of an intended parent, the court should attribute constructive notice of that fact to the artificially inseminated woman. Therefore, the court should respect the donor's intentions and recognize him as the child's legal father.

Paternity by Biology

If the child's conception resulted from an arrangement between his or her mother and a known sperm donor, the child should have a chance to be supported by his or her biological father. In those situations, the known sperm donor's paternity should attach because of biology, and the man should have to take steps to have his parental rights terminated. This would put the artificially conceived child on par with a child conceived as the result of a "one-night stand." Since the known sperm donor supplies the genetic material that results in the child's conception, there should be a rebuttable presumption that he is the legal father of the child. In order to rebut the presumption, the woman or the sperm donor should have to prove that the sperm donor never intended to parent the child. One way for the woman to meet this burden of proof is to present evidence that the donor, by word or deed, waived his parental rights to the child. However, the court should allow the presumption to be rebutted only if it is in the best interests of the child to so permit. Rebuttal should be considered to be in the child's best interests only if there is another person legally obligated or willing to parent the child. Another way to satisfy the "best interests of the child" standard should be for the woman to show that she is financially capable of providing for the child.

Paternity by Function

Courts should treat situations involving the paternity of known sperm donors as they do the ones addressing the paternity of the husband or partner of an artificially inseminated woman. Thus, the court should review the actions the donor took after the child's conception and birth. If the known sperm donor acted as a father to the child, and did so with the permission of the artificially inseminated woman, his paternity should be legally recognized. Nevertheless, since the parties are not married or in a committed relationship, the courts should strictly apply the functional parent doctrine. Therefore, a man should not be deemed to be the father just because he forms a relationship with the child. In some cases, a single woman might permit the sperm donor to play a role in the child's life because she wants her child to have a father figure. Her actions should not result in the sperm donor being established as her child's legal parent. In order to obtain parental status, the sperm donor should take on all the functions of fatherhood, including providing regular financial support, visiting the child on a regular basis, and making decisions with regard to the child's upbringing, and do so with the consent of the artificially inseminated woman.

The proposals in this chapter are meant to assist courts with the difficult task of adjudicating the paternity of the husbands and the partners of the artificially inseminated woman, and that of the non-spousal sperm donors. I am sure that others may disagree with some or all of my proposals. Nonetheless, I hope that my recommendations will add to the conversation about the law's need to address the consequences of the existence of nontraditional families. Legislatures and courts need to take steps to address the unique needs of children conceived by artificial insemination. Those children of science are here to stay, and, in a few decades, they will probably be viewed as any other class of children. Until that time, the legislatures and courts have the obligation to ensure that their needs are being met by the persons who collaborate to conceive them.

Conclusion

I remember as a teenager hearing the chant, "First comes love, then comes marriage, then comes the baby in the baby carriage." The sentiment that inspires that rhyme has faded. People recognize that love and marriage have very little to do with the baby carriage. Children of passion are conceived as the result of sexual intercourse. Love is sometimes present, but not necessary, when adults come together and conceive a child. The identities of the biological parents—of the woman who contributes the egg and of the man who contributes the sperm—are clear. However, it is not always so easy for courts to determine the legal parents. Biology alone is no longer enough to deem a woman a legal mother or a man a legal father. Things are even more complicated when children of science are the children who need to know the identity of their legal parents.

This book is about comparing the legal treatment of children of passion with that of children of science. The establishment of the parent-child relationship is crucially important to all children. Likewise, the status of parent imposes numerous social, moral, and legal obligations on the adult. It is a role that should not be lightly assumed. With regard to children of passion, from the moment they take their first breath, they have legal parents. The biological parents are usually classified as the legal parents unless there are compelling reasons why that should not be the case. Typically, the status of legal parent will not be removed from the biological parent except in situations where there is another person able to prove that he or she is more deserving of the title. At any rate, the child of passion ends up with two legal parents responsible for providing him or her with financial support. Children of science have not been treated as well as children of passion. Instead of ensuring that children of science have two parents, the law is such that those children may end up with one or no legal parent. The consequence is that the children are left without adequate financial support.

In order to promote the best interests of children of science, the law needs to treat them on par with children of passion. Once children are born, society has an obligation to ensure that they are given the financial and emotional support they need. That support must come from the parents. In most cases, children of science have relationships with their mothers that are similar to the relationships enjoyed by children of passion. Legislatures and courts should act to ensure that those children are likewise supported by their paternal parents. One way to achieve that goal is to expand the definition of "father" to include a person who has taken on the role or is willing to take on the role. The "best interests of the child" standard has survived harsh criticism and remains the test courts apply when evaluating issues that impact children. Nonetheless, courts usually do not use the standard to make initial parentage determinations. Parental fitness is not relevant to an adjudication of paternity. Moreover, courts do not consider the child's needs when making paternity determinations. That approach may be appropriate for children of passion because persons have a right to procreate. Thus, legislatures cannot pass laws that prevent certain classes of persons from becoming parents.

With regard to children of science, courts are being called on to adjudicate parentage. Legislatures have enacted statutes setting forth the steps that must be taken for the adults in situations involving children of science to be designated as parents. The legislation relevant to this book controls the adjudication of paternity. Currently, legislatures and courts determine the legal parents of children conceived using scientific methods. In making those initial parentage decisions, those entities focus upon what is in the best interests of the adults. With regard to the inseminated woman's husband, courts and the legislatures are reluctant to burden the man with paternal obligations without his informed consent. That reluctance springs from the desire to protect the man's right not to procreate. In essence, the legislatures and courts are looking out for the man's best interests. Limits are placed upon the rights and responsibilities of sperm donors to protect the couple seeking to be parents from interference and to protect the sperm donor from forced parenthood. The artificially conceived child is left out of the equation. That approach to paternity adjudication needs to change. When making paternity determinations, courts should strive to promote the best interests of the child and to recognize the relationships the child has with the adults in his or her life. As a consequence, science's child will become papa's baby.

Notes

INTRODUCTION

1. This is a reference to the title of a Michael Jackson song.

2. *Anonymous v. Anonymous*, 1991 WL 57753 (N.Y. Sup.) at 2.

3. John A. Gibbons, *Who's Your Daddy? A Constitutional Analysis of Post-Mortem Insemination*, 14 J. Contemp. Health L. & Pol'y 187, 192 (Fall 1997).

4. Marla J. Hollandsworth, *Gay Men Creating Families through Surro-Gay Arrangements: A Paradigm for Reproductive Freedom*, 3 Am. U. J. Gender & L. 183, 204 (Spring 1995).

5. Sheri Gilbert, *Fatherhood from the Grave: An Analysis of Postmortem Insemination*, 22 Hofstra L. Rev. 521, 526–527 (Winter 1993).

6. Barbara K. Padgett, *Illegitimate Children Conceived by Artificial Insemination: Does Some State Legislation Deny Them Equal Protection Under the Fourteenth Amendment?* U. Louisville J. Fam. L. 511,516--517 (1993–1994).

7. Cindy L. Steeb, *A Child Conceived after His Father's Death? Posthumous Reproduction and Inheritance Rights: An Analysis of Ohio Statutes* 48 Clev. St. L. Rev. 137, 140 (2000).

8. *Id.*

9. Inseminating a woman with the sperm of a man who was not her husband was highly controversial. Sandi Varnado, *Who's Your Daddy? A Legitimate Question Given Louisiana's Lack of Legislation Governing Assisted Reproductive Technology*, 66 La. L. Rev. 609, 615–616 (Winter 2006).

10. Karin Mika & Bonnie Hurst, *One Way to Be Born? Legislative Inaction and the Posthumous Child*, 79 Marq. L. Rev. 993, 997 (Summer 1996).

11. Janet J. Berry, *Life after Death: Preservation of the Immortal Seed*, 72 Tul. L. Rev. 231, 236 (Nov. 1997).

12. Barack Obama,"We Need Fathers to Step Up," http://www. parade.com/news/2009 (June 21, 2009).

13. http:www.brainyquote.com (last visited Jan. 31, 2011).

14. http:www.allgreatquotes.com/father-day quotes (last visited Feb. 2, 2011).

15. China A. Rosas, *A Necessary Compromise: Recognizing the Rights of a Donated Generation to Tame the Wild Wild West of California's Sperm Banking Industry*, 37 Sw. U. L. Rev. 393 (2008).

16. Scott J. Shackelford & Lawrence M. Friedman, *Legally Incompetent: A Research Note*, 49 Am. J. Legal Hist. 321, 321 (July 2007).

17. http://www.history.com/topics/father-day (last visited Feb. 10, 2011).

18. An unwed father is a man who has a child with an unmarried woman.

19. See e.g., *Thurnwald v. A.E.*, 163 P.3d 623 (Utah 2007); *In re Cassidy Y.Y.*, 802 N.Y.S. 2d 520 (N.Y.A.D. 3 Dept. 2005); *Doe v. Roe*, 631 S.E. 2d 317 (S.C. App. 2006); *see also* Toni L. Craig, *Establishing the Biological Rights Doctrine to Protect Unwed Fathers in Contested Adoptions*, 25 Fla. St. U. L. Rev. 391, 408–409 (Winter 1998).

20. Katherine L. Tyler, *International Custody Battles: The Not So Curious Case of David Goldman*, 12 J. L. & Fam. Stud. 533, 533 (2010).

21. Mariano Castillo, *Childless Man Freed after Serving Time for Child Support Violations*, http://www.articles.cnn.com (July 15, 2009).

22. http://www.brainyquote.com (last visited Feb. 11, 2011).

23. Tiffany J. Jones, *Neglected by the System: A Call for Equal Treatment For Incarcerated Fathers and Their Children—Will Father Absenteeism Perpetuate the Cycle of Criminality?* 39 Cal. W.-L. Rev. 87, 97–99 (Fall 2002) (discussing the negative impacts of father absenteeism).

24. Linda C. McClain, *"Irresponsible" Reproduction*, 47 Hastings L. J. 339, 387–388 (Jan. 1996). *see also* Julia M. Fisher, *Book Review: Marriage Promotion Policies and the Working Poor: A Match Made in Heaven?* 25 B. C. Third World L. J. 475, 479–483 (Spring 2006) (discussing the economic disadvantages of single parenthood enumerated in David Shipler, *The Working Poor* (New York: Alfred A. Knopf, 2009)).

25. Fisher, *supra* at 481–482.

26. Male infertility factors contribute to approximately 50 percent of all infertility cases, and male infertility accounts for about one-third of all infertility cases. Moreover, recent medical studies indicate that men have to worry about their biological clock because the quality of their sperm deteriorates with age.

27. *Raftopol v. Karma A. Ramey*, 12A.3d.783, 789, (Conn. 2011).

28. C.G.S.A. § 45a–727a (West 2010).

29. Michael V. Hernandez, *A Flawed Foundation: Christianity's Loss of Preeminent Influence on American Law*, 56 Rutgers L. Rev. 625, 674 (Spring 2004).

30. Mallory Simon, *Iowa Voters Oust Justices Who Made Same-Sex Marriage Legal*, www.cnn.com (Nov. 3, 2010).

31. *See G.D.K. v. State of Wyo. Dept. of Family Services*, 92 P. 3d 834, 835 (Wyo. 2004); Ala. Code Ann. § 26-17-204(a) (West, 2008) ("A man is presumed to be the father of a child if: (1) he and the mother of the child are married to each other and the child is born during the marriage.")

32. "'Assisted reproduction' means a method of causing pregnancy other than sexual intercourse. The term includes a. Intrauterine insemination; b. Donation of eggs; c. Donation of embryos; d. In vitro fertilization and transfer of embryos; and e. Intracytoplasmic sperm injection." N.D. Cent. Code § 14-20-02 (2008). "'Artificial insemination' means introduction of semen of a donor . . . into a woman's vagina, cervical canal or uterus through use of instruments or other artificial means." Idaho Code Ann. § 39-5401 (West 2008). This book is limited to artificial insemination because the state statutes dealing with the relevant paternal obligations deal solely with artificial insemination and not other forms of assisted reproduction. *See In re Parentage of J.M.K.*, 119 P.3d 840, 849 (Wash. 2005) (holding that artificial insemination statute did not apply to situations involving in vitro fertilization).

33. This is referred to as heterologous artificial insemination (AID).

34. *See Marriage of Witbeck-Wildhagen*, 667 N.E. 2d at 125) (holding that it is against public policy to require a man to provide financial support for a child his wife conceives by artificial insemination without his consent).

35. *See e.g., R.S. v. R.S.*, 670 P.2d 923 (Kan. Ct. App. 1983) *quoted in In re Baby Doe*, 353 S.E. 2d 877, 879 (S.C. 1986) ("Husband's consent to his wife's impregnation by artificial insemination may be expressed, or it may be implied from conduct which evidences knowledge of the procedure and failure to object.")

36. Carmel B. Sella, *When a Mother is a Legal Stranger to Her Child: The Law's Challenge to the Lesbian Nonbiological Mother*, 1 UCLA Women's L. J. 135, 142–146 (Spring 1991); *see also* Maggie Mantemach, *Where is My Other Mommy: Applying the Presumed Father Provision of the Uniform Parentage Act to Recognize the Rights of Lesbian Mothers and Their Children*, 9 J. Gender Race & Just. 385, 407–408 (Winter 2005).

37. Emily Stork, *Born to No Mother: In Re Roberto D.B. and Equal Protection for Gestational Surrogate Rebutting Maternity*, 16 Am. U. J. Gender Soc. Pol'y & L. 283, 293–307 (2007) (evaluating different tests courts have relied upon to determine the legal mother of a child born as the result of a surrogate arrangement).

38. *R.S. v. R.S.*, 670 P2d 923 (Kan. 1983); *Gursky v. Gursky*, 242 N.Y.S. 2d 406 (1963).

39. *See State ex rel. H. v. P.*, 90 A.D. 2d 434 (1982) (wife estopped from denying husband's paternity).

40. Hopkins *supra* note at 233–234.

41. *See e.g., State v. Frisard*, 694 So. 2d. 1032 (La. App. 5 Cir., 1997).

CHAPTER 1

1. 2 Pa. D. & C.3d 302 (Pa. Com. Pl. 1977).

2. *Id.* at 303.

3. *Id.* at 304.

4. *Id.*

5. *Id.* at 304–305.

6. *Id.*

7. *Id.* at 306.

8. *Id.* at 303.

9. *Id.* at 306.

10. *Id.* at 307.

11. *Id.* at 308.

12. *Id.* at 309.

13. *Id.*

14. *Simpson v. Calivas*, 650 A. 2d 318 (N.H. 1994).

15. *Welsh v. Welsh*, 783 So. 2d 446, 447 (La. App. 5 Cir. 2001).

16. John C. Sheldon & Nancy D. Mills, *In Search of a Theory of Alimony*, 45 Me. L. Rev. 283, 288--289 (1993).

17. Matthew 13:55, New King James Version.

18. Steve N. Peskind, *Who's Your Daddy? An Analysis of Illinois' Law of Parentage and the Meaning of Parenthood*, 35 Loy. U. Chi. 811, 836 (Spring 2004).

19. *Morris v. Davies*, (1837) 5 Clark & F 163, 7 (Eng. Reprint 365).

20. *Goodright v. Moss*, 98 E.R. 1257, 1258 (1777) (establishing Lord Mansfield's Rule).

21. Wyo. Stat. Ann. § 14-2-102 (West 2010).

22. 109 Supt. Ct. 2333 (1989).

23. *Brinkley v. King*, 701 A.2d 176, 180 (Pa. 1997).

24. 71 Cal. Rptr. 399 (Cal. App. 2 Dist., 1998).

25. 940 A2d. 459 (Pa. Super., 2007).

26. *State in Interest of J.W.F. (Schoolcraft)* 799 P.2d 710 (Utah 1990).

27. *Schoolcraft*, 799 P.2d at 713.

28. *Id.*

29. *Id.* at 712.

30. *Id.* at 713.

31. *Teece v. Teece*, 715 P.2d 106 (Utah 1986).

32. *Id.*, 715 P.2d at 107.

33. *Id.* at 106.

34. *Id.*

35. *Lopes v. Lopes*, 518 P.2d 687 (1974).

36. *Id.* 518 P.2d at 688.

37. *Id.*

38. *Id.* at 689.

39. ("It requires but little reflection to appreciate the undesirable effects it would have upon family solidarity to permit the spouses to scandalize each other by accusations of immoral conduct concerning the conception of children born in the family. Of graver moment than the disgrace to themselves, it seems repugnant to one's sense of justice to allow them to stigmatize the innocent child, whose welfare and adjustment will be so crucially affected thereby during his whole lifetime. Yet he is in the anomalous position of being without voice or defense in a dispute in which there is often engendered a great deal of emotion and recrimination; and in which, however the issue may be resolved, cannot do other than have deeply scarring effects upon him.") *Id.*

40. *Pearson v. Pearson*, 182 P.3d 353 (Utah, 2008).

41. *Id.* at 354.

42. *Id.*

43. *Id.* at 355.

44. *Id.* at 356.

45. *Id.* at 358.

46. Deborah A. Ellingboe, *Sex, Lies, and Genetic Tests: Challenging the Marital Presumption of Paternity under the Minnesota Parentage Act*, 78 Minn. L. Rev. 1013, 1023 (April 1994).

47. Debi McRae, *Evaluating the Effectiveness of the Best Interests Marital Presumption of Paternity: Is It Actually in the Best Interests of Children to Divorce the Current Application of the Best Interests of Marital Presumption of Paternity?* 5 Whittier J. Child & Fam. Advoc. 345, 357 (Spring 2006).

48. *Matter of Marriage of Ross*, 783 P. 2d 331, 339 (Kan. 1989).

49. *Evans v. Wilson*, 856 A2d 679 (Md. 2004).

50. *Id.* at 682.

51. *Id.* at 683.

52. *Id.*

53. *Id.* at 684.

54. *Id.* at 688.

55. *Id.* at 692.

CHAPTER 2

1. According to the 2010 U.S. Census, married couples make up only 48 percent of all households.

2. Davis Kingsley, *Illegitimacy and the Social Structure*, 45 Am. J. Sociology 215 (1939), *quoted in* Harry D. Krause, Illegitimacy: Law and Social Policy 1 (Bobbs-Merrill, 1971).

3. The Elizabethan "Poor Laws" established a duty to exhaust parental resources to support the child before the local parish was obligated to provide relief. See Act for Relief of the Poor, 43 Eliz., c. 2, § 1 (1601) *cited in* Child, Family, and State: Problems and Materials on Children and the Law 157 (New York: Aspen Publishers, 2009).

4. Black's Law Dictionary 1099 (8th ed., 2004) ("the son of no one").

5. 1 William Blackstone, Commentaries on the Laws of England 447 (William S. Hein & Co., Inc., 1992).

6. *In re Tyson*, 306 So. 2d 822 (La. App. 1975).

7. *Paker v. Nothomb*, 93 N.W. 851 (Neb. 1903).

8. Juhi Metha, *Prosecuting Teenage Parents under Fornication Statutes: A Constitutionally Suspect Legal Solution to the Social Problem of Teenage Pregnancy*, 5 Cardozo Women's L. J. 121, 128–130 (1998).

9. 409 U.S. 538 (1973).

10. *Wallis v. Smith*, 22 P.3d 682 (N.M. Ct. App. 2001).

11. *Wallis* 22 P.3d at 683.

12. *Id.*

13. *Id.* at 684.

14. *Id.* at 685.

15. *Id.*

16. *Id.*

17. 430 U.S. 762 (1977).

18. *Id.* at 763--764.

19. *Id.* at 764.

20. *Id.*

21. *Id.* at 765.

22. *Id.* The statute allowed non-marital children to inherit by intestate succession only from their mothers without conditions; marital children were permitted to inherit from both their mothers and fathers without conditions .*Id.*

23. *Trimble*, at 768.

24. *Id.* at 766.

25. *Id.*

26. *Id.*

27. *Id.* at 769–770.

28. *Id.*

29. *Id.* at 772–773.

30. *Id.* at 772.

31. *Id.* at 776.

32. 439 U.S. 259 (1978).

33. *Lalli*, at 261.

34. *Id.* at 262–263.

35. *Id.* at 262.

36. *Id.* at 262–263.

37. *Id.* at 268.

38. *Id.* at 271.

39. *Id.* 271–272.

40. *Id.*

41. *Id.* at 274.

42. *Id.* at 271–272.

43. *Id.* at 273.

44. *Id.* at 271–273.

CHAPTER 3

1. The information contained in this chapter expands upon an article I wrote in 2009 entitled *Two Fathers, One Dad: Allocating the Paternal Obligations Between the Men Involved in the Artificial Insemination Process*, 13 Lewis & Clark L. Rev. 949 (Fall 2009).

2. http://www.merriam-webster.com.

3. *Yount v. Johnson*, 915 P2d 341, 346 (N.M. App. 1996) ("Consent is a defense for intentional torts like assault and battery.")

4. Matthew J. Toddy, *Assumption of Risk Merged with Contributory Negligence: Anderson v. Ceccardi*, 45 Ohio St. L .J. 1059, 1060–1062 (1984).

5. *Koapke v. Herfendal*, 660 N.W. 2d 206, 211 (N.D. 2003).

6. Cal. Fam. Code § 7613(a) (West 2010).

7. A.C.A. § 9-10-201(b) (West 2011).

8. *K.S. v. G.S.*, 440 A.2d 64, 68-69 (N.J. Super. 1981).

9. Unif. Parentage Act (2000) § 706(a).

10. Browne Lewis, *Dead Men Reproducing: Responding to the Existence of Afterdeath Children*, 16 Geo. Mason L. Rev. 403, 426–428 (Winter 2006). Posthumously conceived children will be discussed in chapter 5.

11. M.S.A. § 257.56, subd. 1 (West 2011).

12. *In re Marriage of A.C.H. and D.R.H.*, 210 P3d 929 (Or. App. 2009)

13. 667 N.E.2d.122 (Ill. App. 4 Dist. 1996).

14. *Witbeck*, 667 N.E. 2d at 123.

15. *Id.*

16. *Id.*

17. *Id.*

18. *Id.*

19. 750 ILCS 40/3(a) (West 1994), *cited in Witbeck v. Wildhagen*, 667 N.E. 2d at 124.

20. *Witbeck* 667 N.E. 2d at 123.

21. *Id.*

22. *Id.* at 125.

23. *Id.*

24. *Id.*

25. *Id.*

26. *Id.* at 126.

27. *Id.*

28. *Lane*, 912 P2d 290 (N.M. Ct. App. 1996).

29. *Id.* at 292.

30. *Id.*

31. *Id.*

32. *Id,*

33. *Id.* at 293.

34. *Id.* at 292.

35. *Id.* at 294.

36. *Id.*

37. *Id.* at 295, *quoting Vaughn v. United Nuclear Corp.,* 650 P2d 3, 7 (N.M. Ct. App.).

38. *Id.*

39. *Id.*

40. *Lane* at 295.

41. *Id.*

42. *Id.* at 296.

43. *Id.*

44. *Id.*

45. Unif. Statutes of Children of Assisted Conception Act § 3, 9C U.L.A. 370 (2001). *See also Id.* § 3 cmt., 9C U.L.A. 370–71 ("The presumptive paternity of the husband of a married woman who bears a child through assisted conception reflects a concern for the best interests of the children of assisted conception. Any uncertainty concerning the identity of the father of such a child ought to be shouldered by the married woman's husband rather than the child. Thus, the husband (not someone acting on his behalf such as a guardian, administrator, or executor) has the obligation to file an action aimed at denying paternity through lack of consent to the assisted conception rather than the child or mother having an obligation to prove the husband's paternity.")

46. Fla. Stat. Ann. § 742.11(1) (West 2005), *See also K.S.,* 440 A.2d at 68.

47. Ga. Code Ann. § 19-7-21 (2004).

48. Del. Code Ann. tit. 13 § 8-705 (a) (Supp. 2008). Accord Utah Code Ann. §78B-15-705(1) (2008); Wyo. Stat. Ann.§ 14-2-905(a) (2009).

49. Tex. Fam. Code Ann. § 160.705(a) (Vernon 2008) ("Except as otherwise provided by Subsection (b), the husband of a wife who gives birth to a child by means of assisted reproduction may not challenge his paternity of the child unless: (1) before the fourth anniversary of the date of learning of the birth of the child he commences a proceeding to adjudicate his paternity; and (2) the court finds that he did not consent to the assisted reproduction before or after the birth of the child.")

50. *Id.* Accord Del. Code. Ann. tit. 13, § 8-705(b) (Supp. 2008); Utah Code Ann. § 78B-15-705(2) (2008); Wyo. Stat. Ann. § 14-2-905(b) (2009).

51. Unif. Parentage Act (amended 2002) § 705, 9B U.L.A. 64 (Supp. 2009) ("Except as otherwise provided in subsection (b), the husband of a wife who gives birth to a child by means of assisted reproduction may not challenge his paternity of the child unless: (1) within two years after learning of the birth of the child he commences a proceeding to adjudicate his paternity; and (2) the court finds that he did not consent to the assisted reproduction, before or after birth of the child. (b) A proceeding to adjudicate paternity may be maintained at any time if the court determines that: (1) the husband did not provide sperm for, or before or after the birth of the child consent to, assisted reproduction of his wife; (2) the husband and the mother of the child have not cohabited since the probable time of assisted reproduction; and (3) the husband never openly held out the child as his own.")

52. La. Civ. Code Ann. art. 188 (2007).

53. *Id.* at art. 189.

54. *Id.*

55. N.H. Rev. Stat. Ann. §168-B:2(1) (a) (LexisNexis 2001).

56. N.H. Rev. Stat. Ann. § 5-C:30(1) (LexisNexis 2008).

57. N.H. Rev. Stat. Ann. § 168-B:3(II) (LexisNexis 2001).

58. *Id.*

59. *Id.* §168-B:7.

60. "'Informed consent' occurs when a competent person, while exercising care for his or her own welfare, makes a voluntary decision about whether or not to participate in a proposed medical procedure or contractual arrangement that is based on full awareness of the relevant facts." *Id.* §168-B:1(VI).

61. *Id.* §168-B:13 III and (IV).

62. *Id.* §168-B:13(IV)(c).

63. *Id.* § 168-B:3(II).

64. Unif. Parentage Act, amended 2002, 9B U.L.A. 4 (Supp. 2009). The language of the UPA repeatedly refers to a "man" and a "woman." *See, e.g., id.* § 704, 9B U.L.A. 63.

65. Unif. Parentage Act (amended 2002) § 704 (Supp. 2009).

66. Unif. Parentage Act (amended 2002) § 703 (Supp. 2009).

67. *Skinner v. Oklahoma*, 316 U.S. 535 (1942).

68. UPA § 705a (1) & (2).

69. UPA § 705b (1), (2), & (3).

70. UPA § 706 (b).

71. UPA § 706(a).

72. UPA § 707.

73. *Grusky v. Grusky*, 242 N.Y.S. 2d 406, 408 (1963).

74. *Id.* at 408.

75. *Id.*

76. *Id.*

77. *Id.*

78. *Id.* at 409.

79. *Id.* at 410.

80. *Id.*

81. *Id.* at 411.

82. *Id.*

83. *Id.* at 412.

84. *Id.*

85. *Levin v. Levin*, 645 N.E. 2d 601 (Ind. 1994).

86. *Id.* at 603.

87. *Id.*

88. *Id.* at 603–604.

89. *Id.*

90. *Levin*, at 604.

91. *Id.*

92. *Id.* at 604–605.

93. *Michael H. v. Gerald D.*, 491 U.S. 110 (1989).

94. 903 P2d 207 (Mont. 1995).

95. *Id.* at 208.

96. *Id.*

97. *Id.* at 209.

98. *Id.* at 211.

99. *Id.*

100. *Id.*

CHAPTER 4

1. This is the title of a 2010 movie starring Annette Bening and Julianne Moore.

2. *E.g.*, Colo. Rev. Stat. § 19-4-1069 (2) (2008); Tex. Fam. Code Ann. §160.702 (Vernon 2008); Utah Code Ann. §78B-15-702(2008).

3. The donor is not the child's natural father. Ala. Code §26-17-702 (LexisNexis Supp. 2008); Cal. Fam. Code § 7613(b) (West Supp. 2009); 750 Ill. Comp. Stat. 40/3(b) (West 2009); Mo. Ann. Stat. § 210.824(2) (West 2004). The donor is not the child's biological father. Minn. Stat. Ann. § 257.56(2) (West 2003).

4. *E.g.*, Or. Rev. Stat. § 109.239(2) (2007) ("A child born as a result of the artificial insemination shall have no right, obligation, or interest with respect to such donor.")

5. *E.g.*, N.M. Stat. § 40-11-6 (B)-(2006).

6. For example, the Michigan legislature has dealt with the legal consequences of the existence of artificially conceived children by passing a statute stating in relevant part: "A child conceived by a married woman with consent of her husband following the utilization of assisted reproductive technology is considered to be the legitimate child of the husband and wife." Mich. Comp. Laws Serv. § 333.2824(6) (LexisNexis 2005). The statutory provision leads one to conclude that a sperm donor has no obligation to a child conceived using his sperm if the woman is married. Nonetheless, the legislature has not yet addressed the situation where an unmarried woman conceives a child using donated sperm.

7. Anne Reichmann Schiff, *Frustrated Intentions and Binding Biology: Seeking Aid in Law*, 44 Duke L. J. 524, 564 (Dec. 1994).

8. Harvey L. Fisher & Paula K. Garrett, *It Takes Three, Baby: The Lack of Standard, Legal Definitions of "Best Interest of the Child" and the Right to Contract for Lesbian Potential Parents*, 15 Cardozo J. L. & Gender 1, 5–6 (2008).

9. Fla. Stat. Ann. § 742.14 (West 2005).

10. "A donor is not the parent of a child conceived by means of assisted reproduction." Unif. Parentage Act (amended 2002) 703 (Supp. 2009).

11. Unif. Parentage Act cmt. § 703.

12. 127 Cal. App. 4th 319, 25 Cal. Rptr. 3d 482 (2005).

13. *Id.* at 484.

14. *Id.*

15. *Id.*

16. *Id.* at 486.

17. *Id.* at 487–488.

18. *Id.*

19. Wis. Stat. Ann. § 891.40(2) (West 2009).

20. *See* Diane M. Gianelli, *Fertility Doctor's Conviction Fuels Issue of Self-Policing*, American Medical News, March 23, 1992.

21. *See, e.g.,* M.G.L.A. 190B § 2-302 (2010 West).

22. *Straub v. B.M.T.,* 645 N.E. 2d 597 (1994), *rehearing denied* April 12, 1995.

23. Kan. Stat. Ann. 38-1114(f) (West 2011) (emphasis added).

24. N.J. Stat. Ann. § 9:17-44 (b) (West 2011).

25. N.H. Rev. Stat. §168-B:11 (West 2011).

26. C.R.S.A. §19-4-106(2) (West 2011).

27. 775 P.2d 27 (Colo. 1989).

28. *Interest of RC,* 775 P2d at 27.

29. *Id.* at 28.

30. *Id.*

31. *Id.*

32. *Interest of RC* at 28–29.

33. *Id.* at 29.

34. *Id.*

35. *Id.*

36. *Id.* at 33.

37. *Id.* at 29.

38. *Id.*

39. *Id.* at 34.

40. *Id.* at 30.

41. *Id.* at 33.

42. *Id.* at 33–34.

43. *Id.* at 34.

44. *Id.* at 35.

45. *Straub,* 645 N.E. 2d at 597.

46. *See In re K.M.H.,* 169 P3d 1025, 1042 (Kan. 2007). The court held that the failure of the sperm donor to deposit his sperm with a licensed physician did not take the transaction outside of the artificial insemination statute as long as a licensed physician actually performed the procedure. *Id.* In the case, the man delivered his sperm directly to the woman, and she took it to a licensed physician who performed the artificial insemination. *Id.*

47. In at least four states, including Connecticut, Georgia, Oklahoma, and Oregon, it is illegal for someone other than a physician to artificially inseminate a woman.

48. 179 Cal. App. 3d 386, 224 Cal. Rptr. 530 (1986).

49. *Id.* at 389.

50. *Id.*

51. *Id.*

52. *Id.* at 390.

53. *Id.*

54. *Id.*

55. *Id.* at 391.

56. *Id.*

57. *Id.* at 392.

58. *Id.* 393.

59. *Id.*

60. *Id.* at 394.

61. *Id.*

62. *Id.* at 398.

63. *Id.*

64. Martin Richards, *Genes, Genealogies, and Paternity: Making Babies in the Twenty-First Century*, in Freedom and Responsibility in Reproductive Choice 53, 55 (J. R. Spencer & Antje du Bois-Pedain, eds., 2006). Some states still have statutes regulating the use of artificial insemination in animals. *See, e.g.,* Idaho Code Ann § 25-803 (2000) ("It is unlawful for any person to practice artificial insemination of domestic animals unless he shall first obtain a license so to do as provided in this act. Provided, no license shall be required of or by any person to perform artificial insemination upon his own domestic animals.")

65. 923 A.2d 473 (Pa. Super. Ct. 2007).

66. *Jacob*, 923 A.2d at 476.

67. *Id.*

68. *Id.*

69. *Id.* at 480.

70. *Id.*

71. *Id.*

72. *Id.* at 481.

73. *Id.*

74. *Id.* at 482.

75. *Id.*

CHAPTER 5

1. Congress has unsuccessfully sought to pass federal legislation banning cloning. However, a few states do have anti-cloning laws. Elizabeth Price Foley, *The Constitutional Implications of Human Cloning*, 42 Ariz. L. Rev. 647 (Fall 2000) (discussing the executive and legislative responses to the prospect of human cloning).

2. UPC § 2-302.

3. *E.g.,* M.C.A. §-41-3-102 (20) ("'Physical neglect' means either failure to provide basic necessities, including but not limited to appropriate and adequate nutrition, protective shelter from the elements, and appropriate clothing related to weather conditions, or failure to provide cleanliness and general supervision, or both, or exposing or allowing the child to be exposed to an unreasonable physical or psychological risk to the child.") *Id.*

4. *See e.g.,* People in Interest of J.S.N., 371 NW2d 361 (S.D. 1985).

5. LSA-C.C. Art. 186 (West 2011).

6. *See, e.g.,* V.T.C.A. Family Code 160.204 (West 2011).

7. In May of 2010, Barbara Walters hosted an ABC News Special entitled "Born in My Heart: A Love Story." On the show, Walters and others, including Connie Chung and Carole Simpson, spoke about adoption and shared how it changed their lives. http://abcnews.go.com/2020/story?id=123612&page=1#top.

8. *See J.P. v. Missouri Department of Social Services*, 75 S.W. 2d 847 (Mo. App. W. D. 1988) (discussing the jointly sponsored state-federal adoption subsidy program).

9. *Lankford v. Wright*, 489 S.E. 2d 604, 606–607 (N.C. 1997).

10. *Johnson v. Johnson*, 617 NW 2d 97 (2000).

11. *Id.* at 100.

12. *Id.*

13. *Id.* at 101.

14. *Id.* at 107.

15. *Id.*

16. *See Pope v. First Nat. Bank in Dallas*, 658 S.W. 2d 764, 765 (Tex. App. 5. Dist. 1983); *see also Gardner v. Hancock*, 924 S.W. 2d 857 (Mo. 1996) (discussing the difference between the legal doctrines of equitable adoption and adoption by estoppel).

17. *Recent Development, Illegitimates: Definition of "Children" Under Federal Welfare Legislation*, 67 Colum. L. Rev. 984, 991 (May 1967).

18. *Dan Quayle v. Murphy Brown*, www.time.com (June 1, 1992).

19. Lindsay L. Abbate, *What God Has Joined "Let" Man Put Asunder: Ireland's Struggle Between Cannon and Common Law Relating to Divorces*, 16 Emory Int'l L. Rev. 583, 592–593 (Fall 2002).

20. *Montayre v. Montayre*, 22 N.Y.S. 2d 489, 489 (N.Y. Sup. 1940); *see also Jones v. Stautz*, 159 N.Y.S. 2d 903, 905 (N.Y. Dom. Rel. Ct., 1957) ("At common law a husband was under no obligation to support the children of his wife by a former marriage nor was he under a moral obligation to do so; there being no kinship nor blood relationship.")

21. *Moyer v. Moyer*, 471 S.E. 2d 676, 678 (N.C. App. 1996).

22. Michael J. Broyde, *Marital Fraud—Fact Pattern: Jewish Response*, 16 Loy. L. A. Int'l & Comp. L. J. 95, 105–106 (November 1993).

23. 15 § V.S.A. 296.

24. HRS §577-4 (West 2011).

25. *Cumberland County Bd. of Social Services v. W.J. P.*, 755 A2d 1171, 1172 (N.J. Super. A.D. 2000).

26. *Drawbaugh v. Drawbaugh*, 647 A2d 240 (Pa. Super. 1994).

27. *Miller v. Miller*, 478 A2d 351, 355 (N.J. 1984).

28. Some of those theories will be discussed in chapter 6.

29. *Dewey v. Dewey*, 886 P2d 623 (Alaska 1994).

30. Nazeem M. I. Goolam, *The Beginning of Life-Ethical Perspectives*, 18 Med. & L. 577, 587 (1999).

31. *Doornbos v. Doornbos*, Super. Ct. Cook Co. No. 545, 44981(1854) aff'd 139 N.E. 2d 844 (Ill. 1956) (holding that heterologous artificial insemination by a third-party donor, with or with the consent of the husband, constitutes adultery on the part of the mother, and that the child so conceived is not a child born during the marriage and is therefore a non-marital child).

32. Catherine DeLair, *Ethical, Moral, Economic, and Legal Barriers to Assisted Reproductive Technologies Employed by Gay Men and Lesbian Women*, 4 DePaul J. Health Care L. 147, 154 (Fall 2000).

33. Hollie J. Harlow, *Paternalism without Paternity: Discrimination against Single Women Seeking Artificial Insemination by Donor*, 6 S. Cal. L. Rev. & Women's Stud. 173, 193 (Fall 1996).

34. Daniel B. Sinclair, *Assisted Reproduction in Jewish Law*, 30 Fordham Urb. L. J. 71, 77–89 (Nov. 2002).

35. Genesis 16.

36. Martha M. Ertman, *What's Wrong with a Parenthood Market?: A New and Improved Theory of Commoditization*, 82 N.C. L. Rev. 1 (Dec. 2003).

37. This was a 2010 movie starring Jennifer Lopez.

38. I.C. §29-1-2-7(b)(1) & (2)(A)(B) & (3) (West 2010).

39. *See* Browne Lewis, *Children of Men: Balancing the Inheritance Rights of Marital and Non-Marital Children,* 39 Univ. Toledo L. Rev. 1 (Fall 2007) (discussing the steps non-marital children have to take to have the opportunity to inherit from their fathers).

40. *Morrow v. Scott,* 7 Ga. 535 (1849); *see also Pearson v. Carlton,* 18 S.C. 47 (1882).

41. Anne Reichmann Schiff, *Arising from the Dead: Challenges of Posthumous Procreation,* 75 N.C. L. Rev. 901 (March 1997); Browne Lewis, *Graveside Birthday Parties: The Legal Consequences of Forming Families Posthumously,* 60 Case W. Res. L. Rev. 1159 (Summer 2010).

42. *See, e.g., In re Estate of Kievernagel,* 83 Cal. Rptr. 3d 311, 312 (Cal. Cr. App. 2008); *see also* Lewis, *supra* at 403–404.

43. *See, e.g., In re Estate of Kolacy,* 753 A2d 1257 (N.J. Super. Ct. Ch. Div. 2000); *Khabbaz v. Comm'r , Soc. Sec. Admin..,* 903 A.2 1180 (N.H. 2007).

44. *Hecht v. Superior Court,* 20 Cal. Rptr. 2d 275 (Ct. App. 1993).

45. *Id.* at 275.

46. *Id.*

47. *Id.* at 278–279.

48. *Woodward v. Commr. of Social Sec.,* 760 N.E. 2d 257 (Mass., 2002).

49. *Id.* at 260.

50. *Id.*

51. *Id.*

52. *Id.*

53. *Id.* at 261.

54. *Id.*

55. *Id.* at 262.

56. *Id.*

57. *Id.* at 263.

58. *Id.* at 264.

59. *Id.* at 265.

60. *Id.*

61. *Id.* at 266.

62. *Id.* at 265.

63. *Id.* at 266.

64. Marriage ends at death, so children conceived after the death of one of the parties are non-marital. *See Woodward,* 760 N.E. 2d at 266–267, *cited in* Christopher A. Scharman, *Not without My Father: The Legal Status of the Posthumously Conceived Child,* 55 Vand. L. Rev. 1001, 1020 (Apr. 2002).

65. *Woodward,* 760 N.E. 2d at 267.

66. *Id.* at 268.

67. *Id.* at 269.

68. *Id.* at 269–270.

69. *Id.* at 266.

70. *Id.* at 272.

71. *Id.*

72. *See* Susan C. Stevenson-Popp, *"I Have Loved You In My Dreams": Posthumous Reproduction and the Need for Change in the Uniform Parentage Act,* 52 Cath. U. L. Rev. 727,

732 (Spr. 2003) (advocating modifying statutory law to line up with the reasoning of the *Woodward* decision).

73. Christian Eichenlaub, *"Minnesota Nice": A Comparative Analysis of Minnesota's Treatment of Adoption by Gay Couples,* 5 U. St. Thomas L. J. 312, 315–321 (Winter 2008).

74. *See, e.g.,* IC §31-11-1-1 ("(a) Only a female may marry a male. Only a male may marry a female. (b) A marriage between persons of the same gender is void in Indiana even if the marriage is lawful in the place where it is solemnized.") *Id.*

75. Defense of Marriage Act, 110 Stat. § 2416 (1996). The statute passed the House of Representatives by a vote of 342–67 and the Senate by a vote of 85–14.

76. Lynne D. Wardle & Lincoln C. Oliphant, *In Praise of Loving: Reflections on the "Loving Analogy" for Same-Sex Marriage,* 51 How. L. J. 117, 162–164 (Fall 2007).

77. Michael L. Hopkins, Comment, *"What is Sauce for the Gander is Sauce for the Goose": Enforcing Child Support on Former Same-Sex Partners Who Create a Child through Artificial Insemination,* 25 St. Louis U. Pub. L. Rev. 219, 222 (2006).

78. *See In re Parentage of Robinson,* 890 A.2d 1036, 1041 (N.J. Super. Ct. Ch. Div. 2005) (applying artificial insemination statute to same-sex couple who got married in Canada by focusing upon the commitment made by the couple instead of upon their gender).

79. *T.F. v. B.L.,* 813 N.E. 2d 1244, 1246–47 (Mass. 2004).

80. *Id.* at 1247.

81. *Id.*

82. *Id.*

83. *Id.* at 1247.

84. *Id.* at 1248 (She posted a picture and message on the Internet stating, "I hope you all enjoy the pics of my wonderful, beautiful boy.") *Id.*

85. *Id.*

86. *Id.*

87. *Id.* at 1249.

88. *Id.* at 1250.

89. *Id.* at 1252.

90. *Id.*

91. *Id.* at 1252.

92. *Id.* at 1253.

CHAPTER 6

1. *In re C.K.G.,* 173 S.W. 3d 714, 721 (Tenn. 2005).

2. Gary Debele, *Custody and Parenting by Persons Other Than Biological Parents: When Non-Traditional Family Law Collides with the Constitution,* 83 N.D. L. Rev. 1227, 1227–1228 (2007).

3. Andrew Noble, *Intestate Succession for Stepchildren in Pennsylvania: A Proposal for Reform,* 64 U. Pitt. L. Rev. 835, 840–848 (Summer 2003).

4. Margaret Mahoney, *Stepparents as Third Parties in Relation to Their Stepchildren,* 40 Fam. L. Q. 81, 99 (Spring 2006).

5. New International Bible, Genesis 16.

6. 537 A. 2d 1227 (1987).

7. *Id.; see also* Vicki C. Jackson, *Baby M and the Question of Parenthood*, 76 Geo. L. J. 1811 (June 1988).

8. *Baby M*, 537 A. 2d at 1236.

9. *Id.* at 1237.

10. *Id.*

11. *Id.* at 1235.

12. *Id.*

13. *Id.* at 1236.

14. *Id.* at 1237.

15. *Id.*

16. *Id.*

17. *Id.* at 1240.

18. *Id.* at 1259.

19. *Id.* at 1261.

20. *Id.* at 1264.

21. 644 N.E. 2d 760 (1994). For an analysis of *Belsito, see* Dawn Wenk, *Belsito v Clark: Ohio's Battle with "Motherhood,"* 28 Tol. L. Rev. 247 (Fall 1996).

22. *Belsito* 644 N.E.2d at 761.

23. *Id.* at 760.

24. *Id.* at 761.

25. *Id.* at 762.

26. *Id.*

27. *Id.*

28. *Id.* at 763.

29. *Id.* at 766.

30. *Id.* at 763.

31. *Id.* at 766.

32. *Id.*

33. *Id.*

34. *Id.*

35. "The birth test becomes subordinate and secondary to genetics." *Id.* at 767.

36. Marjorie Maguire Shultz, *Reproductive Technology and Intent-Based Parenthood: An Opportunity for Gender Neutrality*, 1990 Wis. L. Rev. 297, 323–27 (1990).

37. *Id.* at 322.

38. *Id.* at 324–325.

39. John Lawrence Hill, *What Does It Mean To Be a "Parent"? The Claims of Biology as the Basis for Parental Rights*, 66 N.Y.U. L. Rev. 353, 413–418 (May 1991).

40. *Id.* at 414.

41. *Id.* at 415.

42. *Id.*

43. *Id.*

44. *Id.* at 416.

45. *Id.* at 417.

46. *Id.*

47. *Id.*

48. 851 P2d 776 (Cal. 1993).

49. *Johnson*, 851 P2d at 778.

50. *Id.*

51. *Id.*

52. *Id.*

53. *Id.* at 778.

54. *Id.*

55. *Id.* at 779.

56. *Id.* at 780.

57. *Id.* at 781.

58. *Id.* at 780.

59. *Id.* at 781. This is consistent with the state's treatment of paternity. *See Michael H. v. Gerald D.*, 491 U.S. 110, 118 (1989) (California law does not permit a child to have two legal fathers).

60. *Id.* at 782.

61. *Id.*

62. *Id.*

63. 61 Cal. App. 4th, 72 Cal. Rptr. 3d 280 (1998).

64. *Id.* at 282.

65. *Id.* at 282–283.

66. *Id.* at 282.

67. *Id.* at 283.

68. *Id.* at 282.

69. *Id.* at 283.

70. *Id.*

71. *Id.* at 284.

72. *Id.* at 290.

73. *Id.* at 282.

74. *Id.*

75. *Id.*

76. *Id.*

77. Joseph Goldstein, Anna Freud, & Albert Solnit, Beyond the Best Interests of the Child 31–34 (New York: The Free Press, 1973).

78. *Id.* at 98.

79. Joseph Goldstein, Anna Freud, & Albert Solnit, Before the Best Interests of the Child 15–18 (New York: The Free Press, 1979).

80. *Id.*

81. Katharine T. Bartlett, *Rethinking Parenthood as an Exclusive Status: The Need for Legal Alternatives When the Premise of the Nuclear Family Has Failed*, 70 Va. La. Rev. 879 (June 1984).

82. *Evans v. McTaggert*, 88 P.3d 1078, 1082 (Alaska 2004).

83. *In re Clifford K.*, 217 W.Va. 625, 619 S.E. 2d 138, 157 (2005).

84. *In re Custody of H.S.H.K.*, 533 N.W. 2d 419, 435–36 (Wis. 1995).

85. S.E. 2d 162 (S.C. 2006).

86. *Id.* at 164.

87. *Id.*

88. *Id.*

89. *Id.* at 165.

90. *Id.*

91. *Id.*

92. *Id.* at 166.

93. *Id.*

94. *Id.*

95. *Id.* at 169.

96. *Id.*

97. *Id.*

98. *Id.*

99. *Id.*

100. *Id.*

101. Naomi Cahn, *Perfect Substitutes or the Real Thing?* 52 Duke L. J. 1077 (April 2003).

102. S.E.2d 162 (S.C. 2006).

103. *Id.* at 170.

104. *Id.*

105. *Id.*

106. *Id.* at 171.

107. *Id.* at 172.

108. *Id.*

109. *Id.*

110. *Id.*

111. Nancy D. Polikoff, *The Deliberate Construction of Families Without Fathers: Is It an Option for Lesbian and Heterosexual Mothers?* 36 Santa Clara L. Rev. 375 (1996).

112. Susan L. Pollet, *Still a Patchwork Quilt: A Nationwide Survey of State Laws Regarding Stepparent Rights and Obligations,* 48 Fam. Ct. Rev. 528 (July 2010).

113. *See* ALI, Principles of the Law of Family Dissolution: Analysis and Recommendation (Principles) (2002).

114. *A.H. v. M.P.,* 857 NE 2d 1061, 1073 (Mass. 2006).

115. Principles, § 2.03(1)(b).

116. *Id.* at §2.03(1)(b)(i).

117. *Id.* at § 2.03(1)(b)(ii)(A).

118. *Id.* at § 2.03(1)(b)(ii).

119. *Id.* at § 2.03(1)(b)(ii)(A).

120. *Id.* at § 2.03(1)(b)(ii)(B).

121. *Id.* at § 2.03(1)(b)(iii).

122. *Id.* at 2.03(1)(b)(iv).

123. An example of the parent by estoppel doctrine will be discussed in chapter 8.

124. *See In re Parentage of M.F.,* 228 P.3d 1270, 1274 (Wash. 2010) (holding that the de facto parent theory did not apply to a situation involving a stepfather because he had a statutory right to adopt his stepchild).

125. *In re R.J.,* 79 Cal. Rptr. 3d 184, 186–187 (Cal. App. 3 Dist. 2008).

126. *In re Parentage of L.B.,* 122 P3d 161, n7 (Wash. 2005).

127. *Smith v. Gordon,* 968 A.2d 1, 8–9 (Del. Supr. 2009); *Kazamierazak v. Query,* 736 So. 2d. 106, 109–110 (Fla. App. 4 Dist., 1999).

128. 13 Del. Code § 8-201(b) (6).

129. 13 Del. Code § 8-201(c) (1–3)

130. ALI, Principles of the Law of Family Dissolution Analysis and Recommendations, Part I. §§§ 2.03(1), 2.04, 2.09, 2.10, 2.13 (Tentative Draft No. 3 1998).

131. 408 N.W. 2d 516 (Mich. App. 1986).

132. *Id.* at 604.

133. *Id.* at 604–605.

134. *Id.* at 605.

135. *Id.* at 605–606.

136. *Id.* at 607.

137. *Id.* at 608–609.

138. *Id.* at 609.

139. *Id.* at 610.

140. *Id.* at 611–612.

141. *Lipnevicius v. Lipnevicius*, 2010WL 3389748 at 2 (Mich. App. 2010).

142. *See, e.g., Gallagher v. Gallagher*, 539 N.W. 2d 479, 481–482 (Iowa 1995) (A husband who was not the biological or adoptive father of a child was recognized as the equitable father because the wife had permitted him to act as the father. The court held that the elements of equitable estoppel leading to an adjudication of equitable parenthood were "(1) a false representation or concealment of a material fact; (2) a lack of knowledge of the true facts on the part of the actor; (3) the intention that the representation or concealment be acted upon; and (4) reliance thereon by the party to whom it is made, to his or her prejudice and injury.") *Id.* at 482.

CHAPTER 7

1. Susan Nauss Exxon, *The Best Interest of the Child: Going beyond Legalese to Empathize with a Client's Leap of Faith*, 24 J. Juv. L. 1, 4–6 (2003–2004).

2. RCWA § 26.09.002 (West 2010).

3. *Ortega v. Bhola*, 869 A2d 1261, 1262 (Conn. App. 2005) ("The guiding principle in determining whether visitation is proper is the best interest of the child.")

4. Ark. Code Ann. §. 9-27-102 (West 2010).

5. Nev. Rev. Stat. Ann. §128.005(2)(c) (West 2010).

6. *Department of Social Services of State ex. Rel. Wright v. Byer*, 687 N.W. 2d 586, 592 (S.D. 2004).

7. 851 P.2d at 788–789.

8. *Id.* at 798.

9. *See, e.g., Watson v. Watson*, 46 So. 3d 218, 221–223 (La. App. 2 Cir. 2010); *In re Pfeuffer*, 837 A.2d 311, 314 (N.H. 2003); *Marshall v. Harris*, 981 So. 2d 345, 348 (Miss. App. 2008).

10. *See, e.g.,* V.T.C.A. Fam. Code § 153.002 ("The best interest of the child shall always be the primary consideration of the court in determining the issues of conservatorship and possession of and access to the child.") *Id.*

11. *See, e.g.,* Ind. Code Ann. § 31-34-19-6 (LexisNexis 2009); Kan. Stat. Ann. § 38-2201(6); *Steed v. Steed*, 877 So. 2d 602 (Ala. Civ. App. 2003).

12. *See, e.g.,* M.C.A. § 40-4-212 (West 2010).

13. *People ex. Rel. AMK*, 68 P.3d 563 (Colo. App., 2003).

14. Conn. Gen. Stat. Ann. § 45a-719 (West 2010).

15. N.D. Cent. Code Ann. § 14-09-06.2(1)(i)–(j); *see also Zimmerman v. Zimmerman*, 569 N.W. 2d 277 (N.D. 1997).

16. *In re Interest of R.P.*, 749 P.2d 49 (Kan. App. 1988); *see also In re Adoption/Guardianship of Alonza D., Jr.*, 987 A 2d 536 (Md. 2010).

17. 705 Ill. Comp. Stat. Ann. § 405/1-3(4.05); N.D. Cent. Code Ann. § 14-09-06.2(1).

18. Mich. Comp. Laws Ann. § 722.23 (West 2010).

19. Conn. Gen. Stat. Ann. § 45a-719.

20. ("The court shall not presume that one parent, because of his or her sex, is better qualified than the other parent to act as a joint or sole legal custodian for a child or as the child's primacy residential parent, nor shall it consider conduct of a proposed sole or joint custodian or primary residential parent that does not affect his or her relationship with the child.") Del. Code. Ann. Tit. 13 §722.

21. Julie E. Artis, *Judging the Best Interests of the Child: Judges' Accounts of the Tender Years Doctrine*, 38 Law & Soc'y Rev. 769, 773–774 (December 2004).

22. Idaho Code § 16-1601.

23. *Price v. Price*, 611 N.W. 2d 425, 430 (S.D. 2000).

24. 611 NW 2d 425, 428 (S.D. 2000).

25. *Id.* at 429.

26. *Id.* at 430.

27. In particular, the court analyzed the following factors relating to parental fitness: "(1) mental and physical health; (2) capacity and disposition to provide the child with protection, food, clothing medical care, and other basic needs; (3) ability to give the child love, affection, guidance, education and to impart the family's religion or creed; (4) willingness to maturely encourage and provide frequent and meaningful contact between the child and the other parent; (5) commitment to prepare the child for responsible adulthood, as well as to insure that the child experiences a fulfilling childhood; and (6) exemplary modeling so that the child witnesses first hand what it means to be a good parent, loving spouse, and a responsible citizen." *Id.*

28. The court evaluated stability by emphasizing the following factors: "(1) the relationship and interaction of the child with the parents, step-parents, siblings and extended families; (2) the child's adjustment to home, school and community; (3) the parent with whom the child has formed a closer attachment, as attachment between parent and child is an important developmental phenomena and breaking a healthy attachment can cause detriment; and (4) continuity, because when a child has been in one custodial setting for a long time pursuant to court order or by agreement, a court ought to be reluctant to make a change if only a theoretical or slight advantage for the child might be gained." *Id.* at 432.

29. *Id.* at 433 (stating that "The primary caretaker can be identified be determining 'which parent invested predominate time, care and consistency in raising the child'").

30. *Id.* at 434.

31. *Id.* at 435.

32. *Id.*

33. *Id.* at 436.

34. Note, *Alternatives to "Parental Right" in Child Custody Disputes Involving Third Parties*, 73 Yale L. J. 151, 157 (1963).

35. *Id.*

36. *Id.* at 162.

37. *Id.*

38. Joseph Goldstein, *Psychoanalysis and Jurisprudence*, 77 Yale L. J. 1053, 1076 (1968).

39. Joseph Goldstein, Anna Freud, & Albert J. Solnit, Beyond the Best Interests of the Child 4 (New York: The Free Press, 1973).

40. *G.S. v. T.B.*, 985 So. 2d 978, 982 (Fla. 2008).

41. 574 N.E. 2d 1055 (Ohio 1991).

42. *Id.* at 1057.

43. *Id.*

44. *Id.* at 1058.

45. *Id.*

46. *Id.*

47. *Id.* at 1059.

48. *Id.*

49. *Id.*

50. That doctrine is discussed in chapter 6.

51. New International Bible, Ecclesiastes 10:9.

52. New International Bible 1 Timothy 6:10.

53. Peter M. Cicchino, *The Problem Child: An Empirical Study and Rhetorical Analysis of Child Poverty in the United States,* 5 J. L. & Pol'y 5, 36–37 (1996); Ron Haskins, *What Works Is Work: Welfare Reform and Poverty Reduction,* 4 N.W. J. L. & Soc. Pol'y 30 (Winter 2009).

54. *In re Marriage of Buzzanca*, 72 Cal. Rptr. 2d 280, 290 (Cal. App. 4th. 1998).

55. Lyneka Little, *Ultra Deadbeat Dad Gets 23 Months in Jail,* at http://www.abcnews.go.com (September 29, 2010).

CHAPTER 8

1. *Miller v. Miller*, 912 A.2d 951, 968 (Vt. 2006), *citing In re B.L.V.B.*, 628 A.2d 1271, 1275–76 (Vt. 1993).

2. Some of the information included in this chapter was originally shared with the readers in Browne Lewis, *Two Fathers, One Dad: Allocating Paternity Between the Men Involved in the Artificial Insemination Process*, 13 Lewis & Clark L. Rev. 949 (Fall 2009).

3. *See* Sarah McGinnis, *You Are Not The Father: How State Paternity Laws Protect (and Fail to Protect) the Best Interests of Children*, 16 Am. U. J. Gender Soc. Pol'y & L. J. 311, 325–330 (2007), contending that giving the court too much discretion in paternity determinations may not be in the best interests of the child.

4. *See C.M. v. C.C.*, 377 A2d 821, 825 (N.J. Juv. & Dom. Rel. 1977): ("It is in a child's best interests to have two parents wherever possible.")

5. Daryl L. Gordon-Ceresky, *Artificial Insemination: Its Effect on Paternity and Inheritance Rights*, 9 Conn. Prob. L. J. 245 (1995).

6. I am using "paternal parent" instead of "father" because I also want my proposal to benefit children conceived by persons in same-sex relationships.

7. *See, e.g.*, Jane Singer, *Marriage, Biology, and Paternity: The Case for Revitalizing the Marital Presumption*, 65 Md. L. Rev. 246, 268–270 (2006); Melanie B. Jacobs, *My Two Dads: Disaggregating Biological and Social Paternity*, 78 Ariz. St. L. J. 809 (Fall 2006); Donald C. Habin, *Daddy Dilemmas: Untangling the Puzzles of Paternity*, 13 Cornell L. J. & Pub.

Pol'y 29 (Fall 2003); Kris Frankling, *"A Family Like Any Other Family": Alternative Methods of Defining Family Law*, 18 N.Y.U. Rev. L. & Soc. Change 1027 (1990/1991).

8. *See* Nancy C. Dowd, *Multiple Parents/Multiple Fathers*, 9 J. L. & Fam. Stud. 231 (2007) ,(advocating the principle of multiple parents).

9. Jeffrey Dodge, *Same-Sex Marriage and Divorce: A Proposal for Child Custody Mediation*, 44 Fam. Ct. Rev. 87 (Jan. 2006).

10. Carmel B. Stella, *When a Mother Is a Legal Stranger to Her Child: The Law's Challenge to the Lesbian Nonbiological Mother*, 1 U.C.L.A. Women's L. J. 135, 142–146 (Spring 1991); *see also* Maggie Mantemach, *Where Is My Other Mommy: Applying the Presumed Father Provision of the Uniform Parentage Act to Recognize the Rights of Lesbian Mothers and Their Children*, 9 J. Gender Race & Just. 385, 407–408 (Winter 2005).

11. Emily Stork, *Born to No Mother: In Re Roberto D.B. and Equal Protection for Gestational Surrogate Rebutting Maternity*, 16 Am. U.K. Gender Soc. Pol'y L. 283, 293–307 (2007) (evaluating different tests courts have relied upon to determine the legal mother of a child born as the result of a surrogate arrangements).

12. Most of the artificial insemination statutes contain a physician requirement.

13. *See Lehr v. Robertson*, 463 U.S. 248, 262 (1983) (The court noted that "The significance of the biological connection is that it offers the natural father an opportunity that no other male possesses to develop a relationship with his offspring. If he grasps that opportunity and accepts some measure of responsibility for the child's future, he may enjoy the blessings of the parent-child relationship and make uniquely valuable contributions to the child's development. If he fails to do so, the Federal Constitution will not automatically compel a State to listen to his opinion of where the child's bests lie.") *Id.*

14. To qualify as a partner, the person must be a part of a civil union or domestic partnership. This designation is not meant to refer to an unmarried man and woman in a long-term relationship.

15. *In re Baby Doe*, 353 S.E. 2d 877 (S.C. 1987); *In re Marriage of Witbeck-Wildhagen*, 667 N.E. 2d 122 (Ill. App. 4 Dist. 1996).

16. *Karin T. v. Michael T.*, 484 N.Y.S. 2d 780 (N.YU. Fam. Ct., 1985).

17. *Lane v. Lane*, 912 P.2d 290 (N.M. App. 1996); *State ex. Rel. H. v. P.*, 90 A2d 434, 457 (1982).

18. *State ex rel. H. v. P.*, 457 N.Y.S. 2d 488 (N.Y.A.D., 1982).

19. *Id.*

20. *Wakeman v. Dixon*, 921 So. 2d 669 (Fla. App. 1 Dist. 2006).

21. Note, Steven M. Cytryn, *What Went Wrong? Why Family Preservation Programs Failed to Achieve Their Potential*, 17 Cardozo J. L. & Gender 81, 81–82 (2010).

22. *See, e.g, People v. Sorensen*, 437 P.2d 495 (Cal. 1968) (in which a woman's husband was convicted for not paying child support for a child his wife conceived using donor sperm with his consent).

23. This means that the person must be a told that if he or she consents to the artificial insemination, he or she will be legally responsible for supporting the child.

24. In various areas of law, the courts attribute constructive knowledge to a person if there is something that they should have known. In most cases, if a reasonable person in the person's circumstance would have inquired further, courts deem the person to have known what he or she would have discovered had he or she made the inquiry.

25. Richard Lewis Browne, *Undeserving Heirs?—The Case of the "Terminated" Parent*, 40 U. Rich. L. Rev. 547, 548 (2006).

26. *Shineovich v. Kemp*, 214 P.3d 29 (Or. App. 2009) (rejecting an argument that the presumption of paternity should be applied to situations involving same-sex couples).

27. 812 P 2d 1014 (Ariz. 1990).

28. *Id.* at 1015.

29. *Id.* at 1016.

30. *Id.* at 1017.

31. *Id.*

32. *Id.* at 1018.

33. *Id.*

34. *Id.*

35. *See, e.g., People v. Sorensen*, 437 P2d 495 (Cal. 1968); *see also* Nancy D. Polikoff, *This Child Does Have Two Mothers: Redefining Parenthood to Meet the Needs of Children in Lesbian-Mother and Other Non-traditional Families*, 78 Geo. L. J. 459, 501–502 (February 1990) (recommending the recognition of parenthood by estoppels in order to protect persons involved in same-sex relationships).

36. *Loranger Const. Corp. v. E.F. Hauserman Co.*, 374 N.E. 2d 306, 308–309 (Mass. App. 1978).

37. *Peluso v. Kistner*, 970 A 2d 530, 532–533 (Pa. Cmwlth. 2009).

38. *Meyer v. Meyer*, 25 So. 3d 39, 43 (Fla. App. 2 Dist., 2009).

39. Michael B. Metzger & Michael J. Phillips, *Promissory Estoppel and Third Parties*, 42 Sw. L. J. 931, 937 (1988); *see also Foote v. Simmonds Precision Products Co., Inc.* 613 A 2d 1277 (Vt., 1992); *Frost Crushed Stone Co., Inc . v. Odell Geer Const. Co., Inc.* 110 S.W. 3d 41, 43 (Tex. App.-Waco, 2002).

40. *Doctors Hosp. 1997, L.P. v. Sambuca Houston, L.P.*, 154 S.W. 3d 634, 636 (Tex. App.-Houston [14 Dist.] 2004).

41. *Skebba v. Kasch*, 724 N.W. 2d 408 (Wis. App. 2006).

42. *Baker v. Ayres and Baker Pole and Post, Inc.*, 170 P3d 1247, 1250 (Wyo. 2007).

43. *U.S. Ecology v. State*, 28 Cal. Rptr. 3d 894, 904 (Cal. App. 4 Dist. 2005).

44. *Moore v. Mo.-Neb. Express, Inc.* 892 SW 2d. 696, 703 (Mo. App. 1994).

45. *Wright v. Newman*, 467 S.E. 2d 533 (Ga. 1996).

46. *Id.* at 535.

47. *Id.*

48. O.C.G.A. § 13-3-44 (a), *cited in Id* at 534.

49. *Id.* at 535.

50. *Id.*

51. *Nugent v. Slaght*, 638 N.W.2d 594, 599 (Wis. App. 2001).

52. 125 S.W. 3d 840 (Ark. Ct. App. 2003).

53. *Brown*, 125 S.W. 3d. at 841.

54. *Id.* at 842.

55. *Id.* at 841.

56. *Id.* at 842.

57. *Brown,* at 842.

58. *Id.*

59. *Brown* at 843.

60. *Id.* at 844.

61. A more expansive discussion of this theory can be found in chapter 6 of this book.

62. *V.C. v. M.J.B.*, 748 A.2d 539, 550 (1999).

63. *Id.* at 552.

64. Bartlett, *supra* note at 946.

65. *Id.* at 946–947.

66. *Id.* at 946.

67. *Id.* at 947.

68. *Id.*

69. *See* Or. Rev. Stat. §109.119 (2007) (acknowledging that a child-parent relationship may be created by establishing emotional ties with a non-biological child).

70. *See* Bartlett, *supra* note at 946–948.

71. *See In re Marriage of Sorensen*, 906 P 2d 838, 841 (Or. Ct. App. 1995) (recognizing the stepmother as the child's psychological parent over the objection of the biological parent).

72. Polikoff, *supra* at 387–388 (presenting the concept of a "functional parent" and calling for statutory reform to protect families with same-sex parents).

73. *Id.* at 387–388.

74. The court should be permitted to decide what is a reasonable period of time on a case-by-case basis.

75. Unif. Parentage Act (1973) 4(a), 9B U.L.A. 393 (2001) ("A man is presumed to be the natural father of a child if . . . (4) while the child is under the age of majority, he receives the child into his home and openly holds out the child as his natural child . . . ").

76. A committed woman is a woman who is in a civil union or a domestic partnership. A committed woman may also be a woman who is in a long-term relationship that is "characterized by an emotional and financial commitment and interdependence." *Braschi v. Stahl Assocs. Co.*, 545 N.E. 2d 49, 54 (N.Y. 1989).

77. This is similar to the honorary trust some states permit persons to establish to ensure that there is someone to take care of their pets after they die. Adam J. Hirsch, *Bequest for Purposes: A Unified Theory*, 56 Wash. & Lee L. Rev. 3, 98 (1999).

78. *See, e.g., In re R.C.*, 775 P.2d 27 (Colo. 1989); *see also Jacob v. Shultz-Jacob*, 923 A 2d 473 (Pa. Super. Ct. 2007).

79. *See In re R.C.*, 775 P2d at 35 (stating that the court will recognize an agreement between a known sperm donor and an unmarried woman that the donor will be treated as the father of the artificially conceived child).

80. *See* N.H. Rev. Stat. Ann. 168-B:11 (LexisNexis 2001) ("A sperm donor may be liable for support only if he signs an agreement with the other parties to that effect."). *See also C.O. v. W.S.*, 639 N.E. 2d 523, 525 (Ohio Ct. Com. Pl. 1994).

81. *T.F. v. B.L.*, 813 N.E. 2d 1244, (Mass. 2004).

82. *See, e.g., Johnson*, 851, P.2d at 782 (holding that the natural mother was the woman who intended to have the child conceived and who intended to parent the child).

83. Melanie B. Jacobs, *Applying Intent-Based Parentage Principles to Non-Legal Lesbian Coparents*, 25 N. Ill. U. L. Rev. 433 (Summer 2005).

84. Shultz, *supra* note at 323.

Index

Best interests of the child (*continued*)
economic, 179–82, 184, 186; equitable parent
doctrine and, 159; family definition and, 12–13;
marital presumption of paternity and, 11, 29–30,
34–40, 79–81, 171; for posthumously conceived
children, 124–25
Best interests of the child standard, 163–67, 214;
application of, 169–72; for artificially conceived
children, 14–17, 166–67, 171–72, 174–82, 184; in
court decisions, 165–67; critique of, 172–74; definition of, 167–69; economic best interests test for,
179–82; for marital children, 166, 170–71; modifications of, 174–82; psychological best interests
test for, 174–79; state statutes mandating, 165–66;
in surrogacy cases, 166–67
Beyond the Best Interests of the Child (Goldstein,
Freud, and Solnit), 144–45
Bible: marital presumption cases in, 27; non-marital
children in, 45
Bilhah, 45
Biology: in artificial insemination cases, 65–66,
69, 72, 75–76, 78–81, 131–37, 210–11, 213; best
interests of child and, 134; expanding paternity
beyond, 185–86; gestational surrogacy and,
140–42; marital presumption priority over,
22–23, 30–31, 38–40; multiple parents sharing,
136–37; in non-marital children paternity cases,
1–2, 41–44, 50, 56; in non-spousal sperm donor
cases, 90; parenthood by, 131–37, 210–11; paternity
by agreement and, 93–94; rebuttal of paternity
based on, 187
Birth control, 50–52
Blood relationships, 131–37
Blood tests. *See* DNA evidence
Brown v. Brown, 200–201
Bullock, Sandra, 21
"'But for' causation," parenthood by intent and, 138–39

California: sperm donor paternity in, 98; surrogacy
cases in, 141–42
Catholic Church: artificial insemination in, 121;
children and marriage in, 117
Child abuse, 174–75
Child-neglect adjudications, 113
Children: classes of, 111, 129; economic costs of,
180–81; government protection of, 163–66; legal
definition of, 111; marriage and, 23–26; poverty
and, 180–81. *See also specific groups of children*
Child support: for adopted children, 115; in artificial
insemination cases, 74, 77–79, 179–82, 206; for
children of same-sex relationships, 127–28; by
estoppel parents, 153, 199–201; by functional parents, 151; for non-marital children, 43, 49–52; by
non-spousal sperm donors, 105–6; paternity by
agreement and, 94; UPA approach to, 74; welfare
reform and, 42–43, 181–82

Christianity: artificial insemination in, 121; non-
marital children and, 116–17
Chung, Connie, 225n7
Churchill, William, 126
Cibrian, Eddie, 22
Citizens Against Paternity Fraud, 22
Clinton, Hillary, 9
Clinton, William, 31
Cloning, 111, 225n1
Colorado, sperm donor paternity in, 91–94
Committed woman, 237n76; artificial insemination
of, 207–8
Confused artificial insemination, 5, 137
Connecticut: artificial insemination in, 224n47; best
interests of the child standard in, 168–69
Consent to artificial insemination, 2, 4, 60–69, 189–
91; best interests of the child and, 65–66, 69, 72,
75–76, 79–81; biology and, 65–66, 69, 72, 75–76,
79–81; constructive, 69; definition of, 60; expira-
tion of, 191; informed, 72, 222n60; posthumously
conceived children and, 125; requirement for,
60–62; by same-sex partners, 189–91; withdrawal
of, 62, 75, 191; written, 62–69, 191
Consent to paternity: by agreement, 90–96, 138–39,
209–10; by husbands or same-sex partners, 189–91
Constructive consent, 69
Constructive knowledge, 192, 235n24
Contraception, 50–52
Contract, parenthood by, 138–39, 209–10
Coolidge, Calvin, 8
Co-parenting agreements, 154
Couple, preservation of, 30–34
Court decisions, best interests of child approach in,
165–67
Covenant, marriage as, 25
Crosby, David, 85
Cuckolded man, 1, 4, 10–11, 21–23; children and
marriage, 23–26; marital presumption and,
26–30; preservation of marriage and, 30–34;
protection of child and, 29–30, 34–40
Custody: of artificially conceived children, 186–87;
by psychological parents, 151
Cypher, Julie, 85

De facto parents, 155–57
Delaware: artificial insemination statute, 71; best
interests of the child standard in, 169; de facto
parents in, 155–56
Department of Agriculture (USDA), child costs
reported by, 180
Dickens, Charles, 44
Disability. *See* Persons with disabilities
Discretion, paternity by, 104–7
Divorce: marital presumption of paternity and,
25–26, 28–29, 34–35, 37; paternity link with,
118–19

DNA evidence: legal parenthood based on, 136–37; marital presumption of paternity and, 29, 38–39, 194–96; multiple biological parents and, 136–37; non-marital children and, 47

Economic best interests of the child, 184, 186; test for, 179–82
Economic dependence, paternity by, 206–7
Economic support. *See* Financial support
Edwards, Elizabeth, 21
Edwards, John, 21
Egg donors, 132
Elie'zer of Damascus, 47
Elizabethan Poor Laws, 219n3; bastardy statues in, 45
Emotional abuse, 174–75
Emotional well-being: of artificially conceived children, 202–4; best interests of the child and, 174–79; paternity importance for, 6–7
Equitable adoption, 114–16
Equitable estoppel: in artificial insemination cases, 77–78, 197–201; child support based on, 200–201; elements of, 200–201
Equitable parent doctrine, 157–59
Estoppel: in artificial insemination paternity cases, 16, 76–79, 197–201; parenthood by, 16, 153–55, 197–201
Etheridge, Melissa, 85
Evans, Brett, 38–39
"Expenditures on Children by Families" (USDA), 180
Extramarital children, 1, 4, 10–11, 21–23; children and marriage, 23–26; marital presumption and, 26–30; preservation of marriage and, 30–34; protection of, 29–30, 34–40; society's treatment of, 117–19

Family: changing definition of, 12–14, 128–29. *See also* Legal child; Parenthood
Family Support Act of 1988, 50
Father-child relationship. *See* Parent-child relationship
Fatherhood. *See* Paternity
Father's Day, 8
Fathers' Rights Movement, 8
Federal Office of Child Support Enforcement, 50
Fertile man, 2–3, 11–12, 83–86, 223n6; fornicating man compared with, 96–97; mandating statutory non-paternity for, 86–90; paternity by discretion for, 104–7; paternity by non-acquiescence for, 97–101; recognizing paternity by agreement for, 90–96; self-insemination and, 101–4; unintended consequences for, 96–97
Financial support: for adopted children, 114–16; for artificially conceived children, 14, 64–65, 69, 74, 77–79, 111, 170–71, 174, 179–84, 186, 189,

203, 206–9; for children by surrogates, 142–44; for children of same-sex relationships, 127–28; economic costs of raising children, 180–81; by estoppel parents, 153; for marital children, 24, 26, 112–14; for non-marital children, 28–29, 42–43, 45–46, 49–52, 116–17; by non-spousal sperm donors, 83, 88–89, 105–6; paternity importance for, 6–9; from psychological parents, 146; for stepchildren, 113–14, 117–19; welfare reform and, 42–43, 181–82
Florida: artificial insemination statute, 70; sperm donor paternity in, 86
Foreman, George, 17
Fornicating man, 1–2, 11, 41–44; child support provided by, 43, 49–52; consequences faced by, 49–56; discouragement of, 48–49; fertile man compared with, 96–97; historical treatment of, 44–49; inheritance and, 43, 45–46, 52–56, 219n22; paternity fraud protection for, 46–48; as sperm donor, 4, 41–44
Forum shopping, 174
Frampton, Carl, 105–6
Fraud: contraceptive, 50–51; paternity, 9, 22, 46–48
Frauenfield, Mark, 194–96
Freud, Anna, 144–45
Freud, Sigmund, 6
Functional parents, 17, 151–53, 204–6, 211

Gallagher v. Gallagher, 232n142
Gay and lesbian partners. *See* Same-sex partners
Gender, parental, 169
Genetic testing. *See* DNA evidence
Georgia, artificial insemination in, 70, 224n47
Gestational surrogacy, 140–42
Goldman, Bruna, 8
Goldman, David, 8
Goldstein, Joseph, 144–45, 176–77
Gomez v. Perez, 49–50
Gordon, Sherman, 52–53
Government, protective role of, 163–66
Grammer, Kelsey, 118
Guardian, for artificially conceived children, 208–9

Hagar, 45, 121, 133
Hatley, Frank, 9
Hawaii, stepparent support obligations in, 119
Health care provider, in artificial insemination process, 97–101, 103–4, 186
Heirs. *See* Inheritance
Heterologous insemination (HI), 5
Hill, John Lawrence, 138–40
Homologous insemination, 5
Hoover, Herbert, 9
Husbands: allocating paternity of, 183–207; consent to artificial insemination by, 2, 4, 60–62, 64–65, 189–91; contributions made by, 189–97;

Husbands (*continued*)
in custody disputes involving artificially conceived children, 186–87; economic dependence
on, 206–7; estoppel paternity of, 197–201; functional paternity of, 204–6; post-conception/post-
birth actions of, 201–7; pre-conception/pre-birth
actions of, 197–201; presumption of paternity of
artificially conceived children, 69–73, 192–97,
235n24; as psychological parents, 202–4. *See also*
Marital presumption of paternity

Idaho, best interests of the child standard in, 169
Illegitimacy, 28; artificial insemination and, 62, 66,
69, 77; historical treatment of, 44–49; non-spou-
sal sperm donation and, 89–90; stigma of, 25,
27–29, 46, 116–17. *See also* Non-marital children
Illinois, non-marital children cases in, 52–53
Implied consent, in artificial insemination cases, 61
Income, best interests of child and, 169, 180–81
Indiana, artificial insemination cases in, 78–79
Infertility, male, 11, 216n26
Informed consent, 72, 222n60
Inheritance: by adopted children, 116; for marital
children, 24, 113; for non-marital children, 43,
45–46, 52–56, 219n22; from non-spousal sperm
donors, 89; paternity importance for, 6; for post-
humously born children, 122–26, 227n64; from
psychological parents, 146; for stepchildren, 132
In loco parentis doctrine, 118–19
In re Adoption of Ridenour, 178–79
In re Interest of R.C., 92–94
In re J. W. F. (Schoolcraft), 35–36
In re Marriage of Buzzanca, 142–44
In re Neiderhiser's Estate, 23–24
Insemination. *See* Artificial insemination
Instruction on Respect for Human Life in its Ori-
gins and on the Dignity of Procreation (Donum
Vitae) (Sacred Congregation for the Doctrine of
Faith), artificial insemination in, 121
Intent, parenthood by, 137–44, 189–90, 210
Inter vivos children, 120–22
In the Matter of Baby M, 133–34
Isaac, 47
Ishmael, 121
Islam, artificial insemination in, 120–21

Jackson, Michael, 9–10
Jacob, 45
Jacobs, William, 23
Jacob v. Shultz-Jacob, 105–6
Jesus, 27
Jewish law, artificial insemination in, 121
Jhordan v. Mary K., 98–101
John, 80–81
Johnson, Elizabeth, 147–51
Johnson v. Calvert, 140–42, 144, 166–67

Johnston, Hugh, 33
Johnston, Levi, 42
Jolie, Angelina, 43
Joseph, 27
Judicial bias, 173
Judicial economy, 9–10
Judicial inefficiency, 173
Judicial uncertainty, 173–74

Kane, Ellen, 123
Kane, William, 123
Kansas, sperm donor paternity in, 91
The Kids Are Alright, 83
Known sperm donors, 16–17, 85–86, 102; agreement
to paternity by, 90–96, 209–10; best interests of
the child marital presumption and, 79–81; child
support paid by, 105–6; married or committed
woman and, 207–8; unmarried or uncommitted
woman and, 209–11
Kutcher, Ashton, 80

Lalli v. Lalli, 54–55
Lane case, 66–69
Law, society's influence over, 3, 13, 111, 183
Legal child, 111; adopted, 112, 114–16; artificially con-
ceived, 119–28; extramarital, 117–19; inter vivos,
120–22; marital, 112–14; non-marital, 112, 116–17;
of same-sex relationships, 126–28; testamentary,
122–26, 227n64
Legal contract, marriage as, 23–25
Legal vasectomy, 86–90
Lehr v. Robertson, 235n13
Lesbian partners. *See* Same-sex partners
Letterman, David, 31
Levin case, 78–79
Lopes v. Lopes, 35–36
Lord Mansfield's Rule, 27–28
Louisiana: artificial insemination statute, 71; non-
marital children in, 46; posthumously born
children in, 113

Mandela, Nelson, 17
Man's rights: in artificial insemination process, 184;
reproductive, 64–65, 74–76, 171–72, 214
Marital children, 3, 10–11, 23–26; benefits to, 22–23;
best interests of, 166, 170–71; financial support
for, 24, 26, 112–14; society's treatment of, 22–23,
28–29, 48–49, 112–14; testamentary, 113–14, 122
Marital presumption of paternity, 1, 4, 10–11, 21–23;
in artificial insemination cases, 4, 59–60, 62, 65,
79–81, 171–72, 192–97, 235n24; best interests of
child and, 11, 29–30, 34–40, 79–81, 171; biology
and, 22–23, 30–31, 38–40; divorce and, 25–26,
28–29, 34–35, 37; DNA technology and, 29, 38–39,
194–96; for extramarital children, 26–30; history
of, 27–28; for marital children, 23–26; preserva-

tion of marriage and, 28–34; reasons for, 26–27; rebuttal of, 22, 27–28, 30–38, 166, 192–96; typical statute of, 29

Marriage: artificial insemination during, 102, 120, 207–8, 223n6; children and, 23–26; decline in, 28–29, 43, 112; discouraging sex without, 48–49; as legal contract, 23–25; parties to, 24–25; as partnership, 25–26; preservation of, 28–34; as religious covenant, 25; validity of, 23–24. *See also* Divorce

Mary, 27, 80–81

Mary K., 98–101

Maryland, artificial insemination statute, 69

Massachusetts: children of same-sex relationships in, 127–28; testamentary children in, 123–26

Maternity: by biology, 132–37; by intent, 137–44

Medical history: of artificially conceived children, 83, 90; of biological fathers, 7

Mental health: best interests of the child and, 174–79; paternity importance for, 6–7

Michael H. v. Gerald D., 30–31

Michigan: best interests of the child standard in, 168–69; equitable parent doctrine in, 157–59; non-spousal sperm donors in, 223n6

Middleton v. Johnson, 147–51

Minnesota, artificial insemination statute, 62

Misrepresenting moms. *See* Paternity fraud

Moore, Demi, 80

Morrison, Essie Lee, 9

Murphy Brown, 117

Neiderhiser, Robert, 23–24

Nevada, best interests of the child standard in, 166

New Hampshire: artificial insemination statute, 71–73; sperm donor paternity in, 91

New Jersey, sperm donor paternity in, 91

Newman, Kim, 199–200

New Mexico, non-marital children cases in, 51

Nicely, Naomi, 23–24

Nixon, Richard, 8

Non-acquiescence, paternity by, 97–101

Non-consenting man, 2, 12, 59–61; consent requirement in artificial insemination cases, 60–62; constructive consent in artificial insemination cases, 69; estoppel in artificial insemination cases, 16, 76–79, 197–201; litigating paternity in cases of, 76–81; marital presumption of paternity and, 79–81; presumption of husband's paternity in artificial insemination cases, 69–73, 192–97, 235n24; states with artificial insemination statutes legislating paternity, 61–69; UPA and, 62, 71, 73–76, 221n51; written consent in artificial insemination cases, 62–69, 191

Non-marital children, 1–3, 11, 41–44; biology and, 1–2, 41–44, 50, 56; de facto parents of, 155; financial support for, 28–29, 42–43, 45–46, 49–52, 116–

17; historical treatment of, 44–49; illegitimacy of, 25, 27–29, 46, 116–17; inheritance by, 43, 45–46, 52–56, 219n22; legal rights of, 49–56; posthumous paternity adjudication and, 122, 227n64; society's treatment of, 22–23, 48–49, 112, 116–17

Non-paternity, presumption of, 86–90, 92–94

Non-spousal sperm donors, 2–3, 83–86, 223n6; financial support by, 83, 88–89, 105–6; mandating statutory non-paternity for, 86–90; married or committed woman and, 207–8; paternity by discretion for, 104–7; paternity by non-acquiescence for, 97–101; recognizing paternity by agreement for, 90–96; self-insemination and, 101–4; unintended consequences for, 96–97; unmarried or uncommitted woman and, 208–11

Obama, Barack, 5–6

Ohio: best interests of the child standard in, 178–79; surrogacy cases in, 134–36

Oklahoma, artificial insemination in, 224n47

Oliver Twist (Dickens), 44

Oregon, artificial insemination in, 224n47

Orman, Suze, 209

Palin, Bristol, 42

Palin, Sarah, 42

Parental fitness, 170, 233n27

Parental rights: best interests of child and, 171; termination of, 113

Parent-child relationship: for artificially conceived children, 184, 202–4; for children of same-sex relationships, 128; equitable parent doctrine and, 157–59; protection of, 34–37; sperm donor paternity and, 106; UPA approach to, 73–74

Parenthood: by agreement, 90–96, 138–39, 209–10; by biology, 131–37, 210–11; by economic dependence, 206–7; by equity, 157–59; by estoppel, 16, 153–55, 197–201; by function, 17, 151–53, 204–6, 211; by intent, 137–44, 189–90, 210; meaning of, 131, 137, 203; by psychology, 17, 144–51, 202–4; types of, 131

Partners. *See* Same-sex partners

Partnership, marriage as, 25–26

Paternity: by consent, 90–96, 189–91, 209–10; definition of, 4, 13–14, 131, 137, 185–86, 214; by discretion, 104–7; divorce and, 118–19; by economic dependence, 206–7; father's emotional stake in, 8; importance of, 5–10; by non-acquiescence, 97–101; presumption of, 69–73, 192–97, 235n24. *See also* Marital presumption of paternity; Parenthood

Paternity fraud, 9; extramarital affairs and, 22; historical protection against, 46–48

Paternity of Adam, 80–81

Pearson, Kelly, 36–37

Pearson, Kimberlee, 36–37

About the Author

BROWNE C. LEWIS is an associate professor and director of the Center for Health Law and Policy at Cleveland-Marshall College of Law. She writes and researches in the areas of biomedical ethics and assisted reproductive technology.